# How to Be
# a Perfect Stranger

## —— VOL. 1 ——

D0094551

# How to Be a Perfect Stranger

## ——VOL. 1 ——

## A Guide to Etiquette in
## Other People's Religious Ceremonies

Edited by Arthur J. Magida
& Stuart M. Matlins

Walking Together, Finding the Way

SKYLIGHT PATHS Publishing

WOODSTOCK, VERMONT

How to Be a Perfect Stranger, Vol. 1: A Guide to Etiquette in Other People's Religious Ceremonies

All rights reserved. No part of this book may be reproduced or transmitted in any form or by any means, electronic or mechanical, including photocopying, recording, or by any information storage and retrieval system, without permission in writing from the publisher.

© 1999 by SkyLight Paths Publishing

**Library of Congress Cataloging-in-Publication Data**

*The Library of Congress cataloged the Jewish Lights Publishing edition as follows:*

Magida, Arthur J.
　　How to be a perfect stranger : a guide to etiquette in other people's
　　religious ceremonies / edited by Arthur J. Magida.
　　　　　p.　　cm.
　　ISBN 1-879045-39-7 (HC)
　　1. Religious etiquette—United States.　2. United States—Religion—
20th century.　I. Title.
　　BJ2010.M34　1995　　　　　　　　　　　　　　　　　95-37474
　　291.3'8—dc20　　　　　　　　　　　　　　　　　　　CIP

H847h
V I

1999 First Quality Paperback Edition, updated & expanded
10 9 8 7 6 5 4 3 2 1

ISBN 1-893361-01-2 (pb)
Manufactured in the United States of America
Cover art by Camille Kress
Cover and text design by Chelsea Dippel

*Walking Together, Finding the Way*
Published by SkyLight Paths Publishing
A Division of LongHill Partners, Inc.
Sunset Farm Offices, Rte. 4 / P.O. Box 237
Woodstock, Vermont 05091
Tel: (802) 457-4000　　Fax: (802) 457-4004

www.skylightpaths.com

# Contents

Acknowledgments 7
Introduction 11
Foreword by Sanford Cloud, Jr., President,
National Conference of Christians and Jews 15

# Acknowledgments

A book such as this is the product of many contributions by many people. It could be no other way given the broad tapestry of religions in America. If nothing else, the willingness of those approached for their wisdom and their knowledge about their specific denominations indicates that American religious leaders are eager to be properly understood—and to properly understand others.

Instrumental in the evolution of *How to Be a Perfect Stranger* were William Shanken and Richard A. Siegel, who developed the original concept and helped get the project into first gear. Stuart Matlins, publisher of SkyLight Paths, developed the methodology for obtaining the information. Arthur J. Magida, editorial director, oversaw the research and writing and provided the impetus for the project. Sandra Korinchak, editorial associate, shepherded the project from start to finish. Michael Schwartzentruber, series editor of Northstone Publishing, compiled the Canadian data and information included in the revised and updated edition.

Each chapter came from information obtained from an extensive questionnaire filled out by clergy and other religious experts coast-to-coast. Without the help of the following, this book would never have become a reality:

Dr. Satyendra Banerjee, priest and past-president,
Bengali Cultural Society of British Columbia

Rabbi Gary M. Bretton-Granatoor, Director of Interreligious Affairs,
Union of American Hebrew Congregations (Reform),
New York, New York

Marj Carpenter, former Mission Interpreter,
Presbyterian Church (USA), Louisville, Kentucky

Glenn Cooper, former Director of Communications,
The Presbyterian Church in Canada, Pictou, Nova Scotia

Scott Dickson, Public Affairs (Canada), Jehovah's Witnesses,
Watch Tower Bible and Tract Society of Canada

Rabbi Moshe Edelman, Associate Director of Regions and
Director of Leadership Development, United Synagogue
of Conservative Judaism, New York, New York

Eugene J. Fisher, Associate Director of the Secretariat for
Ecumenical and Interreligious Affairs of the National Conference
of Catholic Bishops, Washington, D.C.

Ted George, Librarian, Greek Orthodox Cathedral of the
Annunciation, Baltimore, Maryland

Rev. Lance Gifford, Rector, St. John's Episcopal Church,
Baltimore, Maryland

James S. Golding, Editor, The [Greek] Orthodox Observer,
New York, New York

Steven D. Goodman, Professor of Indian and Tibetan Buddhism,
Institute of Buddhist Studies, Berkeley, California

Hoyt Hickman, now retired from the General Board of
Discipleship, United Methodist Church, Nashville, Tennessee

Hans Holznagel, Public Relations Manager,
United Church of Christ, Cleveland, Ohio

Ibrahim Hooper, Council on American-Islamic Relations,
Washington, D.C.

Bede Hubbard, Assistant General Secretary,
Canadian Conference of Catholic Bishops, Ottawa, Ontario

Ralph Janes, Communications Director,
Seventh-day Adventist Church in Canada

Don LeFevre, Manager of Public Affairs Department, The Church
of Jesus Christ of Latter-day Saints, Salt Lake City, Utah

Barbara Liotscos, Consultant for Ministry and Worship,
The Anglican Church of Canada, Toronto, Ontario

Stan Litke, Executive Director, Christian Church
(Disciples of Christ) in Canada, Calgary, Alberta

Rev. David Mahsman, Director of News and Information,
The Lutheran Church–Missouri Synod, St. Louis, Missouri

Mike McDonald, Pulpit Minister, The Church of Christ, Monahans, Texas

Dana Mullen, Clerk–Representative Meeting,
Canadian Yearly Meeting, Ottawa, Ontario

Dr. Paul Nelson, Director for Worship,
Evangelical Lutheran Church in America, Chicago, Illinois

Father Louis Noplos, Assistant Pastor, Greek Orthodox Cathedral
of the Annunciation, Baltimore, Maryland

Sara Palmer, Program Secretary, The Wider Quaker Fellowship,
Philadelphia, Pennsylvania

Mark Parent, Ph.D., Pereaux United Baptist Church,
Pereaux, Nova Scotia

Richard Payne, Dean, Institute of Buddhist Studies,
Berkeley, California

Laurie Peach, Staff Writer, The First Church of Christ, Scientist,
Boston, Massachusetts

Dr. George W. Reid, Director of the Biblical Research Institute,
Seventh-day Adventists, Silver Spring, Maryland

Raymond Richardson, Writing Department,
Jehovah's Witnesses, Brooklyn, New York

Rev. John Roberts, Pastor, Woodbrook Baptist Church,
Baltimore, Maryland

Michael R. Rothaar, Acting Director for Worship,
Evangelical Lutheran Church in America, Chicago, Illinois

John Schlenck, Librarian and Music Director,
Vedanta Society of New York, New York

Bhante Seelawimala, Professor of Theravada Buddhism,
Institute of Buddhist Studies, Berkeley, California

Bruce Smith, Public Affairs, The Church of Jesus Christ
of Latter-day Saints, North York, Ontario

Rabbi David Sulomm Stein, Beit Tikvah Congregation
(Reconstructionist), Baltimore, Maryland

Dr. Suwanda Sugunasiri, President, Buddhist Council of Canada;
Teaching Staff and Research Associate in Buddhist Studies,
Trinity College, University of Toronto

Imam Michael Abdur Rashid Taylor,
Islamic Chaplaincy Services Canada, Bancroft, Ontario

James Taylor, United Church of Canada, co-founder
Wood Lake Books Inc., Okanagan Centre, British Columbia

Dr. David A. Teutsch, President,
Reconstructionist Rabbinical College, Wyncote, Pennsylvania

Juleen Turnage, Secretary of Public Relations,
Assemblies of God, Springfield, Missouri

Jerry Van Marter, Mission Interpreter and International News,
Presbyterian Church (USA), Louisville, Kentucky

Rev. Kenn Ward, editor of *Canada Lutheran*, Winnipeg, Manitoba

Rabbi Tzvi Hersh Weinreb, Shomrei Emunah Congregation
(Orthodox), Baltimore, Maryland

M. Victor Westberg, Manager, Committees on Publications,
The First Church of Christ, Scientist, Boston, Massachusetts

Clifford L. Willis, Director of News and Information,
the Christian Church (Disciples of Christ), Indianapolis, Indiana

# Introduction

We North Americans live in a remarkably fluid society. There is movement between class and race; between the many cultures that form the patchwork known as "American culture"; and between religions, that most personal—and often most deeply embedded—of the institutions that shape us, inform us, inspirit us, enlighten us.

As Americans, we often celebrate the diverse ways we worship God. This pluralism and cross-fertilization, we say, is part of what makes North America special, and it often occurs at the most personal of levels. It is not uncommon, for instance, to be invited to a wedding, a funeral or a religious celebration in the home of a relative or friend of a different faith from one's own. Such exposure to the religious ways of others can give us a deep appreciation for the extraordinary diversity of faith and the variety of ways it surfaces.

Also, as the insightful Catholic writer, Father Andrew M. Greeley, has observed, religion is "a collection of...'pictures'" that we use to give order and meaning to our lives and everything around them. Viewing others' "religious 'pictures'" and noting the contrast between what we see and what we've experienced in our own religious traditions can also deepen and solidify our own faith by making us consider how our tradition speaks to us, comforts us and challenges us.

Yet, we may be uncomfortable or uncertain when we meet "the other" on his or her own turf: What does one do? Or wear? Or say? What should one *avoid* doing, wearing, saying? What will happen during the ceremony? How long will it last? What does each ritual mean? What are the basic beliefs of this particular religion?

Will there be a reception? Will there be food? Will there be grace before we eat? Are gifts expected? When can I leave?

These are just some of the practical questions that arise because of the fundamental foreignness of the experience. *How to Be a Perfect Stranger*

11

addresses these concerns in a straightforward and nonjudgmental manner. Its goal is to make a well-meaning guest feel comfortable, participate to the fullest extent feasible, and avoid violating anyone's religious principles. It is not intended to be a comprehensive primer on theology. It's a guidebook to a land where we may be strangers, but where, on the whole, those on whose celebratory turf we soon will be treading want us to be as comfortable, relaxed and unperturbed as possible.

After all, as the philosopher George Santayana said, "Religion in its humility restores man to his only dignity, the courage to live by grace." And there is nothing more mutually grace-full than to welcome "the stranger"—and for "the stranger" to do his or her homework before entering an unfamiliar house of worship or religious ceremony.

We've all been strangers at one time or another or in one place or another. If this book helps turn the "strange" into the less "exotic" and into the less confusing (but not into the ordinary), then it will have satisfied its goal of minimizing our anxiety and our confusion when face-to-face with another faith—while, at the same time, deepening our appreciation and our understanding of that faith. While we pray and worship in thousands of churches, synagogues, mosques and temples around the country, these denominational fences are not insurmountable. Indeed, these fences come complete with gates. It is often up to us find the key to those gates. We hope that this book helps in the search for that key.

––––––––––––––––––

A few notes on the way in which *How to Be a Perfect Stranger* was compiled and structured:

Each chapter is devoted to a particular religion or denomination; each is organized around that religion's life cycle events, religious calendar and home celebrations.

Basic research was conducted through an extensive questionnaire that was completed in almost all cases by the national office of each religion and denomination. For those denominations whose national office did not respond to the questionnaire, we obtained responses from clergy of that particular faith. To minimize error in nuance, drafts of the entry for each chapter were forwarded for comments to those who had filled out the questionnaire.

*How to Be a Perfect Stranger* is not intended as a substitute for the social common sense that should prevail at social or religious events. For example, if a chapter advises readers that "casual dress" is acceptable at a religious service, this is not to suggest that it is appropriate to show up in Bermuda shorts. Or if a certain denomination allows visitors to use a flash or a video camera, the equipment should not be used in such a way that it disrupts the religious ceremony or disturbs worshippers or other visitors.

The guidelines in this book are just that. They should not be mistaken for firm and unbendable rules. Religious customs, traditions and rituals are strongly influenced by where people live and the part of the world from which their ancestors came to America. As a result, there may be a variety of practices within a single denomination. This book is a general guide to religious practice, and it's important to remember that *particulars* may sometimes vary broadly within individual denominations.

Terms within each chapter are those used by that religion. For example, the terms "New Testament" and "Old Testament" appear in almost every chapter about various Christian denominations. Some Jewish people may find this disconcerting since they recognize only one testament. The purpose is not to offend, but to portray these religions as they portray themselves. The goal of this book, one must remember, is to be "a perfect stranger." And "perfection" might well begin with recognizing that when we join others in celebrating events in their religion's vernacular, we are obliged, as guests, to know the customs, rituals and language of the event.

If the response to this work is positive, we plan to publish subsequent, expanded editions that will include even more religions and denominations. We encourage readers to write to us and suggest ways in which this book could be made more useful to them and to others. Are there additional subjects that future editions should cover? Have important subtleties been missed? We see this book—and the evolution of our unique American society—as an ongoing work-in-progress and welcome your comments. Please write to:

Editors, *How to Be a Perfect Stranger*
SkyLight Paths Publishing
Sunset Farm Offices, Rte. 4
P.O. Box 237
Woodstock, Vermont 05091

# Foreword

The truism that 11:00 on Sunday morning is the most segregated hour in North American life does not refer to race only. For most people, religious practice is an exercise in the familiar. Those of us who participate in congregational worship and observance—and many do in Canada and the United States, the most religiously observant nations in the industrialized West—do so with people who live like us, look like us and pretty much think and believe like us. So while white Americans and Black Americans, for example, do not, as a rule, worship together in large numbers, neither do evangelical and liberal Lutherans, Satmar and Lubavitcher Hasidim, Sunni and Shiite Muslims. Let alone Jews and Presbyterians, or Greek Orthodox and Quakers, or Methodists and Buddhists.

The vitality experienced in these communities is usually enjoyed in isolation: Faith communities in North America often don't have much to do with each other. Many North Americans live in geographic, cultural, economic and social isolation from one another and are ill-prepared to speak honestly across racial, religious and cultural lines. To them, others' ways are strange ways.

Yet, a sense of estrangement is not necessarily a stranger to religious tradition. For example, the earliest writings at the core of the Abrahamic religions—Islam, Christianity and Judaism—use the experience of otherness and isolation from other religious traditions as a pretext to reflect on being strangers in strange lands. Little wonder, then, that many religions exalt the stranger and offer numerous spiritual injunctions about the obligations of hospitality, the right of protection and the general caution, expressed in one form or another, to take care with strangers "lest," as the Christian saint, Paul, wrote in his Letter to the Hebrews (13:2), "we entertain angels unawares."

If the ancient wisdom suggests caution, contemporary circumstances suggest urgency. Indeed, the publication of *How to Be a Perfect Stranger* comes at a time when the airwaves and radio talk shows are dominated by those who would use religious faith as a cover for intolerance, who exploit eternal truths for short-term political gain and who cynically use the spark of faith to ignite culture wars and divide North America into bickering camps.

Having seen how religion can be abused, it is up to us, as citizens, to step out of our isolated communities and into dialogue with those different from ourselves if we are ever to reach the common ground that defines us as citizens, parents, neighbors, and human beings. For shared values can get us past the superficial barriers of language and skin color to catch a glimpse, however fleeting, of the spirit that exists in equal measure in all people. Only around those shared values can we hope to find solutions to many of the problems vexing society as a whole.

For understanding to increase, our differences need not disappear. But they must be understood before we come to know that the values we share are far greater in number and importance than any real or perceived differences. Without that understanding, perception threatens to become reality. Unless we find new ways to talk to each other, we'll be left talking about each other. And we know where that can lead us.

It's time we stopped ignoring the racial, ethnic, cultural and religious fault lines that divide us and our experiences and start finding the way forward for all communities. *How to Be a Perfect Stranger* makes that task seem much more doable and much less daunting. Here, presented in clear, direct prose, is the kind of social, cultural and logistical nuts and bolts you would expect to find in traveller's guides if congregations were your ports of call instead of, say, the island nations of the South Pacific.

*How to Be a Perfect Stranger* is a conscientious labor in the service of intergroup understanding. It expresses as few sermons could fundamental convictions about the value of all creation. It especially conveys truths about those who worship via differing paths than our own. It is a living demonstration of the truth and power of its own central conviction that religious belief can be particular without being intolerant, that it can be fervently held without being divisive, that it can ennoble life with a concern for the common interests of a society reflective of many different traditions.

The editors and researchers of this book have done their work. Now it is time for people of good will to do theirs. *How to Be a Perfect Stranger* shows us the way. For that, we are in its debt.

Sanford Cloud, Jr.

President and CEO,
The National Conference of
Christians and Jews

## Chapter 1 Contents

# Assemblies of God

## I · HISTORY AND BELIEFS

In 1914, when the Assemblies of God was formed, America had, for several years, been in the midst of a major revival movement. Many involved spontaneously spoke "in tongues" (or in a language unknown to those speaking it) and claims were made of divine healing that saved lives. Since many of these experiences were associated with the coming of the Holy Spirit (the empowering quality of God) on the Day of Pentecost, participants in the revival were called Pentecostals.

After mainline churches divorced themselves from the revival phenomenon, about 300 Pentecostal leaders met in Hot Springs, Arkansas. After three days of prayer, they decided to organize themselves not as a new denomination, but as a loose-knit fellowship called the General Council of the Assemblies of God. Two years later, the Council realized the need to establish standards of doctrinal truths.

In part, this Statement of Fundamental Truths asserts that the Bible is divinely inspired and is infallible; the one true God created earth and heaven, redeems humanity from its sins and consists of the Father, the Son (Jesus Christ) and the Holy Spirit; Jesus has always existed and is without beginning or end; humanity was created good and upright, but, by falling into sin, incurred physical and spiritual death; humanity's only hope for salvation from sin and spiritual death is through Christ.

The Assemblies of God is one of the more quickly growing churches in the United States: Since 1960, membership has grown from around 500,000 to more than 1.4 million. The Church is especially keen on using conversion to swell its ranks. In the last decade, the largest number of conversions—61,272—has been in the Church's southwest region (California, Nevada, Arizona and Colorado). Many of these new members are Hispanic-speaking.

**U.S. churches:** 12,000
**U.S. membership:** 1.4 million
*(1998 data from the Assemblies of God)*

**For more information, contact:**

The Assemblies of God
1445 Boonville Ave.
Springfield, MO 65802
(417) 862-2781

Not present in Canada

## II · THE BASIC SERVICE

The Sunday morning service usually begins with singing, Scripture reading or prayer. This is usually followed with hymns, prayer and worship to God, a sermon by the pastor and individuals making either a public commitment to Christ as their Savior or publicly praying for needs and concerns in their lives.

At some point during the service, there will be special prayers for the needs of congregants. Also, the sick may be anointed with oil and prayed for.

Churches observe communion once a month. During this ritual, bread signifying the body of Christ and juice symbolizing his blood are distributed among congregants.

The Assemblies of God encourages various styles of worship: Some congregants may pray silently, some audibly, some may weep openly. Common to most Assemblies of God services is the clapping and raising of hands. This is used as a form of adoration to God. Raised hands during prayer are another expression common to the church and are an outward sign of surrender to God's will.

The service may last about 30 to 60 minutes.

### APPROPRIATE ATTIRE

**Men:** A jacket and tie or more casual attire. No head covering is required.

**Women:** A dress or a skirt and blouse. Clothing need not cover the arms and hems need not reach below the knees (although mini-skirts, shorts and halters are frowned upon). Open-toed shoes and modest jewelry are permissible. No head covering is required.

There are no rules regarding colors of clothing.

## THE SANCTUARY

### What are the major sections of the church?

- *The foyer or lobby:* Where guests and congregants are greeted upon arrival.
- *The main floor:* Where congregants sit.
- *The platform:* Where leaders of the service gather.
- *The pulpit:* Where the service leaders lead prayer or read Scriptures and preach.

## THE SERVICE

### When should guests arrive and where should they sit?

Arrive shortly before the time for which the service has been called. Ushers usually seat guests.

### If arriving late, are there times when a guest should *not* enter the service?

Do not enter during prayers.

### Are there times when a guest should *not* leave the service?

No.

### Who are the major officiants, leaders or participants and what do they do?

- *The pastor,* who leads prayer and delivers a sermon.
- *The minister of music,* who directs the choir and leads the congregation's musical worship.

### What are the major ritual objects of the service?

There are none. Also, most Assemblies of God churches have little, if any, adornment and usually lack statues and stained glass windows. The cross is the most commonly displayed symbol.

### What books are used?

Several translations of the Old and New Testaments are used throughout the Church. Most commonly used is the New International Version of the King James translation of the Bible, which is released by several publishers. The hymnals used also vary from congregation to congregation, although the Church publishes its own hymnal, *Hymns of Glorious Praise* (Springfield, Mo.: Gospel Publishing House, 1991).

### To indicate the order of the service:

A program will be distributed and periodic announcements will be made.

## GUEST BEHAVIOR DURING THE SERVICE

**Will a guest who is not a member of the Assemblies of God be expected to do anything other than sit?**

No. It is entirely optional for guests of other faiths to stand, kneel and sing with congregants and read prayers aloud with them.

**Are there any parts of the service in which a guest who is not a member of the Assemblies of God should *not* participate?**

No.

**If not disruptive to the service, is it okay to:**

◘ **Take pictures?** Possibly.

◘ **Use a flash?** Possibly.

◘ **Use a video camera?** Possibly.

◘ **Use a tape recorder?** Possibly.

(Note: Policies regarding still and video cameras and tape recorders vary with each church. Check with the local pastor before using such equipment during a service.)

**Will contributions to the church be collected at the service?**

Yes.

**How much is customary to contribute?**

If one chooses to give, a contribution between $1 and $5 is appropriate.

## AFTER THE SERVICE

**Is there usually a reception after the service?**

No.

**Is there a traditional form of address for clergy whom a guest may meet?**

Either "Pastor" or "Reverend."

## GENERAL GUIDELINES AND ADVICE

None provided.

## SPECIAL VOCABULARY

**Key words or phrases which might be helpful for a visitor to know:**

◘ *Ordinance:* The Church's term for water baptism and Communion because they were practices ordained or established by Jesus. Many other churches call these practices "sacraments," a term the Assemblies of God rejects because it states that "'sacraments' carries for many people the idea that a spiritual work takes place in a person when the sacrament is received or experienced."

## DOGMA AND IDEOLOGY

**Members of the Assemblies of God believe:**

- Each person may commune directly with God.
- God exists in the Father, the Son (Jesus Christ) and the Holy Spirit (the empowering quality of God).
- As a result of Adam's fall in the Garden of Eden, all people are born in a sinful condition. Children are covered by grace until they reach an age of accountability, but everyone else needs redemption that is provided only through the life, death and resurrection of Jesus. Only by receiving Jesus's forgiveness and accepting Him as Lord can people be forgiven of their sins.
- Divine healing for the sick is provided in Christ's death.
- Baptism endows upon believers:
  1 · The power to witness and serve others.
  2 · A dedication to the work of God.
  3 · A more intense love for Christ.
  4 · Certain spiritual gifts.
- When the Holy Spirit initially fills a believer, that person will speak in an unknown tongue.

**Some pamphlets to which a guest can refer to learn more about the Assemblies of God:**

"The Assemblies of God: The Local Church" and "The Assemblies of God: Our 16 Doctrines." Both are available from the Gospel Publishing House, (800) 641-4310.

# III · HOLY DAYS AND FESTIVALS

- *Christmas*, which always falls on December 25, celebrates the birth of Christ. The traditional greeting is "Merry Christmas."
- *Good Friday*, three days before Easter. Commemorates the crucifixion, death and burial of Jesus.
- *Easter*, which always falls on the Sunday after the full moon that occurs on or after the spring equinox of March 21. Commemorates the death and resurrection of Jesus. The traditional greeting is "Happy Easter."

▣ *Pentecost.* Occurs 50 days after Easter because this is when the Holy Ghost (the spirit of Jesus) descended on His apostles. Celebrates the power of the Holy Spirit and its manifestation in the early Christian church. There is no traditional greeting for this holiday.

## IV · LIFE CYCLE EVENTS

### · Birth Ceremony ·

This ceremony, which is called a Dedication, is based on the biblical account of Jesus calling young children to Him and blessing them. The Church does not believe that the Dedication constitutes salvation, but rather that it lets the child's parents publicly commit themselves to their intentions to raise the child in the teachings of Jesus.

During the Dedication, which is for infants or young children, the pastor asks the parents to pledge to live in such a way that, at an early age, their child will be a Christian. They respond with, "We do." Some pastors also charge the congregation to help the parents by role-modeling Christian living for the child.

The Dedication, which is the same for males and females, usually lasts about three to five minutes. It is part of a larger service (usually a Sunday morning worship service) that lasts from 30 to 60 minutes.

### BEFORE THE CEREMONY

**Are guests usually invited by a formal invitation?**
No. They are usually invited informally and orally by the parents of the newborn.

**If not stated explicitly, should one assume that children are invited?**
Yes.

**If one can't attend, what should one do?**
RSVP orally with regrets.

### APPROPRIATE ATTIRE

**Men:** A jacket and tie or more casual attire. No head covering is required.

**Women:** A dress or a skirt and blouse. Clothing need not cover the arms and hems need not reach below the knees (although mini-skirts, shorts and halters are frowned upon). Open-toed shoes and modest jewelry are permissible. No head covering is required.

There are no rules regarding colors of clothing.

## GIFTS

**Is a gift customarily expected?**
No.

**Should gifts be brought to the ceremony?**
See above.

## THE CEREMONY

**Where will the ceremony take place?**
In the main sanctuary of the church.

**When should guests arrive and where should they sit?**
Arrive shortly before the time for which the service has been called. Ushers will usually seat guests.

**If arriving late, are there times when a guest should *not* enter the ceremony?**
Do not enter during prayers.

**Are there times when a guest should *not* leave the ceremony?**
No.

**Who are the major officiants, leaders or participants at the ceremony and what do they do?**
◪ *The pastor*, who leads the prayer of dedication and makes comments about the infant.

**What books are used?**
None, although the Old and New Testaments are used during the service that includes the Dedication. Most commonly used is the New International Version of the King James translation of the Bible, which is published by several publishers. The hymnals used also vary from congregation to congregation, although the Church publishes its own hymnal, *Hymns of Glorious Praise* (Springfield, Mo.: Gospel Publishing House, 1991).

**To indicate the order of the ceremony:**
A program will be distributed.

**Will a guest who is not a member of the Assemblies of God be expected to do anything other than sit?**
No.

**Are there any parts of the ceremony in which a guest who is not a member of the Assemblies of God should *not* participate?**
No.

**If not disruptive to the ceremony, is it okay to:**
◘ **Take pictures?** Possibly.
◘ **Use a flash?** Possibly.
◘ **Use a video camera?** Possibly.
◘ **Use a tape recorder?** Possibly.

(Note: Policies regarding still and video cameras and tape recorders vary with each church. Check with the local pastor before using such equipment during a service.)

**Will contributions to the church be collected at the ceremony?**
Contributions will be collected as part of the larger service of which the Dedication is just one component.

**How much is customary to contribute?**
If one chooses to give, a contribution between $1 and $5 is appropriate.

### AFTER THE CEREMONY

**Is there usually a reception after the ceremony?**
No.

**Is there a traditional greeting for the family?**
Just offer your congratulations.

**Is there a traditional form of address for clergy whom a guest may meet?**
Either "Pastor" or "Reverend."

## · *Initiation Ceremony* ·

This ceremony, which is the same for males and females, is called a baptism. During it, children who have reached the "age of accountability," which is usually considered to be eight to 10 years of age (although children as young as five or six have been baptized), are fully immersed in the baptismal waters.

Baptism is necessary because all people are born in a sinful condition and it fills one with the purging, cleansing and zeal of the Holy Spirit, the empowering quality of God. Baptism is a public testimony of the death of the individual's sinful nature and of one's new birth in the spirit of Jesus. It endows believers with the power to witness and serve others; a dedication to the work of God; a more intense love for Jesus; and certain spiritual gifts. Baptism, which is performed once for any individual, can occur at any time during one's life.

The baptismal service is usually part of a regular Sunday morning or evening church service. The baptism itself may last about 15 to 30 minutes, depending on the number of persons being baptized.

## BEFORE THE CEREMONY

**Are guests usually invited by a formal invitation?**
They are usually invited informally and orally by the parents of the newborn.

**If not stated explicitly, should one assume that children are invited?**
Yes.

**If one can't attend, what should one do?**
RSVP orally with regrets.

## APPROPRIATE ATTIRE

**Men:** A jacket and tie or more casual attire. No head covering is required.

**Women:** A dress or a skirt and blouse. Clothing need not cover the arms and hems need not reach below the knees (although mini-skirts, shorts and halters are frowned upon). Open-toed shoes and modest jewelry are permissible. No head covering is required.

There are no rules regarding colors of clothing.

## GIFTS

**Is a gift customarily expected?**
No.

**Should gifts be brought to the ceremony?**
See above.

## THE CEREMONY

**Where will the ceremony take place?**
In the main sanctuary of the church.

**When should guests arrive and where should they sit?**
Arrive shortly before the time for which the service has been called. Ushers will usually seat guests.

**If arriving late, are there times when a guest should *not* enter the ceremony?**

Do not enter during prayers.

**Are there times when a guest should *not* leave the ceremony?**

No.

**Who are the major officiants, leaders or participants at the ceremony and what do they do?**

▪ *The pastor*, who performs the baptism.

**What books are used?**

None, although a Bible and hymnal are used during the service which includes the baptism. Several translations of the Old and New Testaments are used throughout the Church. Most commonly used is the New International Version of the King James translation of the Bible, which is released by several publishers. The hymnals used vary from congregation to congregation, although the Church publishes its own hymnal, *Hymns of Glorious Praise* (Springfield, Mo.: Gospel Publishing House, 1991).

**To indicate the order of the ceremony:**

A program will be distributed.

**Will a guest who is not a member of the Assemblies of God be expected to do anything other than sit?**

No.

**Are there any parts of the ceremony in which a guest who is not a member of the Assemblies of God should *not* participate?**

No.

**If not disruptive to the ceremony, is it okay to:**

▪ **Take pictures?** Possibly.
▪ **Use a flash?** Possibly.
▪ **Use a video camera?** Possibly.
▪ **Use a tape recorder?** Possibly.

(Note: Policies regarding still and video cameras and tape recorders vary with each church. Check with the local pastor before using such equipment during a service.)

**Will contributions to the church be collected at the ceremony?**

Contributions will be collected as part of the larger service of which the baptism is just one component.

**How much is customary to contribute?**
If one chooses to give, a contribution between $1 and $5 is appropriate.

## AFTER THE CEREMONY

**Is there usually a reception after the ceremony?**
No.

**Is there a traditional greeting for the family?**
Just offer your congratulations.

**Is there a traditional form of address for clergy whom a guest may meet?**
Either "Pastor" or "Reverend."

## · Marriage Ceremony ·

The Assemblies of God teaches that the family was the first institution ordained by God in the Garden of Eden. The basis for a family is marriage between two consenting adults. Marriage, which is not to be entered into lightly, is said to be "until death do us part."

The marriage ceremony is a ceremony unto itself and may last 30 to 60 minutes.

## BEFORE THE CEREMONY

**Are guests usually invited by a formal invitation?**
Yes.

**If not stated explicitly, should one assume that children are invited?**
No.

**If one can't attend, what should one do?**
RSVP by card or letter with regrets.

## APPROPRIATE ATTIRE

**Men:** A jacket and tie. No head covering is required.

**Women:** A dress. Clothing need not cover the arms and hems need not reach below the knees. Open-toed shoes and modest jewelry are permissible. No head covering is required.

There are no rules regarding colors of clothing.

## GIFTS

**Is a gift customarily expected?**
Yes. Cash or bonds or small household items are most frequently given.

**Should gifts be brought to the ceremony?**
Yes.

## THE CEREMONY

**Where will the ceremony take place?**
In the main sanctuary of the church.

**When should guests arrive and where should they sit?**
Arrive shortly before the time for which the ceremony has been called. Ushers will usually advise guests about where to sit.

**If arriving late, are there times when a guest should *not* enter the ceremony?**
Do not enter during the processional or recessional of the wedding party.

**Are there times when a guest should *not* leave the ceremony?**
No.

**Who are the major officiants, leaders or participants at the ceremony and what do they do?**
◘ *The pastor*, who officiates.

**What books are used?**
Ordinarily, the pastor uses various wedding ceremonies chosen by the bride and groom. These include references to and passages from the Scriptures.

**To indicate the order of the ceremony:**
A program will be distributed.

**Will a guest who is not a member of the Assemblies of God be expected to do anything other than sit?**
Guests of other faiths are expected to stand when other guests rise during the ceremony. It is optional for them to kneel and to sing with the congregants and to join them in reading prayers aloud.

**Are there any parts of the ceremony in which a guest who is not a member of the Assemblies of God should *not* participate?**
No.

**If not disruptive to the ceremony, is it okay to:**
◘ **Take pictures?** Possibly.

◼ **Use a flash?** Possibly.
◼ **Use a video camera?** Possibly.
◼ **Use a tape recorder?** Possibly.

(Note: Policies regarding still and video cameras and tape recorders vary with each church. Check with the local pastor before using such equipment during a service.)

**Will contributions to the church be collected at the ceremony?**
No.

## AFTER THE CEREMONY

**Is there usually a reception after the ceremony?**
Yes. It may be in the same building where the wedding ceremony was held or in a catering hall. Receptions vary from full-course meals to a stand-up reception at which cake, mints, nuts and punch are served. There will be no alcoholic beverages. The reception may last 30 to 60 minutes.

**Would it be considered impolite to neither eat nor drink?**
No.

**Is there a grace or benediction before eating or drinking?**
No.

**Is there a grace or benediction after eating or drinking?**
No.

**Is there a traditional greeting for the family?**
Just offer your congratulations.

**Is there a traditional form of address for clergy who may be at the reception?**
Either "Pastor" or "Reverend."

**Is it okay to leave early?**
Yes, unless it is a formal meal.

## · Funerals and Mourning ·

Members of the Assemblies of God believe that all Christians who have died will one day rise from their graves and meet the Lord in the air. Meanwhile, Christians who are still alive will be raptured (or caught up with those who have risen from their graves) and will also be with the Lord. All who have thus joined with God will live forever.

An Assemblies of God funeral usually begins with singing, Scripture reading or prayer. This is followed with hymns, prayer and worship to God, and a sermon by the pastor.

A ceremony unto itself, the funeral service lasts about 30 to 60 minutes.

### BEFORE THE CEREMONY

**How soon after the death does the funeral usually take place?**
Usually, within two to three days; sometimes, within one week.

**What should someone who is not a member of the Assemblies of God do upon hearing of the death of a member of that faith?**
Telephone or visit the bereaved to offer condolences and sympathies and offer to assist in any way possible.

### APPROPRIATE ATTIRE

**Men:** A jacket and tie. No head covering is required.

**Women:** A dress or a skirt and blouse. Clothing need not cover the arms and hems need not reach below the knees. Open-toed shoes and modest jewelry are permissible. No head covering is required.

Dark, somber colors for clothing are advised.

### GIFTS

**Is it appropriate to send flowers or make a contribution?**
Flowers may be sent to the funeral home or church where the funeral service is held. Contributions may be sent to the home of the bereaved after the funeral.

**Is it appropriate to send food?**
Yes.

### THE CEREMONY

**Where will the ceremony take place?**
Either in a church or a funeral home.

**When should guests arrive and where should they sit?**
Arrive at the time for which the service has been scheduled. Ushers usually advise guests where to sit.

**If arriving late, are there times when a guest should *not* enter the ceremony?**
No.

**Will the bereaved family be present at the church or funeral home before the ceremony?**
Not usually.

**Is there a traditional greeting for the family?**
Just offer your condolences.

**Will there be an open casket?**
Usually.

**Is a guest expected to view the body?**
This is optional.

**What is appropriate behavior upon viewing the body?**
Walk past the casket, then take a seat in the church sanctuary or the room in the funeral parlor where the service will be held.

**Who are the major officiants at the ceremony and what do they do?**
◘ *The pastor*, who delivers a brief sermon and tribute to the deceased.
◘ *Musicians*, who sing one or two songs.

**What books are used?**
The Old and New Testaments. Most commonly used is the New International Version of the King James translation of the Bible, which is released by several publishers.

**To indicate the order of the ceremony:**
A program will be distributed.

**Will a guest who is not a member of the Assemblies of God be expected to do anything other than sit?**
Guests of other faiths are expected to stand when other guests rise during the service. It is optional for them to kneel and to sing with the congregants and to join them in reading prayers aloud.

**Are there any parts of the ceremony in which a guest who is not a member of the Assemblies of God should *not* participate?**
No.

**If not disruptive to the ceremony, is it okay to:**
◘ **Take pictures?** Possibly.
◘ **Use a flash?** Possibly.
◘ **Use a video camera?** Possibly.
◘ **Use a tape recorder?** Possibly.

(Note: Policies regarding still and video cameras and tape recorders vary with each church. Check with the local pastor before using such equipment during a service.)

**Will contributions to the church be collected at the ceremony?**
No.

## THE INTERMENT

**Should guests attend the interment?**
Attendance is optional.

**Whom should one ask for directions?**
An usher or the funeral director.

**What happens at the graveside?**
There are prayers, songs and Scripture readings.

**Do guests who are not members of the Assemblies of God participate at the graveside ceremony?**
No, they are simply present.

## COMFORTING THE BEREAVED

**Is it appropriate to visit the home of the bereaved after the funeral?**
Yes, if one knows the family well.

**Will there be a religious service at the home of the bereaved?**
No.

**Will food be served?**
Possibly.

**How soon after the funeral will a mourner usually return to a normal work schedule?**
A week or two, depending upon individual preference. The Church has no set tradition.

**How soon after the funeral will a mourner usually return to a normal social schedule?**
This is entirely the choice of the bereaved, since the Church has no set tradition. It may be one or two weeks, or more, and is often primarily determined by local cultural traditions.

**Are there mourning customs to which a friend who is not a member of the Assemblies of God should be sensitive?**
No.

**Are there rituals for observing the anniversary of the death?**
No.

## V · HOME CELEBRATIONS

Not applicable to the Assemblies of God.

## Chapter 2 Contents

# 2

# Baptist

## I · HISTORY AND BELIEFS

The Baptist churches descend from the spiritual ferment generated by 17th century English Puritanism. Essentially, Baptists believe in the authority of the Bible, the right to privately interpret it, baptizing only those old enough to profess belief for themselves and strict separation of church and state.

Although there are about two dozen different branches and divisions of Baptist churches in the United States, there are essentially two separate schools of the faith: The General and the Particular. General Baptists believe in a universal atonement in which Christ died for all; Particular Baptists believe in the limited or "particular" death of Christ for believers only.

The movement began in England in the early 17th century. Its founder, John Smyth, moved to Holland in 1607 seeking religious liberty. Some early founders of Massachusetts, including the first president of Harvard, held Baptist beliefs. Although the first Baptist church in the colonies was founded in Providence, Rhode Island, in 1639, Philadelphia became the center of Baptist life during the colonial era.

In 1845, the white Baptist churches had separated into a northern and a southern group, with the northern division opposed to the extension of slavery. After the Civil War, the number of Black churches increased swiftly, mostly because Baptist principles appealed to Blacks and also because the autonomy allowed in individual churches meant that Black Baptist churches could operate without interference from white society. Canadian

Baptists did not suffer from racial disunity but from theological disunity arising out of the Fundamentalist-Modernist controversy of the 1920s.

Today, the two largest Baptist denominations are the Southern Baptist Convention and the National Baptist Convention, U.S.A. Inc. The former has more than 15 million members and its founding in 1845 centered around a missionary impulse. The latter, with about eight million members, is the largest African-American religious association in the United States.

In Canada, three Baptist groups are significant: The Federation Baptists, divided into four conventions; The Fellowship Baptists; and the North American Baptists (German descent).

**U.S. churches:** 91,000
**U.S. membership:** 34 million
*(data from the* 1998 Yearbook of American and Canadian Churches*)*

**For more information, contact:**
The Southern Baptist Convention
901 Commerce St., Suite 750
Nashville TN 37203
(615) 244-2355

The National Baptist Convention, U.S.A., Inc.
1700 World Baptist Center Dr.
Nashville, TN 37207
(615) 228-6292

**Canadian churches:** 3,137
**Canadian membership:** 363,251
*(data from the* 1998 Yearbook of American and Canadian Churches*)*

**For more information, contact:**
Canadian Baptist Federation
7185 Millcreek Drive
Mississauga, ON L5N 5R4
(416) 826-0191

North American Baptists Inc. (Canada)
105 Inglewood Drive
Wetaskiwin, AB T9A 2T3

## I · THE BASIC SERVICE

The sermon is at the heart of the Baptist service. The sermon usually flows from that day's Scriptures' lesson, as do the hymns chosen for that service. The sermon is followed by "the invitation," which asks those present to either become members of the Church or to rededicate themselves to Christ. One or more hymns are sung as congregants or guests come forward to accept "the invitation." The service lasts about one hour.

## APPROPRIATE ATTIRE

**Men:** A suit or sport jacket and tie or more casual attire, depending on the specific church. No head covering is required.

**Women:** A dress or a skirt and blouse. Clothing should cover the arms and hems should reach below the knees. Open-toed shoes and modest jewelry allowed. No head covering is required.

There are no rules regarding colors of clothing.

## THE SANCTUARY

### What are the major sections of the church?

- *The sanctuary:* The part of the church where the altar is located and where ministers lead congregants in prayer. It is usually elevated above the floor level and is invariably at the front of the church.
- *The pulpit or lectern:* The stand at which scriptural lessons and psalm responses are read and the word of God is preached.
- *Seating for congregants:* Seats and sometimes kneeling benches, usually in front and/or to the side of the altar or communion table.
- *Communion table:* The place from which the Lord's Supper is served.
- *Baptistery:* The place for administering baptism.

## THE SERVICE

### When should guests arrive and where should they sit?

Arrive at the time for which the service has been called. Ushers will advise guests and congregants where to sit.

### If arriving late, are there times when a guest should *not* enter the service?

Do not enter while prayers are being recited or while announcements are being made.

### Are there times when a guest should *not* leave the service?

Do not leave during the sermon or during the benediction.

### Who are the major officiants, leaders or participants and what do they do?

- *The pastor,* who presides during the service and preaches.
- *The associate pastor,* who helps the pastor when needed with the service.

▪ *The minister of music*, who leads congregational singing and directs the choir.

▪ *The choir*, which provides music.

▪ *The hostess or usher*, who welcomes visitors and who sometimes makes announcements about church activities.

## What are the major ritual objects of the service?

▪ *Bread and grape juice* (rarely is wine served), which comprise the communion (or the Lord's Supper) and are considered a memorial to the body and blood of Jesus Christ, as well as a reminder of His Second Coming.

▪ *The communion table*, from which the bread and grape juice are offered to congregants. On it may be a crucifix, candles or flowers.

## What books are used?

Several translations of the Bible may be used, especially the King James version, the New International Version and the New Revised Standard Version. All are distributed by several publishers. Most Southern Baptist churches use *The Baptist Hymnal* (Nashville, Tenn.: Convention Press, 1991). Many Canadian Baptist churches use *The Hymnal* (Brantford, ON: Baptist Federation of Canada, 1973).

## To indicate the order of the service:

A program or bulletin will be distributed.

## GUEST BEHAVIOR DURING THE SERVICE

## Will a guest who is not a Baptist be expected to do anything other than sit?

Guests of other faiths are expected to stand, kneel, read prayers aloud and sing with those present, unless this violates their religious beliefs. If one chooses to neither kneel nor stand, remain seated.

## Are there any parts of the service in which a guest who is not a Baptist should *not* participate?

In some churches, communion (or the Lord's Supper) is offered only to members of that congregation.

## If not disruptive to the service, is it okay to:

▪ **Take pictures?** Yes, but only with prior permission of the pastor.

▪ **Use a flash?** Yes, but only with prior permission of the pastor.

▪ **Use a video camera?** Yes, but only with prior permission of the pastor.

▪ **Use a tape recorder?** Yes, but only with prior permission of the pastor.

**Will contributions to the church be collected at the service?**
Yes.

**How much is customary to contribute?**
It is not expected for guests to contribute. If they choose to do so, between
$1 and $5 is appropriate.

## AFTER THE SERVICE

**Is there usually a reception after the service?**
No.

**Is there a traditional form of address for clergy whom a guest
may meet?**
"Pastor" or "Reverend."

**Is it okay to leave early?**
Yes.

## GENERAL GUIDELINES AND ADVICE

None provided.

## SPECIAL VOCABULARY

None provided.

## DOGMA AND IDEOLOGY

**Baptists believe:**
- Jesus Christ is Lord.
- The sacred Scriptures are the sole norm for faith and practice.
- The New Testament church is composed of baptized believers.
- Local congregations are autonomous.
- Religious liberty is guaranteed only by strictly separating church and
  state.

**Some basic books to which a guest can refer to learn more about
the Baptist faith:**

*The Baptist Heritage*, by N. Leon McBeth (Nashville, Tenn.: Broadman Press,
1987).

*The Baptist Way of Life*, by Brooks Hays and John E. Steely (Macon, Ga.:
Mercer University Press, 1993).

## III · HOLY DAYS AND FESTIVALS

▪ *Christmas*, which always falls on December 25, celebrates the birth of Christ. The traditional greeting is "Merry Christmas."

▪ *Easter*, always falls on the Sunday after the full moon that occurs on or after the spring equinox of March 21. Commemorates the death and resurrection of Jesus. The traditional greeting is "Happy Easter."

▪ *Pentecost*. Occurs 50 days after Easter because this is when the Holy Ghost (the spirit of Jesus) descended on His apostles. Celebrates the power of the Holy Spirit and its manifestation in the early Christian church. There is no traditional greeting for this holiday.

▪ *Ash Wednesday*, which occurs 40 days before Easter, commemorates the beginning of Lent, which is a season for preparation and penitence before Easter itself. There is no traditional greeting for this holiday.

▪ *Maundy Thursday*, which falls four days before Easter, commemorates the institution of the Lord's Supper (also known as communion) and Jesus' subsequent arrest and trial. There is no traditional greeting.

▪ *Good Friday*, three days before Easter, commemorates the crucifixion, death and burial of Jesus.

Christmas, Easter and Pentecost are joyful celebrations. Ash Wednesday, Maundy Thursday and Good Friday are somber, penitential commemorations. During the services for these latter three holidays, decorum and discretion are of great importance.

## IV · LIFE CYCLE EVENTS

### · *Birth Ceremony* ·

Baptists practice a child dedication service in which parents present their child and themselves to God in dedication. The congregation is also asked at this time to help the parents nurture their child in the Christian faith. This service usually takes place within the child's first year of life.

### · *Initiation Ceremony* ·

During this ceremony, which is called a baptism, an individual is completely immersed into the baptismal waters. The ceremony represents an active, volitional, public declaration of one's commitment to the Church. One's downward movement in the baptismal waters symbolizes the death of Jesus; the upward movement symbolizes His resurrection.

Baptism occurs at the "age of accountability," which the Church has not defined, but which is assumed to usually occur between the ages of nine to 12 years old. The actual baptism takes about five to ten minutes, although the larger basic service of which it is a part lasts about one hour.

### BEFORE THE CEREMONY

**Are guests usually invited by a formal invitation?**
Guests are usually invited orally, either by telephone or in person.

**If not stated explicitly, should one assume that children are invited?**
Yes.

**If one can't attend, what should one do?**
RSVP with regrets. Gifts are not expected.

### APPROPRIATE ATTIRE

**Men:** A suit or a sport jacket and tie. No head covering is required.

**Women:** A dress. Clothing should cover the arms and hems should reach below the knees. Open-toed shoes and modest jewelry allowed. No head covering is required.

There are no rules regarding colors of clothing.

### GIFTS

**Is a gift customarily expected?**
No.

**Should gifts be brought to the ceremony?**
See above.

### THE CEREMONY

**Where will the ceremony take place?**
In the main sanctuary.

**When should guests arrive and where should they sit?**
Arrive at the time for which the service has been called. Ushers will advise guests and congregants where to sit.

**If arriving late, are there times when a guest should *not* enter the ceremony?**
Do not enter while prayers are being recited or while announcements are being made.

**Are there times when a guest should *not* leave the ceremony?**

Do not leave during the sermon and during the benediction.

**Who are the major officiants, leaders or participants at the ceremony and what do they do?**

◗ *The pastor*, who presides during the service and preaches.

◗ *The associate pastor*, who helps the pastor when needed with the service.

◗ *The minister of music*, who leads congregational singing and directs the choir.

◗ *The choir*, which provides music.

◗ *The hostess or usher*, who welcomes visitors and who sometimes makes announcements about church activities.

**What books are used?**

Several translations of the Bible may be used, especially the King James version, the New International Version, and the New Revised Standard Version. All are distributed by several publishers. Most Southern Baptist churches use *The Baptist Hymnal* (Nashville, Tenn.: Convention Press, 1991). Many Canadian Baptist churches use *The Hymnal* (Brantford, ON: Baptist Federation of Canada, 1973).

**To indicate the order of the ceremony:**

A program or bulletin may be distributed.

**Will a guest who is not a Baptist be expected to do anything other than sit?**

Guests of other faiths are expected to stand, kneel, read prayers aloud and sing with those present, unless this violates their religious beliefs. If one chooses to neither kneel nor stand, remain seated.

**Are there any parts of the ceremony in which a guest who is not a Baptist should *not* participate?**

In some churches, communion (or the Lord's Supper) is offered only to members of that congregation.

**If not disruptive to the ceremony, is it okay to:**

◗ **Take pictures?** Yes, but only with prior permission of the pastor.

◗ **Use a flash?** Yes, but only with prior permission of the pastor.

◗ **Use a video camera?** Yes, but only with prior permission of the pastor.

◗ **Use a tape recorder?** Yes, but only with prior permission of the pastor.

**Will contributions to the church be collected at the ceremony?**

Yes.

**How much is customary to contribute?**
It is not expected for guests to contribute. If they choose to do so, between $1 and $5 is appropriate.

### AFTER THE CEREMONY

**Is there usually a reception after the ceremony?**
There may possibly be a reception. If so, it is usually held in the fellowship hall of the church or at the home of the individual who has been baptized. Light food, such as punch, cookies or cake, may be served. The reception may last up to two hours.

**Would it be considered impolite to neither eat nor drink?**
No.

**Is there a grace or benediction before eating or drinking?**
Yes.

**Is there a grace or benediction after eating or drinking?**
No.

**Is there a traditional greeting for the family?**
Just offer your congratulations.

**Is there a traditional form of address for clergy who may be at the reception?**
"Pastor" or "Reverend."

**Is it okay to leave early?**
Yes.

## · *Marriage Ceremony* ·

Marriage is considered to be a three-way covenant between a woman, a man and God, Who is represented at the marriage ceremony by the pastor, the congregation and the Holy Spirit (the empowering spirit of God). The ceremony takes about 30 to 60 minutes and is a ceremony unto itself.

### BEFORE THE CEREMONY

**Are guests usually invited by a formal invitation?**
Yes.

**If not stated explicitly, should one assume that children are invited?**
No.

**If one can't attend, what should one do?**
RSVP with regrets and send a gift.

## APPROPRIATE ATTIRE

**Men:** A suit or a jacket and tie. No head covering is required.

**Women:** A dress. Clothing should cover the arms and hems should reach below the knees. Open-toed shoes and modest jewelry allowed. No head covering is required.

There are no rules regarding colors of clothing.

## GIFTS

**Is a gift customarily expected?**
Yes. Often appropriate are such household items as sheets, kitchenware or small household appliances.

**Should gifts be brought to the ceremony?**
Send gifts to the home of the newlyweds.

## THE CEREMONY

**Where will the ceremony take place?**
Either in a church or a home.

**When should guests arrive and where should they sit?**
Arrive about 10 minutes before the time for which the ceremony has been called. Ushers will advise guests where to sit.

**If arriving late, are there times when a guest should *not* enter the ceremony?**
Do not enter during the procession or recession of the wedding party.

**Are there times when a guest should *not* leave the ceremony?**
Do not leave before the ceremony has ended.

**Who are the major officiants, leaders or participants at the ceremony and what do they do?**
▪ *The pastor*, who performs the ceremony.
▪ *The bride and groom.*
▪ *Musicians*, who provide music before, during and after the ceremony.

**What books are used?**
Only the pastor uses a text, which is invariably the Bible. Several translations of the Bible may be used, especially the King James version, the New

International Version and the New Revised Standard Version. All are distributed by several publishers. Many Canadian Baptist churches use *The Hymnal* (Brantford, ON: Baptist Federation of Canada, 1973).

**To indicate the order of the ceremony:**
No such guidance is needed for those present since the ceremony is relatively brief and there is no participation by guests.

**Will a guest who is not a Baptist be expected to do anything other than sit?**
No.

**Are there any parts of the ceremony in which a guest who is not a Baptist should *not* participate?**
No.

**If not disruptive to the ceremony, is it okay to:**
- **Take pictures?** Yes, but only with prior permission of the pastor.
- **Use a flash?** Yes, but only with prior permission of the pastor.
- **Use a video camera?** Yes, but only with prior permission of the pastor.
- **Use a tape recorder?** Yes, but only with prior permission of the pastor.

**Will contributions to the church be collected at the ceremony?**
No.

## AFTER THE CEREMONY

**Is there usually a reception after the ceremony?**
Yes. It may be held at the church where the ceremony is conducted or in a home or a catering hall. Depending on the choice of the couple and of the bride's family, a full-course meal may be served. Alcoholic beverages are rarely served. There may be music and dancing. The reception may last more than two hours.

**Would it be considered impolite to neither eat nor drink?**
Yes.

**Is there a grace or benediction before eating or drinking?**
Possibly.

**Is there a grace or benediction after eating or drinking?**
Possibly. If guests arrive and start eating at different times, grace may be said after the meal.

**Is there a traditional greeting for the family?**
Offer your congratulations when you meet the family in the reception line after the service.

**Is there a traditional form of address for clergy who may be at the reception?**
"Pastor" or "Reverend."

**Is it okay to leave early?**
Yes.

## · Funerals and Mourning ·

There are two schools of belief in the Baptist faith about afterlife. One maintains that one enters Paradise immediately after death. This is based on Jesus' words on the cross to the Penitent Thief, "This day shalt be with Me in Paradise" (Luke 23:43). The other school maintains that upon Jesus's Second Coming, a trumpet will sound and the dead will be raised to Paradise. This is based on Paul's writings in First Corinthians (15:32). The funeral service, which is a ceremony unto itself, lasts about 30 to 60 minutes.

### BEFORE THE CEREMONY

**How soon after the death does the funeral usually take place?**
Within one week.

**What should a non-Baptist do upon hearing of the death of a member of that faith?**
Telephone or visit the bereaved to offer condolences and sympathies.

### APPROPRIATE ATTIRE

**Men:** A suit or a sport jacket and tie. No head covering is required.

**Women:** A dress. Clothing should cover the arms and hems should reach below the knees. Open-toed shoes and modest jewelry allowed. No head covering is required.

Dark, somber colors are advised.

### GIFTS

**Is it appropriate to send flowers or make a contribution?**
Flowers may be sent to the home of the bereaved before the funeral or to the church or funeral home where the funeral will take place. Contribu-

tions to a particular charity may be sent to the home of the bereaved before or after the funeral. The amount of the contribution is at the discretion of the donor. Such gifts should be presented to the spouse or adult children of the deceased.

### Is it appropriate to send food?
Food may be sent to the home of the bereaved after the funeral.

## THE CEREMONY

### Where will the ceremony take place?
Either in a church or a funeral home.

### When should guests arrive and where should they sit?
Arrive about 10 minutes before the time for which the ceremony has been called. Ushers will advise guests where to sit.

### If arriving late, are there times when a guest should *not* enter the ceremony?
Do not enter when the bereaved family is entering or during prayers.

### Will the bereaved family be present at the church or funeral home before the ceremony?
No.

### Is there a traditional greeting for the family?
No. Just offer your condolences.

### Will there be an open casket?
Usually.

### Is a guest expected to view the body?
This is optional.

### What is appropriate behavior upon viewing the body?
Join the line of viewers and view the body silently and somberly.

### Who are the major officiants at the ceremony and what do they do?
◗ *The pastor*, who performs the service.
◗ *Musicians*, who provide music before, during and after the service.

### What books are used?
Several translations of the Bible may be used, especially the King James version, the New International Version, and the New Revised Standard Version. All are distributed by several publishers.

**To indicate the order of the ceremony:**

A program or bulletin will be distributed.

**Will a guest who is not a Baptist be expected to do anything other than sit?**

Guests of other faiths are expected to stand, kneel, read prayers aloud and sing with those present, unless this violates their religious beliefs. If one chooses not to kneel or stand, remain seated.

**Are there any parts of the ceremony in which a guest who is not a Baptist should *not* participate?**

No, although, very rarely, communion (or the Lord's Supper) is offered at funeral ceremonies. In some churches, communion is offered only to members of that congregation. In such cases, follow the cues of those present, ask a fellow guest for guidance or ask a pastor for advice before the service begins.

**If not disruptive to the ceremony, is it okay to:**

◙ **Take pictures?** No.

◙ **Use a flash?** No.

◙ **Use a video camera?** No.

◙ **Use a tape recorder?** No.

**Will contributions to the church be collected at the ceremony?**

No.

### THE INTERMENT

**Should guests attend the interment?**

Yes.

**Whom should one ask for directions?**

Either ask the funeral director or follow the funeral procession to the cemetery.

**What happens at the graveside?**

During a brief service, Scriptures are read, prayers are recited and the casket is committed to the ground.

**Do guests who are not Baptists participate at the graveside ceremony?**

No. They are simply present.

## COMFORTING THE BEREAVED

**Is it appropriate to visit the home of the bereaved after the funeral?**

Yes. It is appropriate to do so after the burial. During such visits, happy times during the life of the deceased are recalled and spoken about. A visit of no more than 30 minutes is fitting.

**Will there be a religious service at the home of the bereaved?**

No.

**Will food be served?**

Yes, but no alcoholic beverages. It would be considered impolite for a visitor not to eat. No grace or benediction will be recited before or after eating or drinking.

**How soon after the funeral will a mourner usually return to a normal work schedule?**

Possibly in one week, although there are no doctrinal prescriptions.

**How soon after the funeral will a mourner usually return to a normal social schedule?**

Possibly two months, although there are no doctrinal prescriptions.

**Are there mourning customs to which a friend who is not a Baptist should be sensitive?**

No.

**Are there rituals for observing the anniversary of the death?**

There is usually no formal remembrance in a church, but there are often quiet commemorations of the death within the family of the deceased.

## V · HOME CELEBRATIONS

Not applicable to Baptists.

## Chapter 3 Contents

# 3
# Buddhist

## 1. HISTORY AND BELIEFS

Buddhism was founded in the sixth century B.C. in northern India by Siddhartha Gautama, who was born as the son to a king in what is now southern Nepal. Warned by a sage that his son would become either an ascetic or a universal monarch, the king confined his son to home. A few years after marrying and having a child of his own, Siddhartha escaped from his father's palace around the age of 29. Since he had been sheltered for his entire life from the pains of life, he was shocked when he beheld three men. The first was old and weak; the second was ill and diseased; the last was dead. Each represented different aspects of the impermanence inherent in all forms of earthly existence. He also saw a religious ascetic, who represented the possibility of a solution to these frailties.

Wandering in search of peace, Siddhartha tried many disciplines, including severe asceticism, until he came to the Bodhi Tree (the Tree of Enlightenment). He sat there in meditation until, at the age of 35, he became a Buddha, or one who is enlightened.

In his first sermon after achieving enlightenment, the Buddha spoke of the Four Noble Truths and the Noble Eightfold Path. These succinctly comprise the Buddha's insights into the essential ways of life and how to achieve spiritual liberation. The Buddha died at the age of 80. His last words were for his disciples not to depend on him, but on the *dharma*, or Buddhist teachings.

In subsequent centuries, Buddhism flowered in Asia. Asian immigrants to the United States from the early third of the 19th century to the present have brought Buddhism to America. The first significant influence of

Buddhist values and ideas on American intellectuals seems to have occurred in the 1830s in the writings of the New England transcendentalists. More recently, Buddhism has appealed to members of the "beat" culture of the 1950s, the "counterculture" of the 1960s and the subsequent New Age movement.

In Canada, Buddhism may have arrived as early as the middle of the 19th century when the Chinese arrived, first from California and then from Hong Kong. World Buddhism (i.e., the many cultural Buddhisms from all over the world) began to impact on Canada only after the Canadian multiculturalism policy of the late 1960s. The three major Buddhist centers are Toronto, Vancouver and Montreal.

**U. S. temples:** Not available.
**U.S. membership:** 500,000
*(data from the* 1993 Information Please Almanac*)*

**For more information, contact:**
Buddhist Churches of America
1710 Octavia Street
San Francisco, CA 94109
(415) 776-5600

**Canadian temples:** Not available.
**Canadian membership:** 165,000+
*(data from* Stats Can, *1991)*

**For more information, contact:**
Buddhist Council of Canada
3 Ardmore Road
Toronto, ON  M5P 1V4
(416) 487-2777

## II · THE BASIC SERVICE

There are many varieties of Buddhist congregational gatherings. Some are almost entirely devoted to silent meditation; others bear some resemblance to western worship services, with a sermon by a priest, monk or nun, and announcements by the president or lay leader of the Buddhist temple. Elements most common to Buddhist congregational gatherings are chanting, an incense offering, silent meditation and a sermon or talk by a priest or monk.

The gathering may last one to two hours.

## APPROPRIATE ATTIRE

**Men:** Standards for attire vary widely. A minority of temples expect men to wear a jacket and tie; the vast majority allow much more casual dress. Loose, comfortable, casual clothing is especially recommended for those temples in which members and guests sit on meditation cushions on the floor. (Guests are advised to call the temple prior to the service for details on seating.) No head covering is required in any Buddhist temple.

**Women:** A minority of temples expect a dress or a skirt and blouse. The vast majority allow more casual attire. Loose, comfortable, casual clothing is especially recommended for those temples in which members and guests sit on meditation cushions on the floor. (Guests are advised to call the temple prior to the service for details on seating.) Open-toed shoes and modest jewelry are permissible. No head covering is required in any Buddhist temple.

There are no rules regarding colors of clothing.

## THE SANCTUARY

### What are the major sections of the temple?

The architecture of Buddhist temples varies widely. These elements will be found in many, but not all, temples:

- *The altar:* Contains a statue of the main Buddha for that particular temple. This is at the front of the sanctuary. (Each temple is devoted to one of the hundreds of buddhas in Buddhism.)
- *Side altars:* Contain statues or pictures of the founder of the particular lineage adhered to by a temple. A lineage is a line of teachers and their students who, in turn, also become teachers.
- *Pews or meditation cushions:* Where congregants sit. Some temples have pews; others have pillows on the floor.

## THE SERVICE

### When should guests arrive and where should they sit?

It is customary to arrive early. Where one sits depends on the particular tradition of that temple. If there is a seated meditation, a visitor will probably be directed to a meditation cushion.

### If arriving late, are there times when a guest should *not* enter the service?

Do not enter during meditation.

**Are there times when a guest should *not* leave the service?**

Do not leave during meditation.

**Who are the major officiants, leaders or participants and what do they do?**

◾ *A minister or priest, monk or nun,* who leads the service, including chanting.

◾ *The temple president,* a lay person who may lead the service in some temples in lieu of a monk or priest.

**What are the major ritual objects of the service?**

◾ *An incense burner,* which is usually at the front of the altar and contains an offering of incense. The incense is offered to Buddha and is lit by a priest or monk.

◾ *An ouzo* ("oo-ZOH") *or a mala* ("MAH-lah"), a rosary which is used to count recitations of a mantra, a verbal expression to keep the Buddha in one's mind or to sharpen concentration. The rosary is used by priests and/or monks and by congregants.

◾ *A bell,* used by priests or monks to announce the beginning or end of meditation.

**What books are used?**

All Buddhist traditions and sects quote from the Sutras, which are the collected sayings of the Buddha.

**To indicate the order of the service:**

Periodic announcements may be made by the temple president or instructions may be given by the priest or monk.

## GUEST BEHAVIOR DURING THE SERVICE

**Will a guest who is not a Buddhist be expected to do anything other than sit?**

It is entirely optional for a guest from another faith to chant with the congregation or stand when congregants do so.

**Are there any parts of the service in which a guest who is not a Buddhist should *not* participate?**

No.

**If not disruptive to the service, is it okay to:**

◾ **Take pictures?** Only with prior approval of a priest or monk.

◾ **Use a flash?** Only with prior approval of a priest or monk.

◾ **Use a video camera?** Only with prior approval of a priest or monk.

◾ **Use a tape recorder?** Only with prior approval of a priest or monk.

**Will contributions to the temple be collected at the service?**
Possibly. In some temples, there may be an offertory box near the front door of the temple.

**How much is customary to contribute?**
From $1 to $5.

## AFTER THE SERVICE

**Is there usually a reception after the service?**
There may be a reception in the temple's reception area at which light food may be served. There is usually no alcohol. The reception may last 60 minutes. It is not considered impolite to neither eat nor drink. Some temples have a form of grace before or after eating or drinking.

**Is there a traditional form of address for clergy who may be at the reception?**
Depending on the particular Buddhist denomination, the form of address may be "Reverend," "Lama" or "Roshi."

**Is it okay to leave early?**
Yes.

## GENERAL GUIDELINES AND ADVICE

It is fine not to participate in rituals or meditations if one is uncomfortable about them. Guests who do not participate should sit quietly and still.

A typical mistake that guests should avoid is talking during the service.

## SPECIAL VOCABULARY

**Key words or phrases which might be helpful for a visitor to know:**
- *Gassho* ("GASH-oh"): To place one's hands together in reverence.
- *Osenko* ("oh-SEN-koh"): To burn incense in offering to Buddha.

## DOGMA AND IDEOLOGY

**Buddhists believe:**
- The Four Noble Truths, originally enunciated by the Buddha, comprise the essence of Buddhist teaching and practice:
  1 · All life (birth, aging, death) is suffering.
  2 · Suffering is caused by craving or desire.

3 · Cessation of suffering is possible.

4 · The Noble Eightfold Path can lead to the extinction of suffering.

◪ The Noble Eightfold Path consists of:

1 · Right understanding of the nature of reality.

2 · Right thought, which is free from sensuous desire, ill-will and cruelty.

3 · Right speech, which should be absent of falsehoods, harsh words and useless chatter.

4 · Right action, which includes refraining from killing, stealing and wrong conduct in matters of bodily pleasure, intoxicants and gambling.

5 · Right livelihood, which forbids any conduct contrary to right speech and right action and any trickery or fraud in the service of commerce or one's trade.

6 · Right effort, which seeks to avoid generating new, unwholesome actions and encourages purifying the mind (by avoiding and overcoming unwholesome states of mind, while developing and maintaining wholesome states).

7 · Right mindfulness, or meditative practices that encourage greater alertness and awareness of one's self.

8 · Right concentration, or striving for mental "one-pointedness." Right effort and right mindfulness together develop right concentration—and vice versa.

**A basic book to which a guest can refer to learn more about Buddhism:**

*How the Swans Came to the Lake*, by Rick Fields (Boston: Shambhala Books, 1992).

## III · HOLY DAYS AND FESTIVALS

The three events listed below are celebrated by all Buddhist traditions, but not on the same dates. The examples given below represent the Japanese tradition.

◪ *Nirvana Day*, or *Nehan E* in Japanese. Observed on February 15, which commemorates the death of the Buddha. The Sanskrit word, *nirvana* ("neer-VAH-nah"), means "a blowing out as of a flame," or the extinction of worldly illusions and passions. The doctrine of *nirvana* is closely associated with the condition of *samsara* ("SAHM-sahr-ah"), or recurrent birth-and-death, from which one is finally liberated. *Nirvana* and *samsara* are the themes of the service for Nirvana Day. There is no traditional greeting for this holiday, but guests should be aware that, instead of shaking hands, traditional Buddhists place their palms together in front of their chest and bow slightly when greeting each other.

- *Hanamatsuri Day,* or Buddha Day. Observed on April 8 to celebrate the birth of the Buddha. There is no traditional greeting for this holiday, but guests should be aware that, instead of shaking hands, traditional Buddhists place their palms together in front of their chest and bow slightly when greeting each other.
- *Bodhi Day.* Observed on December 8 as the day on which Siddhartha Gautama vowed to meditate under the Bodhi Tree until attaining enlightenment. There is no traditional greeting for this holiday, but guests should be aware that, instead of shaking hands, traditional Buddhists place their palms together in front of their chest and bow slightly when greeting each other.

## IV · LIFE CYCLE EVENTS

### · Birth Ceremony ·

Not applicable to Buddhism.

### · Initiation Ceremony ·

In certain Japanese Buddhist sects, there is a lay initiation into the faith known as Jukai. It is also a name-giving ceremony. It can occur at any age and is the same for males and females. This is a fairly brief ceremony and is usually part of a larger congregational gathering.

#### BEFORE THE CEREMONY

**Are guests usually invited by a formal invitation?**
Yes.

**If not stated explicitly, should one assume that children are invited?**
No.

**If one can't attend, what should one do?**
RSVP with regrets and send flowers.

#### APPROPRIATE ATTIRE

**Men:** Standards for attire vary widely. A minority of temples expect men to wear a jacket and tie; the vast majority allow much more casual dress. Loose, comfortable, casual clothing is especially recommended for those temples in which members and guests sit on meditation cushions on the floor. (Guests are advised to call the temple prior to the service for details on seating.) No head covering is required in any Buddhist temple.

**Women:** A minority of temples expect a dress or a skirt and blouse. The vast majority allow more casual attire. Loose, comfortable, casual clothing is especially recommended for those temples in which members and guests sit on meditation cushions on the floor. (Guests are advised to call the temple prior to the service for details on seating.) Open-toed shoes and modest jewelry are permissible. No head covering is required in any Buddhist temple.

There are no rules regarding colors of clothing.

## GIFTS

**Is a gift customarily expected?**
No.

**Should gifts be brought to the ceremony?**
See above.

## THE CEREMONY

**Where will the ceremony take place?**
Either in the main sanctuary of the temple or a special area elsewhere in the temple.

**When should guests arrive and where should they sit?**
It is customary to arrive early. Where one sits depends on the particular tradition of that temple. If there is a seated meditation, a visitor will probably be directed to a meditation cushion.

**If arriving late, are there times when a guest should *not* enter the ceremony?**
Do not enter during meditation.

**Are there times when a guest should *not* leave the ceremony?**
Do not leave during meditation.

**Who are the major officiants, leaders or participants at the ceremony and what do they do?**
▪ *The minister or priest*, who leads the service, including chanting.

■ *The temple president,* a lay person who may lead the service in lieu of the minister or priest in some temples.

## What books are used?

All Buddhist traditions and sects quote from the Sutras, which are the collected sayings of the Buddha.

## To indicate the order of the ceremony:

Periodic announcements are usually be made by the temple president or instructions may be given by a priest or monk.

## Will a guest who is not a Buddhist be expected to do anything other than sit?

No. It is entirely optional for a guest from another faith to chant with the congregation or stand when congregants do so.

## Are there any parts of the ceremony in which a guest who is not a Buddhist should *not* participate?

No.

## If not disruptive to the ceremony, is it okay to:

■ **Take pictures?** Only with prior approval of the priest or monk.

■ **Use a flash?** Only with prior approval of the priest or monk.

■ **Use a video camera?** Only with prior approval of the priest or monk.

■ **Use a tape recorder?** Only with prior approval of the priest or monk.

## Will contributions to the temple be collected at the ceremony?

Yes. There is usually an offertory box near the front door of the temple.

## How much is customary to contribute?

From $1 to $5.

### AFTER THE CEREMONY

## Is there usually a reception after the ceremony?

There may be a reception in the temple's reception area at which light food may be served. There is usually no alcohol. The reception may last 60 to 90 minutes.

## Would it be considered impolite to neither eat nor drink?

No.

## Is there a grace or benediction before eating or drinking?

Some temples have a form of grace before eating or drinking.

**Is there a grace or benediction after eating or drinking?**
Some temples have a form of grace after eating or drinking.

**Is there a traditional greeting for the family?**
Just offer your congratulations.

**Is there a traditional form of address for clergy who may be at the reception?**
Depending on the particular Buddhist denomination, the form of address may be "Reverend," "Lama" ("LAH-mah") or "Roshi" ("ROH-shee").

**Is it okay to leave early?**
Yes.

## · *Marriage Ceremony* ·

There is no standard Buddhist marriage ceremony in the United States or Canada. In some cases, the ceremony may be modeled after a standard Protestant wedding service. Regardless of the structure of the ceremony, the overall purpose is to remind those present of the essential Buddhist principle of non-harmfulness to all sentient beings.

The ceremony may last from 15 to 30 minutes.

### BEFORE THE CEREMONY

**Are guests usually invited by a formal invitation?**
Guests will be invited orally, either in person or on the telephone, or through a written invitation.

**If not stated explicitly, should one assume that children are invited?**
The broad variables of Buddhist practice make this impossible to answer. Ask the couple or family members.

**If one can't attend, what should one do?**
RSVP with regrets. Ordinarily, no present is expected.

### APPROPRIATE ATTIRE

**Men:** Standards for attire vary widely. A minority of temples expect men to wear a jacket and tie; the vast majority allow much more casual dress. Loose, comfortable, casual clothing is especially recommended for those temples in which members and guests sit on meditation cushions on the floor. (Guests are advised to call the temple prior to the service for details on seating.) No head covering is required in any Buddhist temple.

**Women:** A minority of temples expect a dress or a skirt and blouse. The vast majority allow more casual attire. Loose, comfortable, casual clothing is especially recommended for those temples in which members and guests sit on meditation cushions on the floor. (Guests are advised to call the temple prior to the service for details on seating.) Open-toed shoes and modest jewelry are permissible. No head covering is required in any Buddhist temple.

There are no rules regarding colors of clothing.

## GIFTS

### Is a gift customarily expected?

No.

### Should gifts be brought to the ceremony?

See above.

## THE CEREMONY

### Where will the ceremony take place?

Either in a temple or outdoors.

### When should guests arrive and where should they sit?

It is customary to arrive early. Where one sits depends on the particular tradition of that temple. Guests should be aware that a temple may have meditation cushions on the floor and not pews in which to sit.

### If arriving late, are there times when a guest should *not* enter the ceremony?

Do not enter during meditation.

### Are there times when a guest should *not* leave the ceremony?

No.

### Who are the major officiants, leaders or participants at the ceremony and what do they do?

◘ *A minister or priest,* who officiates.
◘ *The bride and groom.*

### What books are used?

There are no standard texts for Buddhist wedding ceremonies, although any readings will usually refer to kindness and compassion.

### To indicate the order of the ceremony:

Since the ceremony is fairly brief and only the priest or monk does any recitations, there is little need to indicate the order of the event.

**Will a guest who is not a Buddhist be expected to do anything other than sit?**

Perhaps only to stand when others do.

**Are there any parts of the ceremony in which a guest who is not a Buddhist should *not* participate?**

No.

**If not disruptive to the ceremony, is it okay to:**

◘ **Take pictures?** Only with prior approval of a priest or monk.

◘ **Use a flash?** Only with prior approval of a priest or monk.

◘ **Use a video camera?** Only with prior approval of a priest or monk.

◘ **Use a tape recorder?** Only with prior approval of a priest or monk.

**Will contributions to the temple be collected at the ceremony?**

No.

## AFTER THE CEREMONY

**Is there usually a reception after the ceremony?**

There may be a reception in the temple's reception area or at another site chosen by the newlyweds. Light food may be served, but not meat. There is usually no alcohol. The reception may last 60 minutes.

**Would it be considered impolite to neither eat nor drink?**

No.

**Is there a grace or benediction before eating or drinking?**

Possibly, depending on the particular Buddhist denomination and sect.

**Is there a grace or benediction after eating or drinking?**

Possibly, depending on the particular Buddhist denomination and sect.

**Is there a traditional greeting for the family?**

Just offer your congratulations.

**Is there a traditional form of address for clergy who may be at the reception?**

Depending on the particular Buddhist denomination, the form of address may be "Reverend," "Lama" or "Roshi."

**Is it okay to leave early?**

Yes.

## · Funerals and Mourning ·

According to Buddhist belief, each individual passes through many rein-carnations until they are liberated from worldly illusions and passions. They have then entered *nirvana*, Sanskrit for "a blowing out as of a flame." One enters a new incarnation immediately after death. Although the resulting being is not fully realized for nine months, a new incarnation can be interpreted as entering the womb of a woman.

Three components of any Buddhist funeral ceremony are sharing; the practice of good conduct; and developing a calm mind, or meditation.

A funeral ceremony in several Japanese Buddhist traditions resembles a Christian ceremony in the west, with a eulogy and prayers at a funeral home. It may last one hour and 15 minutes. Cambodian, Thai and Cey-lonese traditions may have up to three ceremonies, each lasting about 45 minutes. (See below for details on these ceremonies.)

### BEFORE THE CEREMONY

**How soon after the death does the funeral usually take place?**

This varies, depending on the specific Buddhist tradition of the bereaved. In certain Japanese traditions, the funeral is usually within one week. In the Buddhist traditions of Cambodia, Ceylon and Thailand, there are three ceremonies. In the first, which is held within two days after death, monks hold a ceremony at the home of the bereaved. In the second, which is held within two to five days after death, monks conduct a service at a funeral home. In the third, which is held seven days after the burial or crema-tion, monks lead a ceremony either at the home of the bereaved or at a temple. This last ceremony, called a "merit transference," seeks to generate good energy for the deceased in his or her new incarnation.

**What should a non-Buddhist do upon hearing of the death of a member of that faith?**

It is usually not considered appropriate to communicate with the bereaved before the funeral.

### APPROPRIATE ATTIRE

**Men:** Standards for attire vary widely. A minority of temples expect men to wear a jacket and tie; the vast majority allow more casual dress. Loose, comfortable, casual clothing is especially recommended for those temples in which members and guests sit on meditation cushions on the floor. (Guests are advised to call the temple prior to the service for details on seating.)

No head covering is required in any Buddhist temple.

**Women:** A minority of temples expect a dress or a skirt and blouse. The vast majority allow more casual attire. Loose, comfortable, casual clothing is especially recommended for those temples in which members and guests sit on meditation cushions on the floor. (Guests are advised to call the temple prior to the service for details on seating.) Open-toed shoes and modest jewelry are permissible. No head covering is required in any Buddhist temple.

In Japanese Buddhist traditions, dark, somber colors for clothing are advised. In Cambodian, Thai or Ceylonese traditions, white colors are advised.

## GIFTS

**Is it appropriate to send flowers or make a contribution?**
It is appropriate to send flowers to the funeral or to make a donation of $5 to $100, depending on one's relation to the deceased. Typically, the bereaved family recommends a specific charity or cause as the recipient of donations.

**Is it appropriate to send food?**
No.

## THE CEREMONY

**Where will the ceremony take place?**
In certain Japanese traditions, the ceremony is usually held at a funeral home. In Cambodian, Thai and Ceylonese traditions, the first ceremony is at the home of the bereaved, the second is at a funeral home and the third is either at the home of the bereaved or at a temple.

**When should guests arrive and where should they sit?**
Arrive at the time for which the service has been called. Sit wherever you wish. If the ceremony is in a funeral home, there will be pews for sitting. If held at the home or the temple of an adherent of the Cambodian, Thai or Ceylonese traditions, sitting will probably be on the floor on meditation cushions.

**If arriving late, are there times when a guest should *not* enter the ceremony?**
No.

**Will the bereaved family be present at the temple or funeral home before the ceremony?**
Yes.

**Is there a traditional greeting for the family?**
Just offer your condolences.

**Will there be an open casket?**
Always.

**Is a guest expected to view the body?**
Yes, because Buddhism deems viewing the body to be a valuable reminder of the impermanence of life.

**What is appropriate behavior upon viewing the body?**
Bow slightly toward the body as a sign of appreciation of its lesson regarding impermanence.

**Who are the major officiants at the ceremony and what do they do?**
- *A minister or priest,* who officiates in the Japanese tradition.
- *A monk,* who officiates in the Cambodian, Thai and Ceylonese traditions.

**What books are used?**
All Buddhist traditions and sects quote from the Sutras, which are the collected sayings of the Buddha.

**To indicate the order of the ceremony:**
Announcements may be made by the priest or monk.

**Will a guest who is not a Buddhist be expected to do anything other than sit?**
Stand when others do so.

**Are there any parts of the ceremony in which a guest who is not a Buddhist should *not* participate?**
No.

**If not disruptive to the ceremony, is it okay to:**
- **Take pictures?** No.
- **Use a flash?** No.
- **Use a video camera?** No.
- **Use a tape recorder?** No.

**Will contributions to the temple be collected at the ceremony?**
No.

## THE INTERMENT

**Should guests attend the interment or cremation?**
If so desired.

**Whom should one ask for directions?**
The funeral director or a monk or priest.

**What happens at the graveside?**
Prayers are recited and the body is committed to the ground.

**Do guests who are not Buddhists participate at the graveside ceremony?**
No.

## COMFORTING THE BEREAVED

**Is it appropriate to visit the home of the bereaved after the funeral?**
Yes.

**Will there be a religious service at the home of the bereaved?**
In Cambodian, Thai and Ceylonese traditions, monks lead a "merit transference" ceremony seven days after the burial or cremation. The purpose is to generate good energy for the deceased in his or her new incarnation.

**Will food be served?**
Yes.

**How soon after the funeral will a mourner usually return to a normal work schedule?**
This totally depends on the individual mourner. There are no religious prescriptions regarding refraining from work.

**How soon after the funeral will a mourner usually return to a normal social schedule?**
Usually not until three months after the death.

**Are there mourning customs to which a friend who is not a Buddhist should be sensitive?**
No.

**Are there rituals for observing the anniversary of the death?**
Japanese, Cambodian, Thai and Ceylonese traditions have a memorial service 90 days after the death. A year after the death, all four traditions have "merit transference" ceremonies, whose purpose is to generate good

energy for the deceased in his or her new incarnation. These may be held either at the home of the bereaved or at a temple. Food will be served, since sharing is an integral part of all Buddhist ceremonies.

## V · HOME CELEBRATIONS

Not applicable to Buddhism.

# Chapter 4 Contents

# 4

# The Christian Church
# (Disciples of Christ)

## I · HISTORY AND BELIEFS

Reacting against the sectarianism common among religions on the American frontier of the early 1800s, the founders of the Christian Church urged a union of all Christians. Two independently developing groups, the "Disciples" and the "Christians," formally united in 1832.

They advocated adult baptism by immersion, weekly observance of the Lord's Supper (more commonly known as communion) and autonomy of local congregations.

The Canadian church traces its heritage to this new American group and to a similar movement within the Scotch Baptist movement in Britain.

One joins the Church after simply declaring his or her faith in Jesus and being baptized by immersion. The highly ecumenical Church was among the founders of the National and the World Councils of Churches. Its secular-oriented programs focus on such issues as helping the mentally retarded, aiding war victims, bolstering farms and improving cities and education.

The Church is highly democratic. Local congregations own their own property and control their budgets and programs. Each congregation votes in the General Assembly that meets every two years.

**U.S. churches:** 3,840
**U.S. membership:** 910,000
*(data from the* 1998 Yearbook of American and Canadian Churches*)*

---

**For more information, contact:**
The Christian Church (Disciples of Christ)
130 East Washington St.
P.O. Box 1986
Indianapolis, IN 46206-1986
(317) 635-3100
cmiller@oc.disciples.org
www.disciples.org

**Canadian churches:** 34
**Canadian membership:** 3,286
*(data from the* 1998 Yearbook of American and Canadian Churches*)*

---

**For more information, contact:**
The Christian Church (Disciples of Christ) in Canada
Box 68048—40 Midlake Boulevard SE
Calgary, AB
(403) 254-8413

## II · THE BASIC SERVICE

The basic worship service is a relatively simple formal liturgy that emphasizes the preaching of God's word and celebration of the Lord's Supper. (The ritual commemorating the Supper is known as Holy Communion). The service includes hymns, psalms, responsive readings, Bible readings, a sermon and, always, the communion liturgy.

Disciples of Christ believe that the Lord's Supper is a celebration and a thanksgiving to God and an affirmation of Christ's spiritual presence.

The service usually lasts less than one hour.

### APPROPRIATE ATTIRE

**Men:** Jacket and tie or slacks and a sport shirt. Attire varies from congregation to congregation. No head covering is required.

**Women:** A dress, skirt and blouse or pants suit are acceptable. Open-toed shoes and modest jewelry are fine. Neither a head covering nor hems below the knees are required.

There are no rules regarding colors of clothing.

## THE SANCTUARY

**What are the major sections of the church?**

◼ *The nave:* Where congregants sit.

◼ *The choir loft:* Where the choir sits.

◼ *The chancel:* Includes the altar and pulpit and seating for clergy. The pastor conducts the worship from this area.

## THE SERVICE

**When should guests arrive and where should they sit?**

It is generally appropriate to arrive a few minutes early to be seated since services typically begin at the hour called. Usually, ushers will help you find a seat.

**If arriving late, are there times when a guest should *not* enter the service?**

Do not enter during spoken or silent prayers. Entry during songs is advised.

**Are there times when a guest should *not* leave the service?**

Do not leave during the message (or sermon), the Scripture reading, prayer and communion.

**Who are the major officiants, leaders or participants and what do they do?**

◼ *The pastor,* who preaches, oversees others who participate in the service and administers the sacraments.

◼ *Elders,* who in some congregations will preside at the table. Their role varies from simply giving a prayer or meditation to the actual administering of the sacraments.

◼ *Liturgists or readers, and assisting ministers,* who assist with prayers and read the scripture lessons.

◼ *An acolyte,* who lights candles, assists with communion and other tasks. This is usually a youth of elementary school age.

◼ *The choir,* which leads the singing.

◼ *Ushers and greeters,* who welcome and seat guests and distribute books.

◼ *The music leader,* who plays the organ, directs the choir and leads singing.

**What are the major ritual objects of the service?**

◼ *The altar,* which symbolizes the presence of God.

◼ *The pulpit,* behind which the pastor stands while preaching.

◼ *The lectern,* where scripture is read.

▪ *The baptismal font,* which is used for baptizing. This is usually near the front of the church.

▪ *A crucifix,* a cross which may have a representation of the body of Jesus Christ on it. This may be on the altar or incorporated in a church's interior design.

▪ *A communion table,* the site from which the Lord's Supper (communion) is served.

### What books are used?

The New Revised Standard Version of the Bible (New York: National Council of Churches' Division of Christian Education, 1989) and *The Chalice Hymnal* (St. Louis, Mo.: Chalice Press, 1995).

### To indicate the order of the service:

Ushers will distribute a program.

## GUEST BEHAVIOR DURING THE SERVICE

### Will a guest who is not a Disciple of Christ be expected to do anything other than sit?

The level of participation depends on whether or not the guest is Christian. Christians will generally be expected to stand and sing with congregants and read prayers aloud. Non-Christians are expected to stand with congregants and are invited to sing and pray with them.

### Are there any parts of the service in which a guest who is not a Disciple of Christ should *not* participate?

No, unless these parts violate or compromise their own religious beliefs. In most, although not all, congregations, it is permissible for visitors to take communion. However, in a minority of congregations this would not be allowed. If possible, check the local practice beforehand.

### If not disruptive to the service, is it okay to:

▪ **Take pictures?** Yes.
▪ **Use a flash?** Yes.
▪ **Use a video camera?** Yes.
▪ **Use a tape recorder?** Yes.

### Will contributions to the church be collected at the service?

Generally, ushers pass an offering plate or basket among the seated congregants. It is the guest's choice whether or not to contribute.

### How much is customary to contribute?

A donation (by cash or check) of $1 to $5 is appropriate.

## AFTER THE SERVICE

**Is there usually a reception after the service?**

Usually, there is a 30- to 60-minute reception in the church's reception area. Light food will be served, but not alcoholic beverages. It is not considered impolite to neither eat nor drink. There is no grace or benediction before or after eating or drinking.

**Is there a traditional form of address for clergy who may be at the reception?**

"Pastor" or "Reverend."

**Is it okay to leave early?**

Yes.

## GENERAL GUIDELINES AND ADVICE

Generally, model your behavior and your movements on that of the other worshippers and follow the instructions of the leaders of the service.

## SPECIAL VOCABULARY

**Key words or phrases which might be helpful for a visitor to know:**

- *Holy Communion:* A rite through which Disciples believe they receive Christ's body and blood as assurance that God has forgiven their sins.
- *Lessons:* Readings from the Bible (or "Scripture"), including the Old Testament (the Hebrew scriptures, written before the birth of Jesus), the Epistle (generally from one of the letters of St. Paul or another New Testament writer) and the Gospel (a reading from Matthew, Mark, Luke or John, the "biographers" of Jesus).

## DOGMA AND IDEOLOGY

**Disciples of Christ believe:**

- Communion is shared weekly and all Christians are welcome to participate in its offering. Disciples believe that Christ is the Host of the table and invite all Christians, regardless of their denomination, to take part. Communion unites Disciples with other Christians.
- Worship is led by lay leaders in conjunction with ordained clergy. Unlike certain other Christian denominations, no confession, or statement that Jesus is the Christ, is required for membership.
- The Law of God, as found, for example, in the Ten Commandments, tells what God expects of us and how we are to live. The Law also shows us

that we fall short of God's expectations and that we are disobedient to God.

◪ The Gospel is the good news of how God remains faithful to His justice, love and mercy, and does not want to see any of us punished or separated from Him because of our sin. The good news (which is what "Gospel" means) is that the eternal Son of God, who is Himself fully God, became a man in the person of Jesus of Nazareth, lived a life of perfect obedience that we cannot live, and suffered God's own punishment for our sin so we don't have to. Instead, we are freely forgiven through Jesus Christ and given eternal life with God as a free gift.

◪ Individuals are encouraged to interpret scripture in light of science, reason, faith and tradition.

## Some basic books to which a guest can refer to learn more about the Disciples of Christ:

*Thankful Praise*, edited by Keith Watkins (St. Louis, Mo.: Chalice Press, 1987).

*Handbook for Today's Disciples* by D. Duane Cummins (St. Louis, Mo.: Chalice Press, 1991).

## III · HOLY DAYS AND FESTIVALS

◪ *Advent*. Occurs four weeks before Christmas. The purpose is to begin preparing for Christmas and to focus on Christ. There is no traditional greeting among church members for this holiday.

◪ *Christmas*. Occurs on the evening of December 24 and the day of December 25. Marks the birth and the incarnation of God as a man. The traditional greeting is "Merry Christmas."

◪ *Lent*. Begins on Ash Wednesday, which occurs six weeks before Easter. The purpose is to prepare for Easter. There is no traditional greeting among church members for this holiday.

Between Lent and Easter, abstention from entertainment and increased giving to the poor is encouraged. Often, there are midweek worship services. Some church members fast, although it not mandated by the Church. Those who fast may choose to abstain from certain foods or from certain meals.

◪ *Easter*. Always falls on the Sunday after the first full moon that occurs on or after March 21. Celebrates the Resurrection of Jesus Christ. The traditional greeting to Disciples of Christ is "Happy Easter!"

◪ *Pentecost Sunday*. The seventh Sunday after Easter. Celebrates the coming of the Holy Spirit, which is the empowering spirit of God in human life. This is often considered the birth of the Christian church. There is no traditional greeting among church members for this holiday.

## IV · LIFE CYCLE EVENTS

### · Birth Ceremony ·

The "blessing and dedication service" acknowledges an infant's presence in the Christian community, and seals a covenant between its parents, sponsors and congregation to guide the child.

The service is part of a larger morning worship service. The entire service usually lasts about one hour.

### BEFORE THE CEREMONY

**Are guests usually invited by a formal invitation?**
They are usually invited by a note or phone call.

**If not stated explicitly, should one assume that children are invited?**
Yes.

**If one can't attend, what should one do?**
RSVP with regrets, either by phone or by sending a note to the parents.

### APPROPRIATE ATTIRE

**Men:** Jacket and tie. No head covering is required.

**Women:** A dress, skirt and blouse, or pants suit are acceptable. Open-toed shoes and modest jewelry are fine. Neither a head covering nor hems below the knees are required.

There are no rules regarding colors of clothing.

### GIFTS

**Is a gift customarily expected?**
While this is entirely optional, such gifts as cash or bonds or baby toys or clothing are certainly appreciated.

**Should gifts be brought to the ceremony?**
No. Bring them to the reception afterward.

## THE CEREMONY

### Where will the ceremony take place?

Just below the chancel area in the main sanctuary of the parents' church. The chancel includes the altar and pulpit and seating for clergy.

### When should guests arrive and where should they sit?

It is generally appropriate to arrive a few minutes early to be seated since services typically begin at the hour called. Usually, ushers will be available to assist you in finding a seat.

### If arriving late, are there times when a guest should *not* enter the ceremony?

Do not enter during prayers.

### Are there times when a guest should *not* leave the ceremony?

Do not leave during the message (or sermon), the scripture reading, prayer and communion.

### Who are the major officiants, leaders or participants at the ceremony and what do they do?

- *The pastor*, who presides.
- *The child's parents.*
- *The child's godparents.*

### What books are used?

The New Revised Standard Version of the Bible (New York: National Council of Churches' Division of Christian Education, 1989) and *The Chalice Hymnal* (St. Louis, Mo.: Chalice Press, 1995).

### To indicate the order of the ceremony:

Ushers will distribute a program.

### Will a guest who is not a Disciple of Christ be expected to do anything other than sit?

The level of participation depends on whether or not the guest is Christian. Christians will generally be expected to stand and sing with congregants and read prayers aloud. Non-Christians are expected to stand with congregants and are invited to sing and pray with them.

### Are there any parts of the ceremony in which a guest who is not a Disciple of Christ should *not* participate?

No, unless they violate or compromise their own religious beliefs.

### If not disruptive to the ceremony, is it okay to:

- **Take pictures?** Yes.

◾ **Use a flash?** Yes.
◾ **Use a video camera?** Yes.
◾ **Use a tape recorder?** Yes.

**Will contributions to the church be collected at the ceremony?**
Generally, ushers pass an offering plate or basket among the seated congregants. It is the guest's choice whether or not to contribute.

**How much is customary to contribute?**
A donation (by cash or check) of $1 to $5 is appropriate.

### AFTER THE CEREMONY

**Is there usually a reception after the ceremony?**
Yes, usually in the church's reception area. This may last about 30 to 60 minutes. Light food is ordinarily served, but not alcoholic beverages.

**Would it be considered impolite to neither eat nor drink?**
No.

**Is there a grace or benediction before eating or drinking?**
No.

**Is there a grace or benediction after eating or drinking?**
No.

**Is there a traditional greeting for the family?**
No. Just offer your congratulations.

**Is there a traditional form of address for clergy who may be at the reception?**
"Pastor" or "Reverend."

**Is it okay to leave early?**
Yes.

## · Initiation Ceremony ·

Baptism by immersion is done for pre- or early adolescents, for adults or for children with parental consent. The sacrament is a symbolic participation in Christ's death, burial and resurrection and also a purifying remission of sin. It is largely based upon Jesus saying in the Gospel of John (3:5) that one can enter the Kingdom of God only if he is "born of water and the Spirit."

For Disciples of Christ, baptism may be done either individually or with one's Sunday School classmates.

## BEFORE THE CEREMONY

**Are guests usually invited by a formal invitation?**
Guests are usually invited by a note or phone call.

**If not stated explicitly, should one assume that children are invited?**
Yes.

**If one can't attend, what should one do?**
Telephone the parents and the adolescent. Offer your congratulations.

## APPROPRIATE ATTIRE

**Men:** Jacket and tie. No head covering is required.

**Women:** A dress, skirt and blouse, or pants suit are acceptable. Open-toed shoes and modest jewelry are fine. Neither a head covering nor hems below the knees are required.

There are no rules regarding color of clothing.

## GIFTS

**Is a gift customarily expected?**
This is entirely optional. Usual gifts are a Bible, a bookmark or something equally modest and fitting to the occasion.

**Should gifts be brought to the ceremony?**
They are usually brought to the reception afterward.

## THE CEREMONY

**Where will the ceremony take place?**
At the baptismal font near the chancel in the main sanctuary of the church. The chancel includes the altar and pulpit and seating for clergy.

**When should guests arrive and where should they sit?**
It is generally appropriate to arrive a few minutes early to be seated since services typically begin at the hour called. Usually, ushers will be available to assist you in finding a seat.

**If arriving late, are there times when a guest should *not* enter the ceremony?**
Do not enter during spoken or silent prayers. Entry during songs is advised.

**Are there times when a guest should *not* leave the ceremony?**
Do not leave during the message (or sermon), the scripture reading, prayer and communion.

**Who are the major officiants, leaders or participants at the ceremony and what do they do?**
◘ *The pastor and/or the elder*, who presides.
◘ The candidate for baptism.

**What books are used?**
The New Revised Standard Version of the Bible (New York: National Council of Churches' Division of Christian Education, 1989) and *The Chalice Hymnal* (St. Louis, Mo.: Chalice Press, 1995).

**To indicate the order of the ceremony:**
Ushers will distribute a program.

**Will a guest who is not a Disciple of Christ be expected to do anything other than sit?**
The level of participation depends on whether or not the guest is Christian. Christians will generally be expected to stand and sing with congregants and read prayers aloud. Non-Christians are expected to stand with congregants and are invited to sing and pray with them.

**Are there any parts of the ceremony in which a guest who is not a Disciple of Christ should *not* participate?**
No, unless they violate or compromise their own religious beliefs.

**If not disruptive to the ceremony, is it okay to:**
◘ **Take pictures?** Yes.
◘ **Use a flash?** Yes.
◘ **Use a video camera?** Yes.
◘ **Use a tape recorder?** Yes.

**Will contributions to the church be collected at the ceremony?**
Generally, ushers pass an offering plate or basket among the seated congregants. It is the guest's choice whether or not to contribute.

**How much is customary to contribute?**
A donation (by cash or check) of $1 to $5 is appropriate.

## AFTER THE CEREMONY

**Is there usually a reception after the ceremony?**
Usually, a 30- to 60-minute reception is held in the church's reception area. Light food is served, but not alcoholic beverages.

**Would it be considered impolite to neither eat or drink?**
No.

**Is there a grace or benediction before eating or drinking?**
No.

**Is there a grace or benediction after eating or drinking?**
No.

**Is there a traditional greeting for the family?**
No. Just offer your congratulations.

**Is there a traditional form of address for clergy who may be at the reception?**
"Pastor" or "Reverend."

**Is it okay to leave early?**
Yes.

## · *Marriage Ceremony* ·

A church wedding is an act of worship in which the couple profess their love for and their commitment to each other before God and ask His blessing on their marriage. The same decorum exercised in any worship service should be exercised in the wedding service.

The ceremony is a ceremony unto itself. In it, the wedding party progresses in, then the pastor reads appropriate lessons from the Bible and asks the bride and groom about their commitment to one another. The pastor delivers a brief homily, wedding vows and rings are exchanged, and the couple are pronounced husband and wife.

The ceremony lasts between 15 and 30 minutes.

### BEFORE THE CEREMONY

**Are guests usually invited by a formal invitation?**
Yes.

**If not stated explicitly, should one assume that children are invited?**
Yes.

**If one can't attend, what should one do?**
RSVP and send a gift.

## APPROPRIATE ATTIRE

**Men:** Jacket and tie. No head covering is required.

**Women:** A dress, skirt and blouse, or pants suit are acceptable. Open-toed shoes and modest jewelry are fine. Neither a head covering nor hems below the knees are required.

There are no rules regarding colors of clothing.

## GIFTS

### Is a gift customarily expected?

Yes, ordinarily cash or items for the household such as small appliances, dishes, towels or blankets.

### Should gifts be brought to the ceremony?

Either bring a gift to the ceremony and place it on the gift table or send it to the home of the newlyweds.

## THE CEREMONY

### Where will the ceremony take place?

In the main sanctuary of the House of Worship. The wedding party will stand near the altar in the chancel, the area in front of the sanctuary that includes the altar and pulpit and seating for clergy.

### When should guests arrive and where should they sit?

It is appropriate to arrive before the time called for the ceremony. An usher will advise you where to sit.

### If arriving late, are there times when a guest should *not* enter the ceremony?

Do not enter during the processional, recessional or during prayer.

### Are there times when a guest should *not* leave the ceremony?

Do not leave during the processional, recessional or during prayer.

### Who are the major officiants, leaders or participants at the ceremony and what do they do?

◘ *The pastor*, who presides.

### What books are used?

The New Revised Standard Version of the Bible (New York: National Council of Churches' Division of Christian Education, 1989) and the worship book with wedding liturgy.

**To indicate the order of the ceremony:**
Ushers will distribute a program.

**Will a guest who is not a Disciple of Christ be expected to do anything other than sit?**
The level of participation depends on whether or not the guest is Christian. Christians will generally be expected to stand and sing with congregants and read prayers aloud. Non-Christians are expected to stand with congregants and are invited to sing and pray with them.

**Are there parts of the ceremony in which a guest who is not a Disciple of Christ should *not* participate?**
No, unless they violate or compromise their own religious beliefs.

**If not disruptive to the ceremony, is it okay to:**
◖ **Take pictures?** Yes.
◖ **Use a flash?** Yes.
◖ **Use a video camera?** Yes.
◖ **Use a tape recorder?** Yes.

**Will contributions to the church be collected at the ceremony?**
No.

### AFTER THE CEREMONY

**Is there usually a reception after the ceremony?**
Yes. It may be at the church, at home or in a catering hall. It may last between one to two hours. Food will be served. Alcoholic beverages may be served if the reception is not held at the church. There will probably be music and dancing.

**Would it be considered impolite to neither eat nor drink?**
No. If you have dietary restrictions, inform your host or hostess in advance.

**Is there a grace or benediction before eating or drinking?**
Guests should wait for the saying of grace before eating.

**Is there a grace or benediction after eating or drinking?**
No.

**Is there a traditional greeting for the family?**
Congratulate the new couple and their parents.

**Is there a traditional form of address for clergy who may be at the reception?**
"Pastor" or "Reverend."

**Is it okay to leave early?**
Yes.

## · *Funerals and Mourning* ·

For Disciples of Christ, death is not the end of life, but the beginning of new life. While Disciples will grieve, they do not mourn as do those who have no hope of ever seeing the deceased again or who are without the sure hope that those who die in faith in Jesus Christ are assured eternal life with God.

The funeral is a service unto itself. A pastor presides. Pall bearers carry or push the casket on rollers into the funeral home or church sanctuary.

The service will last between 15 and 30 minutes. All attending are expected to remain to the end.

### BEFORE THE CEREMONY

**How soon after the death does the funeral usually take place?**
Within one week.

**What should someone who is not a Disciple of Christ do upon hearing of the death of a member of that faith?**
Call the bereaved or visit or send a note to express your sympathy at their loss. Express your concern for them.

### APPROPRIATE ATTIRE

**Men:** Jacket and tie. No head covering is required.

**Women:** A dress or skirt and blouse are acceptable. Open-toed shoes and modest jewelry are fine. No head covering is required.

Dark, somber colors are recommended.

### GIFTS

**Is it appropriate to send flowers or make a contribution?**
It is appropriate to send flowers unless the family expresses otherwise. Send them to the deceased's home or to the funeral home where the funeral will be held.

It is also appropriate to make a donation in memory of the deceased. The family will often announce, either through the funeral home or a classified ad in a local newspaper, the preferred cause or charity for memorial contributions.

There is no standard amount to be donated.

**Is it appropriate to send food?**
You may want to send food to the home of the bereaved for the family and their guests.

## THE CEREMONY

**Where will the ceremony take place?**
Either in the church of the deceased or a funeral home.

**When should guests arrive and where should they sit?**
It is customary to arrive early enough to be seated when the service begins. Someone will tell you where and when to sit.

**If arriving late, are there times when a guest should *not* enter the ceremony?**
Do not enter during the procession or during prayer.

**Will the bereaved family be present at the church or funeral home before the ceremony?**
There is often a visitation at the funeral home the night before the service.

**Is there a traditional greeting for the family?**
Express your sorrow and regrets.

**Will there be an open casket?**
Usually.

**Is a guest expected to view the body?**
This is entirely optional.

**What is appropriate behavior upon viewing the body?**
Stand quietly near the casket, view the body and extend your condolences to the family.

**Who are the major officiants at the ceremony and what do they do?**
◙ *The pastor*, who presides.

**What books are used?**
The New Standard Revised Version of the Bible (New York: National Council of Churches' Division of Christian Education, 1989).

**To indicate the order of the ceremony:**
A program will be distributed.

**Will a guest who is not a Disciple of Christ be expected to do anything other than sit?**

The level of participation depends on whether or not the guest is Christian. Christians will generally be expected to stand and sing with congregants and read prayers aloud. Non-Christians are expected to stand with congregants and are invited to sing and pray with them.

**Are there are any parts of the service in which a guest who is not a Disciple of Christ should *not* participate?**

No, unless these parts violate or compromise their own religious beliefs.

**If not disruptive to the ceremony, it is okay to:**
- **Take pictures?** No.
- **Use a flash?** No.
- **Use a video camera?** No.
- **Use a tape recorder?** No.

**Will contributions to the church be collected at the ceremony?**
No.

## THE INTERMENT

**Should guests attend the interment?**
This is optional. If one decides to do so, join the funeral procession.

**Whom should one ask for directions?**
The funeral director.

**What happens at the graveside?**
The casket is carried to the grave. Prayers and readings are offered. The pastor blesses the earth placed on the casket.

**Do guests who are not Disciples of Christ participate at the graveside service?**
No, they are simply present.

## COMFORTING THE BEREAVED

**Is it appropriate to visit the home of the bereaved after the funeral?**
Yes. More than once is appropriate. The length of the visit depends on one's judgment and sensitivities.

**Will there be a religious service at the home of the bereaved?**
No.

**Will food be served?**

Yes. Wait for grace to be said before eating. It would not be considered impolite not to eat.

**How soon after the funeral will a mourner usually return to a normal work schedule?**

Within three days to a week.

**How soon after the funeral will a mourner usually return to a normal social schedule?**

Within three days to a week.

**Are there mourning customs to which a friend who is not a Disciple of Christ should be sensitive?**

No.

**Are there rituals for observing the anniversary of the death?**

No.

## V · HOME CELEBRATIONS

Not applicable to Disciples of Christ.

# Chapter 5 Contents

# 5
# Christian Science
# (Church of Christ, Scientist)

## I · HISTORY AND BELIEFS

Christian Science was founded in 1879 by Mary Baker Eddy, who was healed of a serious injury in 1866 while reading an account in the New Testament of Jesus' healings. Thirteen years later, she established the Church of Christ, Scientist, in Boston. Mrs. Eddy died in 1910.

The church consists of The Mother Church—the First Church of Christ, Scientist—in Boston and approximately 2,400 branch churches in about 63 countries around the world.

Christian Science theology holds that God created man in His image and likeness. Christian Scientists also believe that God is good and that His creation is all that is real and eternal. This belief is based on the first chapter of Genesis, which states: "So God created man in His own image, in the image of God created He him; male and female created He them....And God saw everything that He had made, and, behold, it was good."

Therefore, Christian Scientists believe that sin, disease and death do not originate in God. Rather, they are considered to be distortions of the human mind.

The church is grounded in the teachings of the King James Bible and relies on spiritual means for healing. According to the church, its spiritual healing "is not popular faith healing or human mind cure. It is not self-hypnosis, mere positive thinking, autosuggestion, or spontaneous remission. Nor is it to be confused with Scientology or New Age thinking....

"Christian Scientists find the Christian healing they experience is the reinstatement of the healing method practiced by Jesus 2,000 years ago.

It is based on understanding the laws of God revealed in the Bible, and conforming to them. These laws are available for all mankind to practice and, thereby, obtain full salvation from sickness as well as sin.

"Christian Science healing involves more than healing sick bodies. It heals broken hearts and minds as well as broken homes, and is directly applicable to all of society's ills."

**U.S. churches:** 2,400
**U.S. membership:** Not available
*(data from the* 1998 Yearbook of American and Canadian Churches*)*

**For more information, contact:**
The First Church of Christ, Scientist
Committee on Publications Office
175 Huntington Avenue
Boston, MA 01945
(617) 450-3301

**Canadian churches:** 94
**Canadian membership:** Not available
No Canadian contact address available.

## II · THE BASIC SERVICE

Christian Science's basic religious service is held on Sunday morning in a Christian Science church. The 60-minute service includes congregational singing, silent and audible prayer, and reading a Lesson-Sermon consisting of passages from the King James Version of the Bible and *Science and Health with Key to the Scriptures,* written by the founder of Christian Science, Mary Baker Eddy.

Communion is held twice a year: On the second Sunday in January and the second Sunday in July, when the congregation kneels for a moment of silent prayer followed by the audible repetition of the Lord's Prayer. No bread or wine is given.

Each church holds a Wednesday evening testimony meeting, in which the First Reader chooses a subject, prepares readings from the King James Bible and Mary Baker Eddy's *Science and Health*, and selects the hymns. The meeting also includes spontaneous sharing of testimonies of healing and remarks on Christian Science by individuals in the congregation.

The public is welcome to Sunday and Wednesday services.

### APPROPRIATE ATTIRE

**Men:** Jacket and tie are not expected. Casual attire is acceptable. No head covering is required.

**Women:** A skirt or blouse, a pants suit or slightly more casual attire are recommended. Arms do not have to be covered by clothing nor do hems need to reach below the knees. Modest jewelry and open-toed shoes are permissible. No head covering is required.

There are no rules regarding colors of clothing.

## THE SANCTUARY

### What are the major sections of the church?

A Christian Science church has no altar. The service is conducted from a platform that has no ritual significance.

## THE SERVICE

### When should guests arrive and where should they sit?

People are welcome whenever they arrive. Usually, an usher will greet latecomers at the door and seat them. If not, guests should sit wherever they wish.

### If arriving late, are there times when a guest should *not* enter the service?

No.

### Are there times when a guest should *not* leave the service?

No.

### Who are the major officiants, leaders or participants and what do they do?

The "pastor" in a Christian Science church is the King James version of the Bible and *Science and Health with Key to the Scriptures* by Mary Baker Eddy. Other than that, there are two primary participants in the service:

- *The First Reader*, elected for a term of one to three years by congregants. He or she conducts the service. Reads mainly from *Science and Health* on Sunday and equally from the King James Bible and *Science and Health* on Wednesday.
- *The Second Reader*, elected by members to read from the Bible at the Sunday Service. He or she shares the platform with the First Reader and presides over the service in the absence of the First Reader.

### What are the major ritual objects of the service?

Simplicity is the mark of a Christian Science service. There are no ritual objects—and few rituals.

### What books are used?

The King James version of the Bible, *Science and Health with Key to the Scrip-*

*tures,* the Christian Science Quarterly and the Christian Science Hymnal.

**To indicate the order of service:**

Refer to the second page of the Christian Science Quarterly, which is provided by ushers. The First Reader may gives cues to the service by saying "Let us sing" or "Let us pray."

## GUEST BEHAVIOR DURING THE SERVICE

**Will a guest who is not a Christian Scientist be expected to do anything other than sit?**

No. The following behavior is optional: Standing, kneeling or singing with the congregation; saying or repeating "The Lord's Prayer," which is the only prayer said orally; contributing to collections; and giving testimony at Wednesday services.

**Are there any parts of the service in which a guest who is not a Christian Scientist should *not* participate?**

No.

**If not disruptive to the service, is it okay to:**
◙ **Take pictures?** Only with permission of an usher.
◙ **Use a flash?** Only with permission of an usher.
◙ **Use a video camera?** Only with permission of an usher.
◙ **Use a tape recorder?** Only with permission of an usher.

**Will contributions to the church be collected at the service?**

Only on Sundays. Collection is taken by ushers after the Lesson-Sermon is read. No one is required to contribute.

**How much is customary to contribute?**

Whatever congregants and guests wish to give. Usually $1 to $5.

## AFTER THE SERVICE

**Is there usually a reception after the service?**

No.

**Is there a traditional form of address for clergy whom a guest might meet?**

No. Christian Science has no clergy.

## GENERAL GUIDELINES AND ADVICE

The congregation stands only while singing hymns. At the end of the third hymn, congregants remain standing while the First Reader reads the "Scientific Statement of Being," passages from I John, and the benediction. After the "Amen," worshippers may leave.

After the second hymn at the Wednesday testimony meeting, worshippers are invited to give testimonies of healing, or just expressions of gratitude to God and Christian Science. Guests are not expected to do this, but may if they wish.

## SPECIAL VOCABULARY

**Key words or phrases which might be helpful for a visitor to know:**

◾ *Mind, Spirit, Soul, Principle, Life, Truth, Love:* When capitalized, these are interchangeable names for God.

◾ *Prayer:* Desire for good; a total turning to and trusting in God; searching to understand the relationship between humans and God.

◾ *Healing:* A realization of God's goodness and the perfection of humanity; regeneration of thought reflected on the body.

◾ *Error:* Mary Baker Eddy's word for "evil"; the opposite of God and good; defined in *Science and Health* as something that "seemeth to be and is not."

◾ *Mortal Mind:* Another name for error or evil; the belief in a mind or life separate from God.

◾ *Matter:* That which appears "real" to the five senses.

◾ *Mortal:* A concept of each person as born and dying. The opposite of the "real" person.

## DOGMA AND IDEOLOGY

**This summary of Christian Science's religious tenets appears in** *Science and Health***:**

1 · As adherents of Truth, we take the inspired Word of the Bible as our sufficient guide to eternal truth.

2 · We acknowledge and adore one supreme and infinite God. We acknowledge His Son, one Christ; the Holy Ghost or divine Comforter; and man in God's image and likeness.

3 · We acknowledge God's forgiveness of sin in the destruction of sin and the spiritual understanding that casts out evil as unreal. But the belief in sin is punished so long as the belief lasts.

4 · We acknowledge Jesus' atonement as the evidence of divine, efficacious Love, unfolding man's unity with God through Christ Jesus the Way-shower; and we acknowledge that man is saved through Christ, through Truth, Life and Love as demonstrated by the Galilean Prophet

in healing the sick and overcoming sin and death.

5 · We acknowledge that the crucifixion of Jesus and His resurrection served to uplift faith to understand eternal life, even the allness of Soul, Spirit and the nothingness of matter.

6 · And we solemnly promise to watch, and pray for that Mind to be in us which was also in Christ Jesus; to do unto others as we would have them do unto us; and to be merciful, just and pure.

**Some basic books or resources to which a guest can refer to learn more about Christian Science:**

*Science and Health with Key to the Scriptures,* by Mary Baker Eddy (Boston: Christian Science Publishing Society).

*Christian Science: A Sourcebook of Contemporary Materials* (Boston: Christian Science Publishing Society, 1993).

Two magazines, the weekly "Christian Science Sentinel" and the monthly "Christian Science Journal." These may be obtained in any Christian Science Reading Room.

A Home Page where people may visit for background or to write and ask for more information. The address is http://www.tfccs.com/

Ask a librarian in a Christian Science Reading Room to help you find appropriate materials. The addresses of these reading rooms can usually be found in your local telephone yellow pages.

## III · HOLY DAYS AND FESTIVALS

Christian Science has no special holidays or festivals.

With the religion's emphasis on the metaphysical, it does not hold a special Christmas service since that would honor the physical nature of Jesus.

A special Thanksgiving service is held on the morning of that holiday. This reflects Mary Baker Eddy's emphasis on gratitude. Similar to a Wednesday testimony meeting, it includes a Lesson-Sermon, silent and audible prayer, and a period for expressions of gratitude. No collection is taken at this service.

## IV · LIFE CYCLE EVENTS

### · *Birth Ceremony* ·

There is no special ceremony for the naming or birth of a child.

## · Initiation Ceremony ·

There is no initiation ceremony. A participant may join the Mother Church and his or her local church as early as the age of 12. But one is not required to do so and may join whenever they feel it is appropriate. On the day one joins the local church, he or she is welcomed by the entire congregation and invited to sign the membership book.

At the age of 20, students graduate from Sunday School and may be informally presented with a copy of *The Mother Church Manual*. Again, there is no formal ceremony.

## · Marriage Ceremony ·

There is no set marriage ceremony. Since Christian Science has no ordained clergy, it has no one who can legally perform a marriage. In accord with the laws where they reside, Christian Scientists may be married by the clergy of another faith.

## · Funerals and Mourning ·

The church does not designate special arrangements or rituals for funerals or mourning. A funeral service is optional.

### BEFORE THE CEREMONY

**How soon after the death does the funeral usually take place?**
Usually about two to four days.

**What should someone who is not a Christian Scientist do upon hearing of the death of a member of that faith?**
Telephone or visit the bereaved or send a condolence card or personal letter.

### APPROPRIATE ATTIRE

**Men:** A jacket and tie. No head covering is required.

**Women:** A dress, a skirt and blouse or a pants suit. Arms do not have to be covered by clothing nor do hems need to reach below the knees. Modest jewelry and open-toed shoes are permissible. No head covering is required.

There are no rules regarding colors of clothing, but slightly subdued colors are preferable.

## GIFTS

**Is it appropriate to send flowers or make a contribution?**

Both flowers to the bereaved family and contributions in the name of the deceased are appropriate. Flowers may be sent to the homes of the bereaved. Contributions are often made to the church of the deceased.

**Is it appropriate to send food?**

Yes, any kind.

## THE CEREMONY

**Where does the ceremony take place?**

Christian Science churches are used only for public worship services. Private funeral or memorial services are arranged by the families concerned and are usually held in their own homes or in funeral homes.

**When should guests arrive and where should they sit?**

Arrive early. Sit wherever you wish.

**If arriving late, are there times when a guest should *not* enter the ceremony?**

No.

**Are there times when a guest should *not* leave the ceremony?**

No.

**Will the bereaved family be present at the church or funeral home before the ceremony?**

This depends on the family's wishes.

**Is there a traditional greeting for the family?**

No.

**Will there be an open casket?**

Rarely. While most Christian Scientists do not have open viewing at the memorial service, this is done at the discretion of the individual.

**Who are the major officiants at the ceremony and what do they do?**

Since the Christian Science church has no clergy, the service is conducted by a Christian Scientist who might be a Reader or a Christian Science practitioner or teacher, or a friend of the deceased.

(A "practitioner" is an experienced Christian Scientist who, on a professional basis, devotes full time to the healing ministry. Individuals enter the public practice of Christian Science as a life work only after demonstrating a consistent ability to heal others through Christian Scientific prayer.)

### What books are used?

The format and content of a Christian Science funeral service are determined by the family or whoever conducts the service. However, the service typically consists of readings from the King James Bible and from *Science and Health with Key to the Scriptures* or some other writing by Mrs. Eddy. Silent prayer, followed by those attending repeating the Lord's Prayer, may also be included. If music is desired, the Christian Science Hymnal contains hymns suitable for funerals.

The service usually includes no personal remarks or eulogy, but the family's wishes are taken into account. If they request, a poem or hymn that is not in the Christian Science Hymnal may be read or sung.

### Will a guest who is not a Christian Scientist be expected to do anything other than sit?

No.

### Are there any parts of the ceremony in which a guest who is not a Christian Scientist should *not* participate?

No.

### If not disruptive to the ceremony, is it okay to:

◘ **Take pictures?** No.
◘ **Use a flash camera?** No.
◘ **Use a video camera?** No.
◘ **Use a tape recorder?** No.

### Will contributions to the church be collected at the ceremony?

No.

## THE INTERMENT

Cremation or burial is solely the bereaved family's decision.

## COMFORTING THE BEREAVED

### Is it appropriate to visit the home of the bereaved after the funeral?

Yes.

### Will there be a religious service at the home of the bereaved?

No.

**Will food be served?**

Sometimes, but not alcoholic beverages.

**How soon after the funeral will a mourner usually return to a normal work schedule?**

This is solely an individual decision. Christian Scientists do not have a prescribed period of mourning or specific customs of mourning.

**How soon after the funeral will a mourner usually return to a normal social schedule?**

This is solely an individual decision. Christian Scientists do not have a prescribed period of mourning or specific customs of mourning.

**Are there rituals for observing the anniversary of the death?**

No.

## V · HOME CELEBRATIONS

Not applicable to Christian Science.

# Chapter 6 Contents

# 6

# Churches of Christ

## I · HISTORY AND BELIEFS

Churches of Christ are autonomous congregations; there are no central governing offices or officers, and Church publications and institutions are either under local congregational control or independent of any one congregation. Members of the Churches of Christ appeal to the Bible alone to determine matters involving their faith and practice.

In the 19th century, Churches of Christ shared a common fellowship with the Christian Churches/Churches of Christ and with the Christian Church (Disciples of Christ). This relationship became strained after the Civil War because of emerging theories of interpreting the Bible and the centralizing of church-wide activities through a missionary society.

The Church teaches that Jesus Christ was divine, that the remission of sins can be achieved only by immersing oneself into Christ, and that the Scriptures were divinely inspired.

**U.S. churches:** 14,000
**U. S. membership:** 2.25 million
*(data from the 1998 Yearbook of American and Canadian Churches)*

**For more information, contact:**
Churches of Christ
P.O. Box 726
Kosciusko, MS 39090

**Canadian churches:** 145
**Canadian membership:** 6,950
*(data from the 1998 Yearbook of American and Canadian Churches)*
No Canadian contact address available.

## II · THE BASIC SERVICE

In most churches, there are a worship service and Bible classes on Sunday morning and another worship service Sunday evening. Both services last about an hour.

On Wednesday evenings, there is a Bible class, which is followed, in some churches, by a brief devotional service.

### APPROPRIATE ATTIRE

**Men:** Jacket and tie are the norm for the Sunday morning service, but are not required. More casual attire, such as slacks or nice jeans and a sport shirt, are appropriate for the Wednesday evening service. No head covering is required.

**Women:** A casual dress is recommended. It is not necessary to cover the arms. Open-toed shoes and modest jewelry permissible. No head covering is required.

There are no rules regarding colors of clothing.

### THE SANCTUARY

**What are the major sections of the church?**
- *The pews,* where members sit for worship.
- *The podium/pulpit area,* where song and prayer leaders and the preacher sit and from where the service is led.

### THE SERVICE

**When should guests arrive and where should they sit?**
Arrive early or at the time called. You may sit in any seat. No usher will seat you.

**If arriving late, are there times when a guest should *not* enter the service?**
It's preferable to enter between songs rather than during them.

**Are there times when a guest should *not* leave the service?**
It's preferable to leave between songs rather than during them.

**Who are the major officiants, leaders or participants and what do they do?**
- *The announcement maker,* who greets congregants and makes announcements during the service.

- *The song leader*, who leads singing.
- *The prayer leader*, who leads prayers.
- *The preacher*, who preaches the sermon.

**What are the major ritual objects of the service?**

- *Grape juice and unleavened bread*, such as thin crackers, are used during communion to symbolize the body and blood of Jesus Christ.

**What books are used?**

A hymnal and a Bible (which includes the Old and New Testaments). Among the more commonly used hymnals are *Majestic Hymnal* (Austin, Tex.: Firm Foundation Publishing, 1959) and *Songs of Faith and Praise* (West Monroe, La.: Alton Howard Publishers, 1993). The church does not endorse a particular translation of the Bible.

Often, several different translations of the Bible are used by congregants at the same service. It is suggested that guests bring their own Bible.

**To indicate the order of the service:**

Sometimes a program is distributed. At other times, prayers and songs are announced by the song leader.

### GUEST BEHAVIOR DURING THE SERVICE

**Will a guest who is not a member of the Churches of Christ be expected to do anything other than sit?**

Guests are expected to sing with congregants during the service, unless the songs being sung are contrary to their religious beliefs. It is optional for them to stand when the congregation rises.

**Are there are any parts of the service in which a guest who is not a member of the Churches of Christ should *not* participate?**

Only members of the Churches of Christ or other Christians take communion. If a visitor is not a Christian or is uncomfortable in partaking of communion, he or should just pass the communion plate to the next person.

**If not disruptive to the service, is it okay to:**

- **Take pictures?** Yes.
- **Use a flash?** Yes, but use sparingly.
- **Use a video camera?** Yes.
- **Use a tape recorder?** Yes.

**Will contributions to the church be collected at the service?**

Usually, there is a collection immediately after communion. It is entirely optional for guests to contribute.

**How much is customary to contribute?**
About $1 to $5.

### AFTER THE SERVICE

**Is there usually a reception after the service?**
No, but there often is a fellowship luncheon immediately after the service. It may last about one hour. Guests are always welcome and are not expected to bring any food.

Often, a church will have a potluck luncheon one Sunday a month. Everyone is invited. Members bring a variety of foods. No alcoholic beverages are served. A prayer is usually said before eating. There is no concluding ritual after eating.

**Is there a traditional form of address for clergy whom a guest may meet?**
Churches of Christ do not have titles for clergy. Ministers or preachers are addressed no differently than are lay members. All church members are considered to be living lives of integrity and each should be trying to live a life as holy as the minister.

**Is it okay to leave early?**
Yes.

### GENERAL GUIDELINES AND ADVICE

None provided.

### SPECIAL VOCABULARY

None provided.

### DOGMA AND IDEOLOGY

**Members of the Churches of Christ believe:**

- Going back to the Bible does not mean establishing another denomination, but rather returning to the original church. Members call themselves "a people of restoration spirit," meaning they want to restore in our time the original New Testament church. They do not consider themselves belonging to a separate denomination, but as members of the church that Jesus established and for which He died.
- Each congregation is independent of every other congregation. The only tie binding the many congregations is a common allegiance to Christ and the Bible.

## III · HOLY DAYS AND FESTIVALS

- Churches of Christ celebrate the death and resurrection of Jesus every week by partaking of communion. Thus, every Sunday is seen as a "holy day."
- Both *Easter* (which is always the Sunday following the first full moon on or after March 21 and which celebrates the resurrection of Jesus Christ) and *Christmas* (which occurs on December 25 and marks the birth and the incarnation of God as Jesus) may be celebrated in churches with a special service or with a special sermon. This reflects the autonomous nature of the Churches of Christ. The traditional greeting for Easter is "Happy Easter" and for Christmas "Merry Christmas."
- Good Friday (the Friday before Easter which commemorates the day on which Jesus was crucified) is not observed because the crucifixion is observed every Sunday in the Churches of Christ.

## IV · LIFE CYCLE EVENTS

### · *Birth Ceremony* ·

Churches of Christ have no birth ceremony.

### · *Initiation Ceremony* ·

The Churches of Christ teaches that children are innocent of sin until they reach an age when they can truly understand right from wrong and make a conscious decision about it. This age is usually considered to be around 13, although it may be as young as 11 or 12.

Baptism is an expression of one's faith in God and to Christ. At this time, a person repents of the sin in his or her life, renounces sinful ways of living and confesses that Jesus is the Son of God. He or she is immersed during baptism as a sign of participating in the death, burial and resurrection of Jesus.

The participant is usually baptized individually, although the ceremony may be done with someone else.

#### BEFORE THE CEREMONY

**Are guests usually invited by a formal invitation?**
Sometimes.

**If not stated explicitly, should one assume that children are invited?**
Yes.

**If one can't attend, what should one do?**
RSVP with regrets, possibly by telephone, and congratulate the person being baptized.

## APPROPRIATE ATTIRE

**Men:** Jacket and tie, if the baptism occurs during worship service. If the baptism is a separate service, dress more casually, for example, in slacks or nice jeans and a sport shirt. No head covering is required.

**Women:** A casual dress if baptism occurs during worship service or if it is a separate service. Open-toed shoes and modest jewelry permissible. No head covering is required.

There are no rules regarding colors of clothing.

## GIFTS

**Is a gift customarily expected?**
No.

**Should gifts be brought to the ceremony?**
See above.

## THE CEREMONY

**Where will the ceremony take place?**
In the church's baptistery. This is usually located behind the pulpit.

**When should guests arrive and where should they sit?**
Arrive early or at the time called. You may sit in any seat. No usher will seat you.

**If arriving late, are there times when a guest should *not* enter the ceremony?**
It's preferable to enter between songs rather than during them.

**Are there times when a guest should *not* leave the ceremony?**
It's preferable to leave between songs rather than during them.

**Who are the major officiants, leaders or participants in the ceremony and what do they do?**
◪ The person being baptized.

◘ The person doing the baptizing.

◘ Often there is a song leader who leads the congregation in singing as preparations for the baptism are being made.

**What books are used?**

A hymnal and a Bible (which includes the Old and New Testaments). Among the more commonly used hymnals are *Majestic Hymnal* (Austin, Tex.: Firm Foundation Publishing, 1959) and *Songs of Faith and Praise* (West Monroe, La.: Alton Howard Publishers, 1993). The church does not endorse a particular version of the Bible.

Often, several different translations of the Bible are used by congregants at the same service. It is suggested that guests bring their own Bible.

**To indicate the order of the ceremony:**

Usually the minister or song leader will give directions.

**Will a guest who is not a member of the Churches of Christ be expected to do anything other than sit?**

You are only expected to sit. It is optional for a guest to sing with the congregation while the participant is changing clothes before and after the baptism.

**Are there are any parts of the ceremony in which a guest who is not a member of the Churches of Christ should *not* participate?**

Only members of the Churches of Christ or other Christians take communion. If a visitor is not a Christian or is uncomfortable in partaking of communion, he or should just pass the communion plate to the next person.

**If not disruptive to the ceremony, is it okay to:**

◘ **Take pictures?** Yes.

◘ **Use a flash?** Yes.

◘ **Use a video camera?** Yes.

◘ **Use a tape recorder?** Yes.

**Will contributions to the church be collected at the ceremony?**

Only if the baptism takes place at the Sunday morning worship. In that case, the collection is part of the worship and not part of the baptism. Collections immediately follow the communion (the passing of the bread and fruit of the vine). Whether guests contribute to this is completely optional.

**How much is customary to contribute?**

About $1 to $5.

## AFTER THE CEREMONY

**Is there usually a reception after the ceremony?**
There is no formal reception after the ceremony.

**Is there a traditional greeting for the family?**
No, simply offer your best wishes.

**Is there a traditional form of address for clergy whom a guest may meet?**
Churches of Christ do not have titles for clergy. Ministers or preachers are addressed no differently than are lay members. All church members are considered to be living lives of integrity and each should be trying to live a life as holy as the minister.

## · *Marriage Ceremony* ·

The Churches of Christ teaches that marriage "originated in the mind of God," who "created woman especially to be a companion for the man....There can be no doubt that God intended for man and woman to marry," since God said, "For this cause shall a man leave his father and mother, and shall cleave unto his wife."

God "officiated" at the marriage between Adam and Eve, and "continues to officiate at all scriptural marriages today."

This is why the church states that marriage is "divine" and that "those who marry not only have obligations to each other, but they also have obligations to God."

Usually, Churches of Christ marriage ceremonies last about 30 minutes.

## BEFORE THE CEREMONY

**Are guests usually invited by a formal invitation?**
Yes. Often, general invitations are published in the church bulletin.

**If not stated explicitly, should one assume that children are invited?**
Yes.

**If one can't attend, what should one do?**
RSVP by phone or card, along with your congratulations. Most friends will send a gift either to a wedding shower or to the couple.

## APPROPRIATE ATTIRE

**Men:** Jacket and tie, although occasionally less formal clothes may be suitable. No head covering is required.

**Women:** Dress modestly. Hems slightly above the knees are fine. Open-toed shoes and modest jewelry permissible. No head covering is required, but hats or scarfs may be worn.

There are no rules regarding colors of clothing.

## GIFTS

### Is a gift customarily expected?
Yes, either for the bridal shower or the wedding itself. Such gifts as small household appliances, sheets or towels or other household goods are appropriate.

### Should gifts be brought to the ceremony?
If you bring a gift to the wedding, place it on the table in the reception area for that purpose. Gifts can also be sent to the home of the newlyweds.

## THE CEREMONY

### Where will the ceremony take place?
In the main sanctuary of the church.

### When should guests arrive and where should they sit?
Arrive early. Sit wherever you wish.

### If arriving late, are there times when a guest should *not* enter the ceremony?
Do not enter the service during the processional.

### Are there times when a guest should *not* leave the ceremony?
Do not leave during the processional.

### Who are the major officiants, leaders or participants at the ceremony and what do they do?
▪ *The minister*, who performs the ceremony.
▪ *Singers*.

### What books are used?
Usually, the minister has a Bible, from which he reads. Other books are usually not used.

**To indicate the order of the ceremony:**
A program will be provided.

**Will a guest who is not a member of the Churches of Christ be expected to do anything other than sit?**
Guests are only expected to enjoy the celebration.

**Are there any parts of the ceremony in which a guest who is not a member of the Churches of Christ should *not* participate?**
No.

**If not disruptive to the ceremony, is it okay to:**
⌁ **Take pictures?** Yes.
⌁ **Use a flash?** Yes.
⌁ **Use a video camera?** Yes.
⌁ **Use a tape recorder?** Yes.

**Will contributions to the church be collected at the ceremony?**
No.

## AFTER THE CEREMONY

**Is there usually a reception after the ceremony?**
There is often a reception in the same building as the ceremony. It lasts about one hour. There may be finger foods, fruit, vegetables and dip. Alcohol in any form is discouraged, as is smoking inside the building.

**Would it be considered impolite to neither eat nor drink?**
No.

**Is there a grace or benediction before eating or drinking?**
Sometimes a prayer is said before eating.

**Is there a grace or benediction after eating or drinking?**
No. But usually after the reception, rice or bird seed are thrown at the newlyweds when they leave. (Bird seed has generally replaced rice because of ecological concerns.)

**Is there a traditional greeting for the family?**
No, just offer your congratulations.

**Is there a traditional form of address for clergy who may be at the reception?**
Churches of Christ do not have titles for clergy. Ministers or preachers are addressed no differently than are lay members. All church members are

considered to be living lives of integrity and each should be trying to live a life as holy as the minister.

## · Funerals and Mourning ·

Members of the Churches of Christ believe that, upon death, the souls of those who are faithful Christians are taken to a place called Paradise to await the Final Judgment. The souls of those who are unfaithful or are not Christians are taken to a place called Tartarus to await judgment. On Judgment Day (which is the second coming of Jesus), the faithful will be taken to heaven and the unfaithful to hell.

The funeral service usually lasts about 30 minutes.

### BEFORE THE CEREMONY

**How soon after the death does the funeral usually take place?**
Usually within two to three days. If family members cannot arrive for the funeral immediately, it may be delayed for four or five days. But this is rare.

**What should someone who is not a member of the Churches of Christ do upon hearing of the death of a member of that faith?**
Visit or telephone the bereaved before the funeral.

### APPROPRIATE ATTIRE

**Men:** Jacket and tie. No head covering is required.

**Women:** A dress or skirt and blouse. Hems slightly above the knees are fine. Open-toed shoes and modest jewelry are permissible. No head covering is required.

There are no rules regarding colors of clothing, but black or other somber colors or patterns are recommended.

### GIFTS

**Is it appropriate to send flowers or make a contribution?**
Flowers, plants and cards are appropriate. They may be sent upon hearing the news of the death or shortly thereafter. They may be sent to the home of the deceased before or after the funeral, or to the funeral home before the funeral.

Contributions are not customary unless the family indicates they are appropriate.

**Is it appropriate to send food?**

Yes, to the home of the bereaved before or after the funeral.

## THE CEREMONY

**Where will the ceremony take place?**

At a church or a funeral home.

**When should guests arrive and where should they sit?**

Arrive early. Register upon entry. No one will tell guests where to sit. Sit wherever there is an available seat.

**If arriving late, are there times when a guest should *not* enter the ceremony?**

Do not enter when the family is entering.

**Will the bereaved family be present at the church or funeral home before the ceremony?**

Yes, but there is no formal receiving line before the service.

**Is there a traditional greeting for the family?**

Express your condolences.

**Will there be an open casket?**

Usually.

**Is a guest expected to view the body?**

This is optional.

**What is appropriate behavior upon viewing the body?**

Most will pause briefly to look one last time at their friend or loved one. Occasionally, someone may pat the hand of the deceased or place a flower in the casket.

**Who are the major officiants at the ceremony and what do they do?**

▪ *One or more ministers* will deliver eulogies.
▪ *Singers* will lead songs.

**What books are used?**

A hymnal and a Bible (which includes the Old and New Testaments). The most commonly used hymnal is *Songs of the Church*. Others are *Majestic Hymnal* (Austin, Tex.: Firm Foundation Publishing, 1959) and *Songs of Faith and Praise* (West Monroe, La.: Alton Howard Publishers, 1993). The church does not endorse a particular version of the Bible.

Often, several different translations of the Bible are used by congregants at the same service. It is suggested that guests bring their own Bible.

**To indicate the order of the ceremony:**
The minister or funeral director will explain any involvement by those present and cue them should they be asked to do anything, such as view the body.

**Will a guest who is not a member of the Churches of Christ be expected to do anything other than sit?**
Guests can sing with the congregation, if the words are not contrary to their religious beliefs. Otherwise, nothing is expected of them.

**Are there any parts of the ceremony in which a guest who is not a member of the Churches of Christ should *not* participate?**
No.

**If not disruptive to the ceremony, is it okay to:**
◙ **Take pictures?** No.
◙ **Use a flash?** No.
◙ **Use a video camera?** No.
◙ **Use a tape recorder?** Yes.

**Will contributions to the church be collected at the ceremony?**
No.

### THE INTERMENT

**Should guests attend the interment?**
Their attendance is optional.

**Whom should one ask for directions?**
The funeral director.

**What happens at the graveside?**
There is prayer, readings from the scriptures, and the minister gives comments about the deceased.

**Do guests who are not members of the Churches of Christ participate at the graveside ceremony?**
No. They are simply present.

### COMFORTING THE BEREAVED

**Is it appropriate to visit the home of the bereaved after the funeral?**
Yes, either after the service at the cemetery or later.

**Will there be a religious service at the home of the bereaved?**

No.

**Will food be served?**

Possibly, but no alcoholic beverages.

**How soon after the funeral will a mourner usually return to a normal work schedule?**

Usually, the bereaved can be expected to return to work after one week of mourning.

**How soon after the funeral will a mourner usually return to a normal social schedule?**

Social occasions are usually avoided for about one month after the death, but this depends on the individual mourner.

**Are there rituals for observing the anniversary of the death?**

There is no formal ritual, although occasionally friends or relatives may call or visit each other on the anniversary of the death.

## V · HOME CELEBRATIONS

Not applicable for the Churches of Christ.

# Chapter 7 Contents

# Episcopalian and Anglican

## I · HISTORY AND BELIEFS

The Episcopal/Anglican Church is derived from the Church of England and shares with it traditions of faith as set forth in its *Book of Common Prayer*.

The English settlers who settled in Jamestown, Virginia, in 1607 brought the seeds of the Episcopal Church to America. After the American Revolution, the Church became independent from the Anglican Church and adopted the name of the Protestant Episcopal Church in the United States of America. This was shortened in 1967 when the Episcopal Church became the Church's official alternate name.

To many Americans after the Revolution, the Church was suspect because it had been closely linked with the British Crown and because many of its leaders and members had sided with England during the war. But extensive missionary efforts in the fledgling nation's new territories (as well as in Africa, Latin America and the Far East) and an eventual network of dioceses from the Atlantic to the Pacific helped it to finally establish its own identity.

In Canada, the first known service was performed by a chaplain in Sir Martin Frobisher's expedition in Frobisher Bay on September 2, 1578. In subsequent years, Anglicanism spread as a result of immigration from the British Isles and the coming of Loyalists, many of whom were Anglicans, after the American Revolution.

The Church is a fairly non-doctrinaire institution. It teaches that the Holy Scriptures were written by people, and inspired by the Holy Spirit (the empowering spirit of God), and that reason helps members penetrate to the full depths of God's truths. It does not control interpretation

119

and practice, and urges members to make responsible moral decisions under the guidance of scripture, tradition and ordained ministry and in response to sincere prayer.

The Episcopal/Anglican Church is democratically structured. Each diocese, which consists of a group of parishes (or churches), is presided over by a bishop, who is democratically elected by a diocesan synod.

According to *The Book of Common Prayer*, "the duty of all Christians is to follow Christ, to come together week by week for corporate worship; and to work, pray and give for the spread of the Kingdom of God."

**U.S. churches:** 7,415
**U.S. membership:** 2.5 million
*(data from the 1998 Yearbook of American and Canadian Churches)*

**For more information, contact:**
The Episcopal Church Center
815 Second Avenue
New York, NY 10017
(212) 867-8400
www.ecusa.anglican.org

**Canadian churches:** 2,390
**Canadian membership:** 740,262

**For more information, contact:**
Anglican Church House
600 Jarvis Street
Toronto, ON  M4Y 2J6
(416) 924-9192

## II · THE BASIC SERVICE

To Episcopalians/Anglicans, worship is a joyous response to God's love, an expression of hope for salvation, a chance to praise God and receive strength and forgiveness, and a way to share faith with other believers.

Ordinarily, the Sunday morning Episcopal/Anglican service lasts between 30 and 60 minutes.

### APPROPRIATE ATTIRE

**Men:** Jacket and tie or more casual clothing. No head covering required.

**Women:** Dress or a skirt and blouse or a pants suit. Open-toed shoes and jewelry are permissible. No head covering required.

There are no rules regarding colors of clothing.

## THE SANCTUARY

### What are the major sections of the church?

- *The sanctuary:* The part of the church where the altar is located and where ministers lead congregants in prayer. It is set off from the body of the church by a distinctive structural feature, such as an elevation above the floor level or by ornamentation. It is usually at the front of the church, but may be centrally located.
- *The pulpit or lectern:* The stand at which scriptural lessons and psalm responses are read and the word of God is preached.
- *Seating for congregants:* Seats and kneeling benches, usually in front and/or to the side of the altar.
- *Baptistery or font:* The place for administering baptism. Some churches have baptisteries adjoining or near their entrance. This position indicates that through baptism, one is initiated, or "enters," the church.
- *Aumbry light:* A lamp that burns continuously in a small box or niche in which the communion sacrament that had not been totally consumed during services is kept. This communion bread and wine may be brought, for instance, by the priest to a congregant who has been hospitalized. The light symbolizes the presence of Christ. The aumbry box is usually either along the wall near the altar or on a table at the rear of the altar.

## THE SERVICE

### When should guests arrive and where should they sit?

It is customary to arrive early. An usher will indicate where to sit. There are usually no restrictions on where to sit.

### If arriving late, are there times when a guest should *not* enter the service?

Check with the ushers.

### Are there times when a guest should *not* leave the service?

No, but guests should plan to remain for the entire service.

### Who are the major officiants, leaders or participants and what do they do?

- *A priest*, who presides, preaches and celebrates communion.
- *A lector*, who reads from the Old Testament and/or the Epistles or apostolic letters, which are a part of the New Testament.
- *A deacon*, who reads from the Gospels, which record the life and ministry of Jesus.

■ *A lay minister*, or chalicist, who assists with the distribution of communion.

■ *An intercessor*, who reads the "prayers of the people," which are petitions, intercessions and thanksgivings by the congregation.

## What are the major ritual objects of the service?

■ *Bread and wine*, which are consecrated into the body and blood of Jesus Christ.

■ *The chalice and paten*, which hold, respectively, the consecrated wine and bread.

■ *The altar*, or table where the bread and wine are consecrated.

■ *The gospel book or Bible*, which may be processed into the midst of the congregation before the gospel is read.

## What books are used?

A hymnal and *The Book of Common Prayer* (New York: Church Hymnal Corp., 1986). In Canada, *The Book of Alternative Services* (Toronto: The Anglican Book Center, 1985) may be used. Occasionally, the Bible lessons are included in the program.

## To indicate the order of the service:

A program will be provided.

### GUEST BEHAVIOR DURING THE SERVICE

## Will a guest who is not Episcopalian/Anglican be expected to do anything other than sit?

They are expected to stand and kneel with the congregation, read prayers aloud and sing with congregants, if this does not compromise their personal beliefs. If one does not wish to kneel, sit when congregants do so. The only behavior that would be considered "offensive" would be not to stand for the reading of the Gospel.

## Are there any parts of the service in which a guest who is not Episcopalian/Anglican should *not* participate?

Yes. Do not receive communion or say any prayers contradictory to the beliefs of your own faith. Only baptized Christians may receive communion.

## If not disruptive to the service, is it okay to:

■ **Take pictures?** No.

■ **Use a flash?** No.

■ **Use a video camera?** No.

■ **Use a tape recorder?** No.

**Will contributions to the church be collected at the service?**

Yes. The offertory takes place about midway through the service. Ushers usually pass the plate for offerings.

**How much is customary to contribute?**

The customary offering is from $1 to $10.

## AFTER THE SERVICE

**Is there usually a reception after the service?**

Yes, in the church's reception area. It may last less than 30 minutes. Usually food and light beverages are served. It is not impolite to refrain from eating. Usually there is no blessing before or after eating or drinking.

**Is there a traditional form of address for clergy who may be at the reception?**

"Mr.," "Miss" or "Mrs." is usually sufficient.

**Is it okay to leave early?**

Yes.

## GENERAL GUIDELINES AND ADVICE

Episcopalians/Anglicans are quite diverse—socially, racially and ethnically. Generally, they rejoice in this diversity and celebrate it. Most consider their church an extension of their family life. What represents "good manners" at home would be considered "good manners" in church. Politeness is the key.

Appearing overly reserved or non-communicative—which can imply disapproval—is a typical mistake that guests can avoid. Conviviality implies acceptance and approval.

## SPECIAL VOCABULARY

**Key words or phrases which might be helpful for a visitor to know:**

- *Gospel:* As used during worship, this means a reading from one of the accounts of the life of Jesus as written in the New Testament by four of his apostles.
- *Sermon:* An explication of the Gospel text that is read during the service.
- *Communion or Eucharist:* The common meal instituted by Jesus Christ at the Last Supper.
- *Morning (or Evening) Prayer:* A worship service that includes prayer and possibly a sermon, but not communion.

## DOGMA AND IDEOLOGY

### Episcopalians/Anglicans believe:

▪ While interpretation of Church teachings may vary from parish to parish, an essential Episcopalian/Anglican belief is that God has three prime qualities as reflected in the Holy Trinity: The Father (Who is infinite, good and omnipotent); The Son (Jesus Christ, Whose life, death and resurrection liberated humanity from sin and death); and The Holy Spirit (God's power of love appearing within men and women in mysterious and unexpected ways).

▪ The Episcopal/Anglican Church recognizes our sinfulness and God's love for His creation as demonstrated by Jesus, Whose life and death affirms our salvation and is celebrated with praise and thanksgiving.

▪ *The Book of Common Prayer* states that private worship alone is inadequate and that religion is a fellowship. Episcopalians/Anglicans must relate to the entire Church through their respective parish and local church community.

### Some basic books to which a guest can refer to learn more about the Episcopal/Anglican faith:

*What Makes Us Episcopalians* by John Booty (New York: Morehouse, 1982).

*So You Think You're Not Religious?* by James R. Adams (Cambridge, Ma.: Cowley, 1989).

*This Anglican Church of Ours* by Patricia Bays (Winfield, B.C.: Wood Lake Books, 1995).

---

## III · HOLY DAYS AND FESTIVALS

---

▪ *Christmas*, which always falls on December 25, celebrates the birth of Christ. The traditional greeting is "Merry Christmas."

▪ *Easter*, which always falls on the first Sunday after the full moon that occurs on or after the spring equinox of March 21. Commemorates the death and resurrection of Jesus. The traditional greeting is "Happy Easter."

▪ *Pentecost*, which occurs 50 days after Easter because this is when the Holy Ghost (the spirit of Jesus) descended on His apostles. Celebrates the power of the Holy Spirit and its manifestation in the early Christian church. There is no traditional greeting for this holiday.

▪ *Ash Wednesday*, which occurs 40 days before Easter, commemorates the beginning of Lent, which is a season for preparation and penitence before Easter itself. There is no traditional greeting for this holiday.

- *Maundy Thursday*, which falls four days before Easter. Commemorates the institution of the Eucharist (also known as Communion) and Jesus' subsequent arrest and trial. There is no traditional greeting.
- *Good Friday*, three days before Easter. Commemorates the crucifixion, death and burial of Jesus.

Christmas, Easter and Pentecost are joyful celebrations. Ash Wednesday, Maundy Thursday and Good Friday are somber, penitential commemorations. During the services for these latter three holidays, decorum and discretion are of great importance.

## IV · LIFE CYCLE EVENTS

### · Birth Ceremony ·

Baptism is administered once to each person, usually as an infant. During the 30- to 60-minute ceremony, which is part of a larger Sunday morning service, a priest pours water on the head of the child or immerses the child into water. This symbolizes the washing away of sins. The Holy Trinity is also called upon to strengthen the new church member.

Baptism is a pledge of repentance and obedience to divine will. It also initiates the individual into the Christian community and into the larger family of the children of a loving God.

### BEFORE THE CEREMONY

**Are guests usually invited by a formal invitation?**
Yes.

**If not stated explicitly, should one assume that children are invited?**
Yes.

**If one can't attend, what should one do?**
RSVP with regrets and send a gift.

### APPROPRIATE ATTIRE

**Men:** Jacket and tie or more casual clothing. No head covering required.

**Women:** Dress or a skirt and blouse or a pants suit. Open-toed shoes and jewelry are permissible. No head covering required.

There are no rules regarding colors of clothing.

## GIFTS

### Is a gift customarily expected?
No. If you attend, your presence is the gift. If you cannot attend, sending a gift would be appropriate.

### Should gifts be brought to the ceremony?
See above.

## THE CEREMONY

### Where will the ceremony take place?
Some churches have a special baptistery, which is usually near or adjoins the church entrance. In more modest churches, the font (which holds the water for baptism) is near the church entrance.

### When should guests arrive and where should they sit?
Arrive early. Ushers will indicate where to sit.

### If arriving late, are there times when a guest should *not* enter the ceremony?
Check with the ushers.

### Are there times when a guest should *not* leave the ceremony?
Guests should plan to stay for the entire service.

### Who are the major officiants, leaders or participants in the ceremony and what do they do?
- *A priest*, who will baptize the child.
- *The child's parents.*
- *Sponsors*, who will speak for the child and agree to aid in the child's upbringing.

### What books are used?
A hymnal and *The Book of Common Prayer* (New York: Church Hymnal Corp., 1986). In Canada, *The Book of Alternative Services* (Toronto: The Anglican Book Center, 1985) may be used. Occasionally, the Bible lessons are included in the program.

### To indicate the order of the ceremony:
A program will be distributed by ushers.

### Will a guest who is not Episcopalian/Anglican be expected to do anything other than sit?
They are expected to stand and kneel with the congregation, read prayers aloud and sing with congregants, if this does not compromise their per-

sonal beliefs. If one does not wish to kneel, sit when congregants do so. The only behavior that would be considered "offensive" would be not to stand for the reading of the Gospel.

### Are there any parts of the ceremony in which a guest who is not Episcopalian/Anglican should *not* participate?

Do not receive communion or say any prayers contradictory to the beliefs of your own faith. Only baptized Christians may receive communion.

### If not disruptive to the ceremony, is it okay to:

◙ **Take pictures?** No.
◙ **Use a flash?** No.
◙ **Use a video camera?** No.
◙ **Use a tape recorder?** No.

### Will contributions to the church be collected at the ceremony?

Yes. The offertory takes place about midway through the service. Ushers usually pass the plate for offerings.

### How much is customary to contribute?

The customary offering is from $1 to $10.

## AFTER THE CEREMONY

### Is there usually a reception after the ceremony?

Possibly. It is solely at the discretion of the parents. If so, it will probably last less than 30 minutes. Food and light beverages will be served.

### Would it be considered impolite to neither eat nor drink?

No.

### Is there a grace or benediction before eating or drinking?

Usually there is no blessing prior to eating.

### Is there a grace or benediction after eating or drinking?

No.

### Is there a traditional greeting for the family?

No, simply offer your best wishes.

### Is there a traditional form of address for clergy who may be at the reception?

"Mr.," "Miss" or "Mrs." is usually sufficient.

### Is it okay to leave early?

Yes.

## · *Initiation Ceremony* ·

Confirmation is conferred, by a bishop, on an early adolescent (or occasionally on an adult who seeks church membership). It strengthens the commitment made by Christians at baptism, which occurs shortly after birth, and initiates one into the adult life of the church.

Episcopalians/Anglicans also believe that confirmation gives them courage to witness Christ in the world and to selflessly serve each other.

Teens participate in the ceremony with members of their confirmation class. The ceremony, which lasts between 30 and 60 minutes, is part of a larger Sunday morning service.

### BEFORE THE CEREMONY

**Are guests usually invited by a formal invitation?**
No.

**If not stated explicitly, should one assume that children are invited?**
Yes.

**If one can't attend, what should one do?**
RSVP with regrets and send a gift.

### APPROPRIATE ATTIRE

**Men:** Jacket and tie or more casual clothing. No head covering required.

**Women:** Dress or a skirt and blouse or a pants suit. Open-toed shoes and jewelry are permissible. No head covering required.

There are no rules regarding colors of clothing.

### GIFTS

**Is a gift customarily expected?**
Yes. This is usually a modest present, more of a token of affection.

**Should gifts be brought to the ceremony?**
Usually they are brought to the reception afterwards.

### THE CEREMONY

**Where will the ceremony take place?**
In the main sanctuary of the confirmand's church.

**When should guests arrive and where should they sit?**

Arrive early. Ushers will help you with seating.

**If arriving late, are there times when a guest should *not* enter the ceremony?**

Check with the ushers.

**Are there times when a guest should *not* leave the ceremony?**

Guests should plan to remain for the entire service.

**Who are the major officiants, leaders or participants in the ceremony and what do they do?**

◨ *The bishop,* who alone has the authority to confirm.

**What books are used?**

A hymnal and *The Book of Common Prayer* (New York: Church Hymnal Corp., 1986). In Canada, *The Book of Alternative Services* (Toronto: The Anglican Book Center, 1985) may be used. Occasionally, the Bible lessons are included in the program.

**To indicate the order of the ceremony:**

A program will be distributed by ushers.

**Will a guest who is not Episcopalian/Anglican be expected to do anything other than sit?**

They are expected to stand and kneel with the congregation, read prayers aloud and sing with congregants, if this does not compromise their personal beliefs. If one does not wish to kneel, sit when congregants do so. The only behavior that would be considered "offensive" would be not to stand for the reading of the Gospel.

**Are there any parts of the ceremony in which a guest who is not Episcopalian/Anglican should *not* participate?**

Do not receive communion or say any prayers contradictory to the beliefs of your own faith. Only baptized Christians may receive communion.

**If not disruptive to the ceremony, is it okay to:**

◨ **Take pictures?** No.
◨ **Use a flash?** No.
◨ **Use a video camera?** No.
◨ **Use a tape recorder?** No.

**Will contributions to the church be collected at the ceremony?**

Yes. The offertory takes place about midway through the service. Ushers usually pass the plate for offerings.

**How much is customary to contribute?**
The customary offering is from $1 to $10.

## AFTER THE CEREMONY

**Is there usually a reception after the ceremony?**
Yes, in the church's reception area. It ordinarily lasts less than 30 minutes. Usually food and light beverages are served.

**Would it be considered impolite to neither eat nor drink?**
No.

**Is there a grace or benediction before eating or drinking?**
Usually there is no blessing prior to eating.

**Is there a grace or benediction after eating or drinking?**
No.

**Is there a traditional greeting for the family?**
No, simply offer your best wishes.

**Is there a traditional form of address for clergy who may be at the reception?**
"Mr.," "Miss" or "Mrs." is usually sufficient.

**Is it okay to leave early?**
Yes.

## · *Marriage Ceremony* ·

The Episcopal/Anglican Church believes that, through the sacrament of marriage, God joins together man and woman in physical and spiritual union.

The marriage ceremony may either be a ceremony unto itself or part of a Holy Communion service. It may last between 30 and 60 minutes.

## BEFORE THE CEREMONY

**Are guests usually invited by a formal invitation?**
Yes.

**If not stated explicitly, should one assume that children are invited?**
No.

**If one can't attend, what should one do?**
RSVP with your regrets and send a gift.

## APPROPRIATE ATTIRE

**Men:** Jacket and tie or more casual clothing (depending on the style of the wedding. This may be indicated in the invitation.) No head covering required.

**Women:** Dress or a skirt and blouse or a pants suit. Open-toed shoes and jewelry are permissible. No head covering required.

There are no rules regarding colors of clothing.

## GIFTS

**Is a gift customarily expected?**
Yes, costing between $20 and $40.

**Should gifts be brought to the ceremony?**
Yes, or they can be sent to the home.

## THE CEREMONY

**Where will the ceremony take place?**
Depending on the wishes of the couple being married, it may be in the main sanctuary of a church, in another part of the church, in a home or banquet hall, or in another setting of their choice.

**When should guests arrive and where should they sit?**
Arrive early. Depending on the setting, ushers may show guests where to sit.

**If arriving late, are there times when a guest should *not* enter the ceremony?**
Check with the ushers.

**Are there times when a guest should *not* leave the ceremony?**
Guests should plan to remain for the entire service.

**Who are the major officiants, leaders or participants at the ceremony and what do they do?**
Depending on the setting and the wishes of the couple, there may be:
- *A priest*, who presides, preaches and celebrates communion.
- *A lector*, who reads from the Old Testament and/or the Epistles or apostolic letters, which are a part of the New Testament.
- *A deacon*, who reads the Gospel, which records the life and ministry of Jesus.
- *A lay minister*, or chalicist, who assists with the distribution of communion.

◾ *An intercessor*, who reads the "prayers of the people," which are petitions, intercessions and thanksgivings by the congregation.

**What books are used?**

*The Book of Common Prayer* (New York: Church Hymnal Corp., 1986) and a hymnal. In Canada, *The Book of Alternative Services* (Toronto: The Anglican Book Center, 1985) may be used. Occasionally, the Bible lessons are included in the program.

**To indicate the order of the ceremony:**

A program will be provided.

**Will a guest who is not Episcopalian/Anglican be expected to do anything other than sit?**

They are expected to stand and kneel with the congregation, read prayers aloud and sing with congregants, if this does not compromise their personal beliefs. If one does not wish to kneel, sit when congregants do so. The only behavior that would be considered "offensive" would be not to stand for the reading of the Gospel.

**Are there any parts of the ceremony in which a guest who is not Episcopalian/Anglican should *not* participate?**

Do not receive communion or say any prayers contradictory to the beliefs of your own faith. Only baptized Christians may receive communion.

**If not disruptive to the ceremony, is it okay to:**

◾ **Take pictures?** No.

◾ **Use a flash?** No.

◾ **Use a video camera?** No.

◾ **Use a tape recorder?** No.

(Photos and videos are usually taken after the ceremony.)

**Will contributions to the church be collected at the ceremony?**

No.

## AFTER THE CEREMONY

**Is there usually a reception after the ceremony?**

There is usually a reception that may last one to two hours. It may be at a home or at a catering facility. Food and beverages may be served and there may be dancing and music.

**Would it be considered impolite to neither eat nor drink?**

No.

**Is there a grace or benediction before eating or drinking?**
Not normally, but there may be a blessing if the reception is a "sit-down" affair.

**Is there a grace or benediction after eating or drinking?**
No.

**Is there a traditional greeting for the family?**
Extend your congratulations and best wishes.

**Is there a traditional form of address for clergy who may be at the reception?**
"Mr.," "Miss" or "Mrs." is usually sufficient.

**Is it okay to leave early?**
Yes, but usually only after toasts have been made and the wedding cake is cut and served.

## · Funerals and Mourning ·

In the Episcopal/Anglican Church, a funeral service can be either part of a larger service or a ceremony unto itself. If it is part of a larger service, that service is called a "requiem," which includes a Holy Communion service.

Episcopalians/Anglicans believe that Christ will come and judge all, the living and dead. Some will be consigned to heaven, where they will spend eternal life in the enjoyment of God. Others will be consigned to hell, where they will spend eternal death in the rejection of God.

### BEFORE THE CEREMONY

**How soon after the death does the funeral usually take place?**
Usually within two to three days.

**What should a non-Episcopalian/Anglican do upon hearing of the death of a member of that faith?**
Telephone or visit the bereaved. There is no specific "ritual" for calling or expressing sympathy to someone who is mourning.

### APPROPRIATE ATTIRE

**Men:** Jacket and tie. No head covering is required.

**Women:** A dress. Clothing should be modest, with arms covered and hems below the knee. Open-toed shoes and modest jewelry are permissible. No head covering is required.

Somber colors are recommended for clothing.

## GIFTS

**Is it appropriate to send flowers or make a contribution?**
Frequently, obituary notices will indicate if flowers are appropriate and may list specific charities for which contributions can be made in memory of the deceased.

**Is it appropriate to send food?**
Ask the bereaved.

## THE CEREMONY

**Where will the ceremony take place?**
At a church or a funeral home.

**When should guests arrive and where should they sit?**
Arrive early. Sit wherever you choose.

**If arriving late, are there times when a guest should *not* enter the ceremony?**
No.

**Will the bereaved family be present at the church or funeral home before the service?**
Yes.

**Is there a traditional greeting for the family?**
No.

**Will there be an open casket?**
Rarely.

**Is a guest expected to view the body?**
This is entirely optional.

**What is appropriate behavior upon viewing the body?**
A moment of silent prayer.

**Who are the major officiants at the ceremony and what do they do?**
◾ *A priest*, who leads the service.

**What books are used?**
*The Book of Common Prayer* (New York: Church Hymnal Corp., 1986) and a hymnal. In Canada, *The Book of Alternative Services* (Toronto: The Anglican Book Center, 1985) may be used. Occasionally, the Bible lessons are

included in the program.

**To indicate the order of the ceremony:**
A program will be provided.

**Will a guest who is not Episcopalian/Anglican be expected to do anything other than sit?**
They are expected to stand and kneel with the congregation, read prayers aloud and sing with congregants, if this does not compromise their personal beliefs. If one does not wish to kneel, sit when congregants do so.

**Are there any parts of the ceremony in which a guest who is not Episcopalian/Anglican should *not* participate?**
Do not receive communion or say any prayers contradictory to the beliefs of your own faith. Only baptized Christians may receive communion.

**If not disruptive to the ceremony, is it okay to:**
◘ **Take pictures?** No.
◘ **Use a flash?** No.
◘ **Use a video camera?** No.
◘ **Use a tape recorder?** No.

**Will contributions to the church be collected at the ceremony?**
No.

### THE INTERMENT

**Should guests attend the interment?**
Yes, especially if the deceased was a close friend.

**Whom should one ask for directions?**
The funeral director or another guest.

**What happens at the graveside?**
The body is committed to the ground. If there has been a cremation, the ashes are either buried or put in a vault.

**Do guests who are not Episcopalian/Anglicans participate at the graveside ceremony?**
No. They are simply present.

### COMFORTING THE BEREAVED

**Is it appropriate to visit the home of the bereaved after the funeral?**
Yes, although there is no specific "ritual" for calling or expressing sympa-

thy to someone who is mourning. Nor is there a "ritual" that guides the behavior of the mourners.

**Will there be a religious service at the home of the bereaved?**
No.

**Will food be served?**
This is at the discretion of the bereaved.

**How soon after the funeral will a mourner usually return to a normal work schedule?**
One week.

**How soon after the funeral will a mourner usually return to a normal social schedule?**
This is entirely at the discretion of the bereaved.

## V · HOME CELEBRATIONS

Not applicable for Episcopalians/Anglicans.

## Chapter 8 Contents

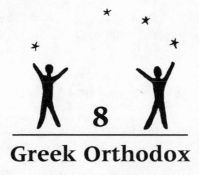

# Greek Orthodox

## I · HISTORY AND BELIEFS

The Orthodox Church was essentially an outgrowth of the Great Schism over doctrinal issues between east and west in the Christian world in the year 1054. This caused a complete breakdown in communication between the Roman Catholic Church, based in Rome, and the Orthodox church, which remained under the jurisdiction of the Patriarch of Constantinople (present day Istanbul).

The word "Greek" is used not just to describe the Orthodox Christian people of Greece and others who speak Greek, but to refer to the early Christians who originally formed the initial Christian church and whose members spoke Greek and used Greek thought to find appropriate expressions of the Orthodox faith.

The term "Orthodox" is used to reflect adherents' belief that they believe and worship God correctly.

Essentially, Orthodox Christians consider their beliefs similar to those of other Christian traditions, but believe that the balance and integrity of the teachings of Jesus' twelve apostles have been preserved inviolate by their church.

Greek Orthodoxy holds that the eternal truths of God's saving revelation in Jesus Christ are preserved in the living tradition of the church under the guidance and inspiration of the Holy Spirit, which is the empowering spirit of God and the particular endowment of the church. While the Bible is the written testimony of God's revelation, Holy Tradition is the all-encompassing experience of the church under the guidance and direction of the Holy Spirit.

The first Greek Orthodox community in the Americas was founded in 1864 in New Orleans by a small colony of Greek merchants. In 1892, the first permanent community of Greek Orthodox in the United States was founded in New York. This is now known as the Archdiocesan Cathedral of the Holy Trinity and See of the Archbishop of North and South America.

There are now about seven million Orthodox Christians in the Western Hemisphere.

**U.S. churches:** 500
**U.S. membership:** 1.5 million
*(data from the Greek Orthodox Diocese of America)*

**For more information, contact:**
The Greek Orthodox Archdiocese of America
8-10 East 79th Street
New York, NY 10021
(212) 570-3500

**Canadian churches:** 76
**Canadian membership:** 350,000
*(data from the* 1998 Yearbook of American and Canadian Churches*)*

**For more information, contact:**
Greek Orthodox Diocese of Toronto (Canada)
27 Teddington Park Avenue
Toronto, ON  M4N 2C4
(416) 322-5055

## II · THE BASIC SERVICE

Greek Orthodox services take place every Sunday. They usually last from one and a half to two hours.

### APPROPRIATE ATTIRE

**Men:** Jacket and tie. A headcovering is not required.

**Women:** Dresses are recommended, as are clothing that covers the arms and hems that reach below the knee. A headcovering is not required. Open-toed shoes and modest jewelry may be worn.

There are no rules regarding colors of clothing.

## THE SANCTUARY

**What are the major sections of the church?**

◘ *The narthex*, where one enters.

◘ *The nave*, where one worships and participates in the services.

◘ *The solea*, where one receives communion and other sacraments.

◘ *The altar*, which is reserved for ordained individuals only.

## THE SERVICE

**When should guests arrive and where should they sit?**

It is customary to arrive early. Ushers will advise guests on where to sit.

**If arriving late, are there times when a guest should *not* enter the service?**

Do not enter during scripture readings and priestly blessings.

**Are there times when a guest should *not* leave the service?**

Yes, during scripture readings and priestly blessings.

**Who are the major officiants, leaders or participants and what do they do?**

The priest or bishop, who conducts the entire service.

**What are the major ritual objects of the service?**

◘ *Icons*, two-dimensional artistic images of saints.

◘ *A gold-covered New Testament*.

◘ *Censer*, an incense burner holder with bells. Smoke from the incense represents prayers being carried to heaven.

◘ *Chalice*, a gold covered cup with a tall stem. Held by a priest or bishop and contains the holy Eucharist, the bread and wine, which after being consecrated by clergy become transubstantiated into the body and blood of Christ.

**What books are used?**

Several books may be used, such as *The Divine Liturgy of St. John Chrysostom* (Brookline, Ma.: Holy Cross Orthodox Press, 1985).

**To indicate the order of service:**

A program will be distributed to congregants and guests.

## GUEST BEHAVIOR DURING THE SERVICE

**Will a guest who is not Greek Orthodox be expected to do anything other than sit?**

Yes. Stand when the congregants arise. Kneeling with them is appropriate only if it does not violate a visitor's own religious beliefs. Remain seated when congregants kneel.

**Are there any parts of the service in which a guest who is not Greek Orthodox should *not* participate?**

Yes. Holy communion. This is the high point of the service. Occurs after a priest or bishop advances toward the congregation from the altar, holds up the chalice and says, "With faith and reverence, draw near." Congregants then go forward to receive communion.

**If not disruptive to the service, is it okay to:**
◘ **Take pictures?** Yes.
◘ **Use a flash?** Yes.
◘ **Use a video camera?** Yes.
◘ **Use a tape recorder?** Yes.

**Will contributions to the church be collected at the service?**

Yes. Trays are passed through the congregation at end of the service.

**How much is customary to contribute?**

About $5.

## AFTER THE SERVICE

**Is there usually a reception after the service?**

A 30- to 60-minute reception is usually held in a room or hall adjoining the main sanctuary. Light food, such as coffee and pastry, is ordinarily served. There are no alcoholic beverages.

**Is there a traditional form of address for clergy who may be at the reception?**

Yes. It is "Father."

**Is it okay to leave early?**

Yes.

## GENERAL GUIDELINES AND ADVICE

Most Greek Orthodox churches have books or pamphlets in every pew that explain the service and that follow it word for word. Also, since about 50 percent of the service is in English, guests who are not Greek Orthodox should not anticipate a service that is predominantly in another language.

## SPECIAL VOCABULARY

**Key words or phrases which might be helpful for a visitor to know:**

- *Kyrie eleison* ("KEE-ree-ay ay-LAY-ee-son"), "Lord have mercy."
- *Irini pasi* ("EE-ree-nay PAH-see"), "Peace be with you."
- *See kyrie* ("see KEE-ree-ay"), "To you, oh Lord."

## DOGMA AND IDEOLOGY

**The Greek Orthodox:**

- Believe in the Holy Trinity (the Father, the Son and the Holy Spirit).
- Do not recognize the Pope as the church's final authority.
- Do not, as do some Christian denominations, consider the Eucharist, the ritual meal of bread and wine that occurs during the service, to be symbolic. After consecration, it is the body and blood of Christ.

**A basic book to which a guest can refer to learn more about the Greek Orthodox Church:**

*The Greek Orthodox Church* by Bishop Kalistos Ware (New York: Penguin Books, 1980).

---

# III · HOLY DAYS AND FESTIVALS

- *New Year*, September 1. Marks the beginning of the church's new year. There is no special greeting to church members for this holiday. A traditional greeting is "Happy New Year."
- *Christmas,* December 25. Marks the birth of Jesus Christ. Church members traditionally greet each other with "Christ is born! Glorify Him!" Non-Greek Orthodox can greet church members with "Merry Christmas." The holiday is preceded by a 40-day fast in which one abstains from eating meat and dairy products.
- *Epiphany*, January 6. Marks the baptism of Jesus Christ. The traditional greeting among church members is "Christ is born! Glorify Him!" No traditional greeting for non-Greek Orthodox.
- *Easter*. Date of observance varies, although it usually occurs in April. Observes the resurrection of Jesus Christ. The holiday is preceded by a 49-day fast in which one abstains from eating fish, meat and dairy products. The traditional greeting among church members is "Christ is risen!" The response to this is "Truly He is risen!" Non-Greek Orthodox can greet church members with "Happy Easter."

■ *Pentecost.* Date of observance varies, but it usually occurs in early June. Marks the day on which the Holy Spirit, the empowering presence of God, descended upon the twelve disciples of Jesus Christ 50 days after Easter. On the eve of Pentecost, the church commemorates those who have departed from this life, praying that they may prove worthy through our prayers and by the grace of the Holy Spirit. There is no traditional greeting for this holiday.

## IV · LIFE CYCLE EVENTS

### · Birth Ceremony ·

The ceremony celebrating the birth of a child is the same for a male and female infant. It marks initiation into the church, forgiveness of sins and the beginning of the Christian life.

The all-in-one service incorporates Chrismation (known in other faiths as confirmation), Baptism and First Communion. During the baptism, the child is anointed with oil on the forehead, cheek, hands and feet. The communion emphasizes the fullness of participation in the sacramental life of the church. During it, the child is given wine and bread which, after consecration by a priest, have become the blood and body of Jesus Christ.

The 30- to 60-minute ritual is a ceremony unto itself and not part of a larger service.

### BEFORE THE CEREMONY

**Are guests usually invited by a formal invitation?**
Yes.

**If not stated explicitly, should one assume that children are invited?**
Yes.

**If one can't attend, what should one do?**
RSVP with regrets. Possibly send a present.

### APPROPRIATE ATTIRE

**Men:** Jacket and tie. A headcovering is not required.

**Women:** Should wear clothing that covers the arms and hems that reach below the knees. A headcovering is not required.

There are no rules regarding colors of clothing.

## GIFTS

**Is a gift customarily expected?**

Yes. Cash, bonds or stocks totalling about $50 to $100 are appropriate.

**Should gifts be brought to the ceremony?**

Either send gifts to the home of the parents or give them to the parents at the ceremony.

## THE CEREMONY

**Where will the ceremony take place?**

In the main sanctuary of the parents' church.

**When should guests arrive and where should they sit?**

Arrive early. An usher will advise a guest where to sit.

**If arriving late, are there times when a guest should *not* enter the ceremony?**

Do not enter during scripture readings and priestly blessings.

**Are there times when a guest should *not* leave the ceremony?**

No.

**Who are the major officiants, leaders or participants at the ceremony and what do they do?**

- *The priest*, who baptizes the child.
- *The godparents*, who assist in the ceremony. The new parents usually choose them from relatives or close friends.

**What books are used?**

Several books may be used, such as *The Divine Liturgy of St. John Chrysostom* (Brookline, Ma.: Holy Cross Orthodox Press, 1985).

**To indicate the order of the ceremony:**

A program will be distributed.

**Will a guest who is not Greek Orthodox be expected to do anything other than sit?**

Yes. Stand when the congregation does.

**Are there any parts of the ceremony in which a guest who is not Greek Orthodox should *not* participate?**

No.

**If not disruptive to the ceremony, is it okay to:**

- **Take pictures?** Yes.

◧ **Use a flash?** Yes.
◧ **Use a video camera?** Yes.
◧ **Use a tape recorder?** Yes.

**Will contributions to the church be collected at the ceremony?**
No.

### AFTER THE CEREMONY

**Is there usually a reception after the ceremony?**
There is often a formal reception lasting one to two hours. It may be in the same building as the ceremony, at the parents' home, or at a catering hall. Food will be served, including alcoholic beverages. There may be music and dancing.

**Would it be considered impolite to neither eat nor drink?**
No.

**Is there a grace or benediction before eating or drinking?**
Yes. An invocation is recited to bless the food.

**Is there a grace or benediction after eating or drinking?**
No.

**Is there a traditional greeting for the family?**
Yes: "May the child live a blessed life." Or simply offer your congratulations.

**Is there a traditional form of address for clergy who may be at the reception?**
Yes. It is "Father."

**Is it okay to leave early?**
Yes, whenever one wishes.

## · *Initiation Ceremony* ·

Baptism serves as one's initiation into the church. Greek Orthodoxy has no ritual ceremonies for adolescents.

## · *Marriage Ceremony* ·

To Greek Orthodox, marriage is a sacrament of union between man and woman, who enter it to be mutually complemented and to propagate the human race. The 30- to 60-minute marriage ceremony is a ceremony unto itself and not part of a larger service.

## BEFORE THE CEREMONY

**Are guests usually invited by a formal invitation?**
Yes.

**If not stated explicitly, should one assume that children are invited?**
No.

**If one can't attend, what should one do?**
RSVP with regrets and send a gift.

## APPROPRIATE ATTIRE

**Men:** Jacket and tie. A headcovering is not required.

**Women:** A dress or a skirt and blouse. Clothing should cover the arms and hems should reach below the knees. A headcovering is not required. Open-toed shoes and modest jewelry may be worn.

There are no rules regarding colors of clothing.

## GIFTS

**Is a gift customarily expected?**
Yes. Appropriate gifts are cash or bonds valued at $50 to $500, or gifts chosen from bridal registries in shops.

**Should gifts be brought to the ceremony?**
They should be either sent to the home or brought to the reception and placed on the gift table.

## THE CEREMONY

**Where will the ceremony take place?**
In the main sanctuary of the church chosen by the celebrants and their family.

**When should guests arrive and where should they sit?**
Arrive early. An usher will advise guests where to sit.

**If arriving late, are there times when a guest should *not* enter the ceremony?**
Do not enter during scripture readings and priestly blessings.

**Are there times when a guest should *not* leave the ceremony?**
No.

**Who are the major officiants, leaders or participants at the ceremony and what do they do?**

◘ *The priest,* who officiates.

◘ *The bride and groom.*

◘ *The best man and maid of honor,* who participate and assist during the ceremony.

**What books are used?**

Only the priest uses a book.

**To indicate the order of the ceremony:**

A program will be distributed.

**Will a guest who is not Greek Orthodox be expected to do anything other than sit?**

Yes. Stand when the congregation does.

**Are there any parts of the ceremony in which a guest who is not Greek Orthodox should *not* participate?**

No.

**If not disruptive to the ceremony, is it okay to:**

◘ **Take pictures?** Yes.

◘ **Use a flash?** Yes.

◘ **Use a video camera?** Yes.

◘ **Use a tape recorder?** Yes.

**Will contributions to the church be collected at the ceremony?**

No.

### AFTER THE CEREMONY

**Is there usually a reception after the ceremony?**

There is often a formal reception lasting two hours or more. There will be a toast to the newlyweds, a meal, music and dancing. The reception may be in the same building as the ceremony, at the parents' home, or at a catering hall.

**Would it be considered impolite to neither eat nor drink?**

No.

**Is there a grace or benediction before eating or drinking?**

Yes. An invocation is recited to bless the food.

**Is there a grace or benediction after eating or drinking?**

No.

**Is there a traditional greeting for the family?**
Yes: "May you prosper." Or simply offer your congratulations.

**Is there a traditional form of address for clergy who may be at the reception?**
Yes: "Father."

**Is it okay to leave early?**
Yes, anytime.

## · Funerals and Mourning ·

The Greek Orthodox Church believes that death is the separation of the soul (the spiritual dimension of each human being) from the body (the physical dimension of each human being). Upon death, we immediately begin to experience a foretaste of heaven and hell. This experience, known as the partial judgment, is based on the general character of our lives regarding behavior, character and communion with God.

At some unknown time in the future, teaches the church, Jesus Christ will return and inaugurate a new era in which His kingdom shall be established. The final judgment will then occur. In our resurrected existence, we will either live eternally in heaven in communion with God, or eternally in hell and out of communion with God.

The 30- to 60-minute Greek Orthodox funeral ceremony is not part of a larger service.

### BEFORE THE CEREMONY

**How soon after the death does the funeral usually take place?**
Within one week; most often within two to three days.

**What should a non-Greek Orthodox do upon hearing of the death of a member of that faith?**
Telephone or visit the family of the deceased, or send cards and/or flowers. If visiting, one should express condolences. It is traditional for Greek Orthodox to say to the bereaved, "May you have an abundant life" and "May their memory be eternal."

### APPROPRIATE ATTIRE

**Men:** Jacket and tie. A headcovering is not required.

**Women:** A dress or a skirt and blouse or a pants suit. Neither clothing that covers the arms, hems that extend below the knees or a headcovering are required. Open-toed shoes and modest jewelry may be worn.

There are no rules regarding colors of clothing, but navy blue or black clothes are recommended for both men and women.

## GIFTS

### Is it appropriate to send flowers or make a contribution?
Flowers may be sent either to the home of the bereaved upon hearing the news or to the funeral itself. Contributions of $50 or more can be made to a fund or charity designated by the family of the deceased.

### Is it appropriate to send food?
No. However, the family of the deceased usually provides a "mercy meal" after the funeral for relatives and friends. This may be held in a restaurant, a church hall or a private home.

## THE CEREMONY

### Where will the ceremony take place?
In a church.

### When should guests arrive and where should they sit?
It is customary to arrive early. Ushers will advise guests where to sit.

### If arriving late, are there times when a guest should *not* enter the service?
No.

### Will the bereaved family be present at the church before the service?
Yes.

### Is there a traditional greeting for the family?
Yes: "Memory Eternal." Or offer your condolences.

### Will there be an open casket?
Usually.

### Is a guest expected to view the body?
This is optional.

### What is appropriate behavior upon viewing the body?
Pause briefly in front of the casket. Traditionally, when Greek Orthodox view the body, they bow in front of the casket and kiss an icon or cross placed on the chest of the deceased. Such rituals are optional for guests who are not Greek Orthodox.

**Who are the major officiants at the ceremony and what do they do?**

The priest, who leads the service.

**What books are used?**

Several books may be used, such as *The Divine Liturgy of St. John Chrysostom* (Brookline, Ma.: Holy Cross Orthodox Press, 1985).

**Will a guest who is not Greek Orthodox be expected to do anything other than sit?**

Yes: Stand when the congregation does and pay respects to the bereaved family.

**Are there any parts of the ceremony in which a guest who is not Greek Orthodox should *not* participate?**

No.

**If not disruptive to the ceremony, is it okay to:**
- **Take pictures?** No.
- **Use a flash?** No.
- **Use a video camera?** No.
- **Use a tape recorder?** No.

**Will contributions to the church be collected at the ceremony?**

No.

## THE INTERMENT

**Should guests attend the interment?**

Yes.

**Whom should one ask for directions?**

The funeral director.

**What happens at the graveside?**

There is a five-minute prayer ceremony and each person present places one flower on the casket. The flowers usually come from those sent to the church for the funeral and then conveyed to the cemetery with the casket.

## COMFORTING THE BEREAVED

**Is it appropriate to visit the home of the bereaved after the funeral?**

Yes, briefly.

**Will there be a religious service at the home of the bereaved?**
No.

**Will food be served?**
Yes.

**How soon after the funeral will a mourner usually return to a normal work schedule?**
The bereaved usually stays home from work for one week.

**How soon after the funeral will a mourner usually return to a normal social schedule?**
The bereaved usually avoids social gatherings for two months.

**Are there mourning customs to which a friend who is not Greek Orthodox should be sensitive?**
Widows may wear black for up to two years.

**Are there rituals for observing the anniversary of the death?**
A memorial service is held on the Sunday closest to the 40th day after the death. Subsequent memorial services are held on the annual anniversaries of the death.

## V · HOME CELEBRATIONS

### · *The Home Blessing* ·

**When does it occur?**
Either on January 6, the Epiphany, which is the traditional date for having one's home blessed annually; or, shortly after moving into a new home.

**What is its significance?**
Holy water is used to sanctify the home, just as Jesus' baptism sanctified the waters of the River Jordan and all creation.

**What is the proper greeting to the celebrants?**
"Congratulations."

### BEFORE THE CEREMONY

**Are guests usually invited by a formal invitation?**
Yes.

**If not stated explicitly, should one assume children are invited?**
No.

**If one can't attend, what should one do?**
Telephone the celebrants with your regrets.

## APPROPRIATE ATTIRE

**Men:** Jacket and tie. A headcovering is not required.

**Women:** A dress or a skirt and blouse or a pants suit. It is not required to wear clothing that covers the arms or hems that extend below the knees or to cover one's head. Open-toed shoes and modest jewelry may be worn. A headcovering is not required.

There are no rules regarding colors of clothing.

## GIFTS

**Is a gift customarily expected?**
This is entirely optional.

**If one decides to give a gift, is a certain type of gift appropriate?**
The usual sort of housewarming gift, which should be brought to the house when you arrive.

## THE CEREMONY

The home blessing ceremony lasts between 15 and 30 minutes. It is customary to arrive early. The major officiate is the priest, who blesses the home.

**What are the major ritual objects of the ceremony?**
- *The cross*, which represents Christ's victory over death through His resurrection.
- *Water*, which is a vehicle for sanctification.
- *A basil flower*, which is used to sprinkle water in the air in the configuration of a cross in each room throughout the house as the priest recites blessings.

**What books are used?**
Prayerbooks may be distributed.

**Will a guest who is not Greek Orthodox be expected to do anything other than sit?**
Yes. Stand when the celebrants rise.

**Are there any parts of the ceremony in which a guest who is not Greek Orthodox should *not* participate?**
No.

**If not disruptive to the ceremony, is it okay to:**
◘ **Take pictures?** Yes.
◘ **Use a flash?** Yes.
◘ **Use a video camera?** Yes.
◘ **Use a tape recorder?** Yes.

## EATING AND DRINKING

**Is a meal part of the celebration?**
Yes. It is served after the ceremony.

**Will there be alcoholic beverages?**
Possibly.

**Would it be considered impolite to neither eat nor drink?**
No.

**Is there a grace or benediction before eating or drinking?**
Yes. An invocation is recited to bless the food.

**Is there a grace or benediction after eating or drinking?**
No.

**At the meal, will a guest be asked to say or do anything?**
No.

**Will there be:**
◘ **Dancing?** No.
◘ **Music?** No.

## GENERAL GUIDELINES AND ADVICE

None provided.

## Chapter 9 Contents

# Hindu

## I · HISTORY AND BELIEFS

There are extraordinary differences between Hindu culture and beliefs and the prevailing Judeo-Christian religions and cultures in North America. Yet, from the Transcendentalists in New England in the early 19th century through the beatniks of the 1950s and the spiritual seekers of today, Hinduism has held a fascination for many thousands of North Americans. Most of these were either influenced tangentially by Hinduism or became actual practitioners of certain aspects of it for a while. But today, the vast majority of Hindus in the United States and Canada are immigrants from Asia, especially from India.

Unlike other religions, Hinduism has no founder and no common creed or doctrine. Generally, it teaches that God is both within being and object in the universe—and transcends every being and object; that the essence of each soul is divine; and that the purpose of life is to become aware of that divine essence. The many forms of worship ritual and meditation in Hinduism are intended to lead the soul toward direct experience of God or Self.

In general, the different gods and goddesses in Hinduism are different ways of conceiving and approaching the one God beyond name and form. Different forms of worship through images, symbols and rituals are helpful to different kinds of persons. Some do not need external worship. The goal is to transcend these forms and the world as it is ordinarily perceived and to realize the divine presence everywhere.

**U.S. temples:** Not available.
**U.S. membership:** 1 million
*(1995 data from The Vedanta Society)*

157

**For more information, contact:**

The Vedanta Society of New York
34 West 71st Street
New York, NY 10023
(212) 877-9197

**Canadian temples:** Not available
**Canadian membership:** 100,000+
*(data from the* 1992 Corpus Almanac & Canadian Sourcebook*)*

**For more information, contact:**

Vendanta Society of Toronto
120 Emmett Avenue
Toronto, ON  M6M 2E6
(416) 240-7262

Bengali Society of British Columbia
9211 Arvida Drive
Richmond, B.C.  V7A 4K5
(604) 271-9283

## II · THE BASIC SERVICE

Hindu temples are understood to be the residence of a particular god or goddess, or many gods and goddesses. At their center is a small room where a main image of that deity is kept.

Hindu services differ from typical congregational services in North America. Usually, Hindus recite prayer or are engaged in rituals at their own pace. In North America, however, some Hindu groups have attempted to modify Hindu customs so they conform more closely to North American practices, such as meeting at certain times on Sundays.

During the typical *puja*, or ritual worship that is held before a specific deity, the god is treated as a "guest" and the devotee is its "host." Prayers are directed to it, flowers are draped around or near it and incense is lit near it. It may even be bathed in special oils. The intention is to offer the best things to the "guest."

During the service, sacramental food called *prasad* may be served to those present. Guests who wish to abstain may do so without offending congregants. During the ritual called *bhog*, which is performed prior to eating, the food is blessed. No alcoholic beverages or non-vegetarian dishes are served as part of *prasad*.

## APPROPRIATE ATTIRE

**Men:** Dress casually. No head covering is required.

**Women:** Dress casually. Not required are a head covering, clothing that covers the arms or hems that reach below the knees. Open-toed shoes and modest jewelry are permissible.

There are no rules regarding colors of clothing.

## THE SANCTUARY

### What are the major sections of the temple?

There are many variables in Hindu temple architecture, especially in North America. But generally, both here and in India, there is a large room called a *natmandir*, where worshippers sit or stand. This faces a smaller section where the deity of the temple resides and where rituals honoring it are performed.

## THE SERVICE

### When should guests arrive and where should they sit?

Arrive at the time for which the service is called. Sit wherever you wish on the floor, as do the congregants.

### If arriving late, are there times when a guest should *not* enter the service?

No.

### Are there times when a guest should *not* leave the service?

No.

### Who are the major officiants, leaders or participants and what do they do?

- *Priests*, who conduct the service.

### What are the major ritual objects of the service?

- *Statues or pictures* that represent any of the thousands of Hindu deities.
- *Narayana shalagram*, a black round stone that symbolizes totality.
- *Flowers*, which may be placed in front of a picture or statue of the temple's deity.
- *Incense*, which is usually burned near the deity to perfume the air.
- *Water from the Ganges River*, the river in India that is holy to Hindus. Often brought to the United States and Canada by traveling Hindus.

◘ *Lamps with five wicks dipped in clarified butter,* and rotated near the deity by the worshippers.

**What books are used?**

The *Bhagavad-Gita*, the epic Sanskrit poem that relates the dialogue between the human Arjuna and the god, Lord Krishna. It consists of 700 two-line stanzas in 18 chapters in which Krishna expounds on the nature of reality. Also used are various scriptures favored by each Hindu sect. Readings from the Vedas and Upanisads and commentaries on the scriptures are regularly performed instead of sermons.

**To indicate the order of the service:**

Periodic announcements will be made by a co-priest.

## GUEST BEHAVIOR DURING THE SERVICE

**Will a guest who is not a Hindu be expected to do anything other than sit?**

No.

**Are there any parts of the service in which a guest who is not a Hindu should *not* participate?**

Guests of other faiths are welcome to participate in any aspects of the service if these do not compromise or violate their own religious beliefs.

**If not disruptive to the service, is it okay to:**

◘ **Take pictures?** Yes, with permission of the priest.

◘ **Use a flash?** Yes, with permission of the priest.

◘ **Use a video camera?** Yes, with permission of the priest.

◘ **Use a tape recorder?** Yes, with permission of the priest.

**Will contributions to the temple be collected at the service?**

Yes.

**How much is customary to contribute?**

There is no usual amount, although $1 to $5 would be appropriate.

## AFTER THE SERVICE

**Is there usually a reception after the service?**

No.

**Is there a traditional form of address for clergy whom a guest may meet?**

"Swamiji" ("SWAH-mee-jee") if a monk, "Panditji" if a priest.

## GENERAL GUIDELINES AND ADVICE

Remove your shoes before entering the main sanctuary.

Silence is expected from all present during the ceremony, except during chanting.

## SPECIAL VOCABULARY

### Key words or phrases which might be helpful for a visitor to know:

- *Prasad* ("PRAH-sahd"), sacramental food.
- *Mantras* ("MAHN-tras"), repeated prayers.
- *Murti* ("MOOR-ty"), a statue or picture representing a deity.
- *Thakur* ("TAH-koor"), Lord or God.

## DOGMA AND IDEOLOGY

### Hindus believe:

- Humans are cast in a recurring cycle of birth and rebirth called *samsara*. *Karma*, the consequences of one's actions, determines one's lot in a future reincarnation from one lifetime to another.
- The Path of Desire, or the attractions of worldly success, is ephemeral and seductive.
- The Path of Renunciation, which comes after one realizes the short-comings of the Path of Desire, can lead to exhilaration and confidence in life's higher calling. The path includes discipline (of every form) and pre-ferring difficult, time-consuming accomplishments to those that are easy and quick.
- Four *yogas*, or disciplines, comprise four paths to enlightenment, or dis-cerning the true nature of reality:

  *Janana yoga*, marshalling the powers of the intellect to cut through the veils of illusion. Includes meditative practices.

  *Bhakti yoga*, directing one's love toward God.

  *Karma yoga*, selfless service toward others.

  *Raja yoga*, which incorporates the above yogas into a unified discipline that addresses the body, mind and emotions. Included in *Raja Yoga* is *hatha yoga*, which disciplines and subdues the body.

### Some basic books to which a guest can refer to learn more about Hinduism:

*The Essentials of Hinduism*, by Swami Bhaskarananda (Seattle, Wa.: Viveka Press, 1994).

*The Upanishads* and *The Bhagavad-Gita*, both of which are available in numerous translations from several publishers.

---

## III · HOLY DAYS AND FESTIVALS

The specific date of Hindu holidays vary from year to year in relation to the western secular calendar because the Hindu calendar is lunar-based.

◾ *Shiva Ratri*, an all-night worship of God as the god Shiva. Shiva's primary qualities are creation and destruction, and compassion and renunciation. This holiday usually occurs in late winter. There is no traditional greeting for this holiday.

◾ *Duhsehra/Durga Puja*, celebrates the triumph of good over evil. Usually occurs in early autumn. There is no traditional greeting for this holiday.

◾ *Rama Navami*, worship of Rama, who (along with the god Krishna) is regarded as God incarnate. This usually occurs in the spring. There is no traditional greeting for this holiday.

◾ *Krishna Janmashtami*, the birthday celebration of Krishna, who (along with Rama) is regarded as God incarnate. Krishna is perhaps the most widely worshipped Hindu deity. This holiday occurs in the late summer. There is no traditional greeting for this holiday.

---

## IV · LIFE CYCLE EVENTS

### · *Birth Ceremony* ·

The naming ceremony occurs when a newborn is six to eight months old. It is called the "rice eating ceremony" because it marks the first time the child has eaten solid food. Held at the child's home, it is a ceremony unto itself.

#### BEFORE THE CEREMONY

**Are guests usually invited by a formal invitation?**
Yes.

**If not stated explicitly, should one assume that children are invited?**
Yes.

**If one can't attend, what should one do?**
RSVP with regrets and send a gift.

## APPROPRIATE ATTIRE

**Men:** Dress casually. No head covering required.

**Women:** Dress casually. Not required are a head covering, clothing that covers the arms or hems that reach below the knees. Open-toed shoes and modest jewelry are permissible.

There are no rules regarding colors of clothing.

## GIFTS

### Is a gift customarily expected?
Yes. Such gift items as clothes or toys are usual. Less common are cash or bonds.

### Should gifts be brought to the ceremony?
Bring gifts to the ceremony itself and place them in the hands of the parents.

## THE CEREMONY

### Where will the ceremony take place?
Usually in a home. Less frequently in a temple.

### When should guests arrive and where should they sit?
Arrive at the time called for the ceremony to begin. Sit wherever you wish.

### If arriving late, are there times when a guest should *not* enter the ceremony?
No.

### Are there times when a guest should *not* leave the ceremony?
No.

### Who are the major officiants, leaders or participants at the ceremony and what do they do?
If the ceremony is held at home, a priest may perform the ritual, but in some cases senior members of the family officiate. If held at a Hindu temple, a priest officiates.

### What books are used?
No standard books are used for the ceremony.

### To indicate the order of the ceremony:
The service is so brief that few, if any, directions are needed for those present.

**Will a guest who is not a Hindu be expected to do anything other than sit?**
No.

**Are there any parts of the ceremony in which a guest who is not a Hindu should *not* participate?**
Guests of other faiths are welcome to participate in any aspects of the service if these do not compromise or violate their own religious beliefs.

**If not disruptive to the ceremony, is it okay to:**
◨ **Take pictures?** Yes, with permission of the priest.
◨ **Use a flash?** Yes, with permission of the priest.
◨ **Use a video camera?** Yes, with permission of the priest.
◨ **Use a tape recorder?** Yes, with permission of the priest.

**Will contributions to the temple be collected at the ceremony?**
No.

## AFTER THE CEREMONY

**Is there usually a reception after the ceremony?**
A reception is usually held both before and after the ceremony, often in the same place as the ceremony itself. Traditional Indian food will be served. No alcoholic beverages will be served. There will be singing and, possibly, music.

*Prasad*, or food offered to a deity, is given to the child before others are fed.

**Would it be considered impolite to neither eat nor drink?**
No.

**Is there a grace or benediction before eating or drinking?**
No.

**Is there a grace or benediction after eating or drinking?**
No.

**Is there a traditional greeting for the family?**
No. Just offer your congratulations.

**Is there a traditional form of address for clergy who may be at the reception?**
"Swamiji" ("SWAH-mee-jee") if a monk, "Panditji" if a priest.

**Is it okay to leave early?**
No.

## · *Initiation Ceremony* ·

There is an initiation ceremony only for males of the priest class. This is called the "sacred thread ceremony" and occurs between the ages of eight and 12. It is strictly private and is a ceremony unto itself.

In this ritual, the boy is initiated into the priesthood. Thereafter, he is regarded as having had his second, or spiritual, birth.

## · *Marriage Ceremony* ·

Hindu marriages are generally arranged by the parents or guardians of the bride and groom. In those rare cases where males and females choose their own partners, permission must be obtained from both sets of parents. No premarital dating or free mixing is allowed between males and females of marriageable age.

A Hindu marriage has seven major ceremonies:

- *Vagdana*, the verbal contract about the marriage between the fathers or guardians of the bride and groom.
- *Kanya Sampradana*, the giving away of the daughter to the groom by her father or guardian.
- *Varana*, welcoming the bride and groom.
- *Panigrahana*, ritualistic holding of each other's hands by the bride and groom.
- *Saptapadi*, a seven-step walking ritual by the bride and groom.
- *Laj homa*, creation of the holy fire that symbolizes the formless divinity. The bride and groom circle it four times and offer a parched paddy as oblation.
- *Sindur dam*, the groom puts red vermilion on the forehead and the furrow of the parted hair of the bride.

Marriage ceremonies are usually held after sunset and before sunrise.

### BEFORE THE CEREMONY

**Are guests usually invited by a formal invitation?**
Yes.

**If not stated explicitly, should one assume that children are invited?**
Yes.

**If one can't attend, what should one do?**
RSVP with regrets and send a gift.

## APPROPRIATE ATTIRE

**Men:** Dress casually. No head covering is required.

**Women:** Dress casually. Not required are a head covering, clothing that covers the arms or hems that reach below the knees. Open-toed shoes and modest jewelry are permissible.

There are no rules regarding colors of clothing.

## GIFTS

**Is a gift customarily expected?**
Yes, usually household items.

**Should gifts be brought to the ceremony?**
Yes.

## THE CEREMONY

**Where will the ceremony take place?**
In any area that is covered. This could be a temple, a home, a catering hall or outside under a canopy.

**When should guests arrive and where should they sit?**
Arrive at the time specified for the ceremony to begin. Sit wherever you wish.

**If arriving late, are there times when a guest should *not* enter the ceremony?**
No.

**Are there times when a guest should *not* leave the ceremony?**
No.

**Who are the major officiants, leaders or participants at the ceremony and what do they do?**
▪ *Priests*, who officiate.
▪ *Parents and/or guardians*, who exchange verbal contracts about the marriage. Also, the bride's father gives her to the groom.
▪ *Bride and groom.*

**What books are used?**
Only the priests use books.

**To indicate the order of the ceremony:**
Ordinarily, neither a program is distributed nor are periodic announce-

ments made by the officiating priests. The ceremony just proceeds, although in the United States and Canada, the priest may occasionally explain the ceremony to guests who are not Hindus.

**Will a guest who is not a Hindu be expected to do anything other than sit?**
No.

**Are there any parts of the ceremony in which a guest who is not a Hindu should *not* participate?**
No.

**If not disruptive to the ceremony, is it okay to:**
- **Take pictures?** Yes.
- **Use a flash?** Yes.
- **Use a video camera?** Yes.
- **Use a tape recorder?** Yes.

**Will contributions to the temple be collected at the ceremony?**
No.

## AFTER THE CEREMONY

**Is there usually a reception after the ceremony?**
There is a reception before and after the ceremony. Traditional Indian foods are served. It may last for many hours.

**Would it be considered impolite to neither eat nor drink?**
Yes.

**Is there a grace or benediction before eating or drinking?**
No.

**Is there a grace or benediction after eating or drinking?**
No.

**Is there a traditional greeting for the family?**
No. Just offer your "congratulations."

**Is there a traditional form of address for clergy who may be at the reception?**
"Swamiji" ("SWAH-mee-jee") if a monk, "Panditji" if a priest.

**Is it okay to leave early?**
Yes.

## · *Funerals and Mourning* ·

Although the physical body dies, *atman* ("AHT-mahn"), or the individual soul, has no beginning and no end. It may, upon death, pass into another reincarnation, the condition of which depends on the *karma*, or consequences of one's actions, reaped during the life that just ended, as well as during previous lifetimes.

But if, over many lifetimes, the deceased has realized the true nature of reality, the individuality of the soul will be lost upon death and it will become one with Brahman, the One, All-Encompassing soul.

### BEFORE THE CEREMONY

**How soon after the death does the funeral usually take place?**
Usually within 24 hours.

**What should a non-Hindu do upon hearing of the death of a member of that faith?**
Telephone or visit the bereaved and offer your condolences.

### APPROPRIATE ATTIRE

**Men:** Dress casually. No head covering is required.

**Women:** Dress casually. Not required are a head covering, clothing that covers the arms or hems that reach below the knees. Open-toed shoes and modest jewelry are permissible.

Wear white clothing. Black is not appropriate.

### GIFTS

**Is it appropriate to send flowers or make a contribution?**
It is appropriate to personally bring flowers to the home of the deceased upon hearing of the death. In Hinduism, there is no concept of a "funeral home," so the body remains at the home until taken to the place of cremation, which is usually 24 hours after death. Flowers are placed at the feet of the deceased.

Donations are not customary.

**Is it appropriate to send food?**
No.

## THE CEREMONY

**Where will the ceremony take place?**
At the place of cremation.

**When should guests arrive and where should they sit?**
Arrive at the time for which the ceremony has been called. Sit wherever you wish.

**If arriving late, are there times when a guest should *not* enter the ceremony?**
No.

**Will the bereaved family be present at the place of cremation before the ceremony?**
Yes.

**Is there a traditional greeting for the family?**
No. Just offer your condolences.

**Will there be an open casket?**
Always.

**Is a guest expected to view the body?**
Yes.

**What is appropriate behavior upon viewing the body?**
Look reverently upon the body and do not touch it.

**Who are the major officiants at the ceremony and what do they do?**
◪ *Priests* or senior members of the family.

**What books are used?**
Special books containing mantras for funeral services. Only the priests use these.

**To indicate the order of the ceremony:**
Ordinarily, neither a program is distributed nor are periodic announcements made by the officiating priests. The ceremony just proceeds, although in the United States and Canada, the priest may occasionally explain the ceremony to guests who are not Hindus.

**Will a guest who is not a Hindu be expected to do anything other than sit?**
No.

**Are there any parts of the ceremony in which a guest who is not a Hindu should *not* participate?**

Guests of other faiths are welcome to participate in any aspects of the service if these do not compromise or violate their own religious beliefs.

**If not disruptive to the ceremony, is it okay to:**
▪ **Take pictures?** No.
▪ **Use a flash?** No.
▪ **Use a video camera?** No.
▪ **Use a tape recorder?** No.

**Will contributions to the temple be collected at the ceremony?**
No.

## THE CREMATION

**Should guests attend the cremation?**
If they wish to.

**Whom should one ask for directions?**
Ask family members.

**What happens at the cremation?**
The last food offering is symbolically made to the deceased and then the body is cremated. The cremation ceremony is called *mukhagni* ("moo-KAHG-nee").

**Do guests who are not Hindus participate at the cremation ceremony?**
No. They are simply present.

## COMFORTING THE BEREAVED

**Is it appropriate to visit the home of the bereaved after the funeral?**
Yes. Visit the bereaved before the *shraddha* ("SHRAHD-hah") ceremony, which occurs 10 days after the death for members of the Bhrahmin caste and 30 days after the death for members of other castes. The ceremony is intended to liberate the soul of the deceased for its ascent to heaven. Visitors are expected to bring fruit to the home of the bereaved.

**Will there be a religious service at the home of the bereaved?**
The *shraddha* ceremony is performed at home. Guests are usually invited to it by phone.

**Will food be served?**

Varies according to tradition.

**How soon after the funeral will a mourner usually return to a normal work schedule?**

In 10 to 30 days, depending on when the *shraddha* ceremony is performed.

**How soon after the funeral will a mourner usually return to a normal social schedule?**

After the *shraddha* ceremony, which occurs 10 to 30 days after the death.

**Are there mourning customs to which a friend who is not a Hindu should be sensitive?**

For 10 to 30 days after the death, depending on when the *shraddha* ceremony is performed, mourners dress, eat and behave austerely.

**Are there rituals for observing the anniversary of the death?**

Yes. These are performed by a priest in a temple. There is no name for these rituals.

## V · HOME CELEBRATIONS

Worship in the home is a paramount aspect of Hindu ritual. This is a private ceremony that centers around the small shrine for a god and goddess found in most Hindu homes.

# Chapter 10 Contents

# 10
# Islam

## I · HISTORY AND BELIEFS

Muslims trace their spiritual ancestry to Ishmael, the son that Abraham, the first patriarch of the Jews, had by Hagar, who was his wife's maid. Seeking to continue his line, Abraham had taken Hagar for a second wife when Sarah had not been able to bear any children. But after Sarah had her son, Isaac, she insisted that Abraham banish Ishmael and Hagar from the tribe. The Quran, Islam's holy book, states that Ishmael went to Mecca, a city in what is now Saudi Arabia. His descendants became Muslims, while descendants of Isaac became Jews.

Muhammad, who is regarded as the last and final prophet of Allah (God), was born in Mecca in approximately 570 A.D. As a young man, he sought solitude in a cave on the outskirts of Mecca, where, according to Muslim belief, he received revelation from God. The basic creed that Muhammad taught is that the one God in heaven demands morality and monotheistic devotion from those He has created.

Initially, Muhammad's message was widely rejected, especially by Mecca's elite, which felt threatened by its egalitarian teachings. But by the time he died in 632 A.D., most of Arabia had embraced Islam.

Muslims revere the Quran, the bible of Islam, as the earthly cornerstone of their faith.

Islam teaches that the Old and New Testaments were also authentic revelations from God and recognizes as prophets all those who were prophets in the Old and New Testaments, including Abraham, Moses, David and Jesus.

With about one billion Muslims around the globe, Islam is the fastest growing religion in the world. Every country in the world has at least a small Muslim community. There are now Muslims in nearly every town in the United States, with more substantial numbers in larger cities, especially in the East and Midwest and on the West Coast. In Canada, there are Muslims in every major city, with substantial numbers in the provinces of Ontario, Alberta and British Columbia.

**U.S. mosques:** 1,000
**U.S. membership:** 6 million
*(1995 data from the American Muslim Council)*

**For more information, contact:**
The American Muslim Council
1212 New York Avenue NW, Suite 400
Washington, DC 20005
(202) 789-2262

**Canadian Islamic Centers and Organizations:** 150
**Canadian membership:** 450,000
*(1996 data from the Muslim World League)*

**For more information contact:**
Islamic Society of North America–Canada
219 Beverly Street
Toronto, ON  M5T 1Z4
(416) 977-2057
isna@isnacanada.com

Muslim World League
191 the West Mall #1018
Etobicoke, ON  M9C 5K8
(416) 622-2184

## II · THE BASIC SERVICE

While Muslims are required to pray five times a day—daybreak, noon, mid-afternoon, sunset and evening—this can be done either in a mosque or wherever individual Muslims may be. Prayer, which is in Arabic, is preceded with *wadu* ("WAH-doo"), washing with water that cleanses the body (hands, mouth, face and feet) and spirit. Congregants then face Mecca and, depending on the time of day, do two to four prostrations (*raka'ah*, pronounced "RAH-kah"). Each *raka'ah* begins with the declaration, "God is most great," and consists of bows, prostrations and the recitation of fixed prayers. At the end of prayer, the *taslim* ("TAHS-lihm"), or "peace greeting," "Peace be upon all of you and the mercy and the blessings of God," is repeated twice.

On Friday, *jumma* ("JUH-mah"), the noon prayer, is a congregational prayer and is recited at a central mosque designated for that purpose. In a mosque, men and women form separate lines for prayer, extending from one side of the mosque's main sanctuary to the other. The tight ranks symbolize unity and equality within the Muslim community. Each gender has its own line to maintain modesty and concentration during the physical movements of standing, bowing and prostration. Their separation does not indicate relative superiority or inferiority. This *jumma* lasts between 30 and 60 minutes.

## APPROPRIATE ATTIRE

**Men:** Casual shirt and slacks. Head covering is not required.

**Women:** A dress or skirt and blouse are recommended. Clothing should cover arms and hems should reach below the knees. A scarf is required to cover the head. Women may wear open-toed shoes and/or modest jewelry.

There are no rules regarding colors of clothing, but openly wearing crosses, Stars of David, jewelry with the signs of the zodiac and pendants with faces or heads of animals or people is discouraged.

## THE SANCTUARY

### What are the major sections of the mosque?

- *The entrance,* where shoes are removed since they are not worn inside a mosque.
- *A musallah* ("muh-SAL-ah"), or prayer room, where prayers are recited. Every *musallah* is oriented toward Mecca, toward which Muslims face during prayers. The prayer room is open and uncluttered to accommodate lines of worshippers who stand and bow in unison. There are no pews or chairs. Members of the congregation sit on the floor. Some mosques have a balcony in the *musallah* reserved for women. Other mosques accommodate men and women in the same *musallah*, or they may have totally separate areas for men and women.
- *The qiblah* ("KIHB-lah"), the direction to which the imam, or prayer leader, faces while praying. In the United States, Muslims face the northeast toward Mecca; in Canada, Muslims face the southeast.
- *A mihrab* ("MEE-rahb"), or niche that indicates which wall of the mosque faces toward Mecca. The *mihrab* is often decorated with Arabic calligraphy. Its curved shape helps reflect the voice of the imam, the prayer leader, back toward the congregation.

▣ Facilities to perform *wadu* ("WAH-doo"), or washings with water of the hands, face and feet. These are done prior to prayers as a way to purify one's self before standing in front of God. *Wadu* facilities range from wash basins to specially designed areas with built-in benches, floor drains and faucets.

▣ *A multi-purpose room*, used for seminars and lectures.

## THE SERVICE

**When should guests arrive and where should they sit?**

Arrive early. Some congregants arrive as much as 30 to 60 minutes before the service starts. Non-Muslim guests will be advised to sit separately from Muslims since Islamic practice forbids them from joining the prayer line. Like the rest of the worshippers in the mosque, guests sit on the prayer rug on the floor.

**If arriving late, are there times when a guest should *not* enter the service?**

No.

**Are there times when a guest should *not* leave the service?**

Do not leave when congregational prayer is being conducted.

A congregational prayer is offered in a group. Muslims are encouraged to pray in groups in mosques, although many pray as individuals and families at home.

**Who are the major officiants, leaders or participants and what do they do?**

▣ *An imam* ("EE-mahm"), who leads the prayers and delivers a sermon.
▣ *A muazzin* ("MOO-ah-zin"), who calls the faithful to prayer.

**What are the major ritual objects of the service?**

None.

**What books are used?**

None, since prayers are memorized. (This means that praying individually means learning the proper rituals in advance. Newcomers to the faith pray in groups and follow the lead of the imam.)

**To indicate the order of the service:**

Periodic announcements are made by a *muazzin*, who calls the *Adhan* ("AHD-han") and the *Iqamah* ("IK-ah-mah"). The *Adhan*, which is aired through public loudspeakers, alerts people that the time of prayer has started. The *Iqamah* is intended to alert mosque worshipers that congregational prayer is about to begin.

## GUEST BEHAVIOR DURING THE SERVICE

**Will a guest who is not a Muslim be expected to do anything other than sit?**
No.

**Are there any parts of the service in which a guest who is not a Muslim should *not* participate?**
No.

**If not disruptive to the service, is it okay to:**
◘ **Take pictures?** No.
◘ **Use a flash?** No.
◘ **Use a video camera?** No.
◘ **Use a tape recorder?** Yes.

(Note: Different Islamic centers have different policies regarding such matters as cameras and tape recorders. If you wish to use such equipment during the service, check in advance with an official of the mosque or center.)

**Will contributions to the mosque be collected at the service?**
Some mosque leaders pass boxes to collect donations; others mount boxes in mosques for voluntary contributions. Non-Muslims are not expected to make a contribution since that would be perceived as having imposed an obligation upon guests and, thus, violate the traditional generosity shown toward guests in Islamic culture.

**How much is customary to contribute?**
This is entirely at the discretion of each person. Perhaps $1 to $5 maximum.

## AFTER THE SERVICE

**Is there usually a reception after the service?**
No.

**Is there a traditional form of address for clergy whom a guest may meet?**
An imam may be directly addressed by the title of "imam" or by his name.

**Is it okay to leave early?**
Yes.

## GENERAL GUIDELINES AND ADVICE

Guests will observe Muslims making two *raka'ah* of prayer upon entering the mosque. This is a way to "greet" and honor the mosque. A full *raka'ah* consists of recitations during one standing, one bowing, and two prostrating motions (separated by a short sitting). Each prayer time requires a specific number of *raka'ah*. For example, dawn prayer consists of two *raka'ah*, noon consists of four and sunset of three. Visiting Non-Muslims should not perform *raka'ah* since the ritual is reserved for Muslims.

Worshippers and guests must not talk when the imam delivers a sermon.

Women should cover their hair with a scarf before entering *musallah*, or the prayer area of a mosque. Some mosques have a separate area for women. When there is no separate room for women, they pray behind the men.

## SPECIAL VOCABULARY

**Key words or phrases which might be helpful for a visitor to know:**

- *Salat* ("SAH-laht"): "Prayer."
- *As Salaam Alaikum* (ahs SAH-lahm ah-LAY-koom"): "Peace Be Upon You." A common greeting between Muslims.
- *Wa Alaikum Salaam* (wah ah-LAY-koom SAH-lahm"): "And Upon You the Peace." A common response to the above greeting.
- *Salla Allahu Alayhi Wa Salaam* ("SAH-lah ah-LAH-hoo ah-LAY-hee wah SAH-lahm"): "May the peace and blessings of Allah be upon him." This is said when any prophet of God is mentioned.
- *Allah Subhana Wa Tala* ("AH-lah SOOB-hah-nah wah TAH-lah"): "God, Who is highly glorified and honored."
- *Raka'ah* ("RAH-kah"): A unit of prayer ritual that consists of motions and verbal recitations.

## DOGMA AND IDEOLOGY

**Muslims believe:**

- One becomes a Muslim by saying and believing the *shahadah* ("SHAH-hah-dah"): "There is no god but God and Muhammad is the Messenger of God."
- A Muslim prays five times a day. The prayers take 5 to 10 minutes. Muslims pray communally at noon on Friday. Muslims face Mecca during their prayers as a sign of unity. But they do not "pray" to Mecca; they pray to God.
- A tax on assets is gathered by the community and distributed according to need. Called the *zakat*, it is generally 2½ percent of one's income.
- Muslims abstain from food, drink and sexual activity from sunrise to sunset during the lunar month of Ramadan.

◾ A Muslim must make the *hajj* ("hahj"), or pilgrimage to Mecca, at least once in his or her lifetime if physically and financially able. The *hajj* symbolizes unity and equality. Muslims of different races, wealth, status and gender gather in Mecca for *hajj*, and all are equal before God.

**Some basic books to which a guest can refer to learn more about Islam:**

The Quran ("koo-RAHN"), of which there are several English translations. A good translation is by Yusuf Ali · This can be found in mosques and Islamic bookstores.

*Islam: The Straight Path*, by John L. Esposito (New York: Oxford University Press, 1992).

---

## III · HOLY DAYS AND FESTIVALS

◾ *Ramadan* ("RAH-mah-dahn"), which occurs during all of Ramadan, the ninth month of the Islamic calendar. (Since Muslims follow the lunar calendar, Ramadan starts about ten days earlier in the solar calendar every year.) From sunrise to sunset, all adult Muslims whose health permits are to abstain from food, drink, smoking and sexual activity. Ramadan is a time for reflection and spiritual discipline, to express gratitude for God's guidance and to atone for past sins. It is recommended that each Muslim read the entire Quran during this month.

The traditional greeting for this holiday is *"Ramadan Mubarak"* ("RAH-mah-dahn moo-BAR-ahk"), meaning, "May God give you a blessed month." The traditional response is *"Ramadan Karim"* ("RAH-mah-dahn KAH-reem"), meaning, "May God give you a generous month."

◾ *Id al-Fitr* ("id AHL-fih-ter"), or the Feast of the Breaking of the Fast, which is celebrated at the end of Ramadan to mark the completion of fasting. The holiday lasts for three days, during which family members gather to feast and exchange presents. In many Muslim countries, it is a national holiday. It is also a time for attending mosque and paying the special alms for the poor, *zakat al-fitr*, required by Islamic law.

The traditional greeting for this holiday is *"Id Mubarak"* ("id moo-BAR-ahk"), which means "[May God make it a] blessed feast." The response is *"Id Karim"* ("id KAH-reem"), which means "[May God make it a] kind feast."

◾ *Id al-Adha* ("id uhl-AHD-hah"), which occurs two to three months after Ramadan and commemorates Abraham's obedience to God when He told him to sacrifice his son, Isaac, and Isaac's submission to the sacrifice. The holiday is marked by slaughtering animals to feed the poor.

The traditional greeting for this holiday is *"Id Mubarak"* ("id moo-BAR-ahk"), which means "[May God make it] a blessed feast."

◾ *Lailat ul-Qadr* ("LIE-laht ul-KAH-dur"), the last 10 days of Ramadan, during which special prayers are offered. This commemorates the "Night of Power" when the Prophet Muhammad first received God's revelation. Although the revelation occurred upon one particular night, it is celebrated during 10 days since the exact night is unknown. All that is known is that the revelation occurred during the last 10 days of Ramadan. During *Lailat ul-Qadr*, Muslims sometimes seclude themselves in their mosque, leaving only when necessary. There is no traditional greeting for these days.

◾ *al-Isra Wal Miraj* ("al-IZ-rah wahl MEE-rahj"), "The Night Journey and The Ascension," which is observed on the 27th day of Rajab, which is the seventh month of the Muslim lunar calendar. The holiday commemorates the night when the Prophet Muhammad is believed to have made a miraculous journey from Mecca to the Aqsa Mosque in Jerusalem, where he then traveled to the heavens where God commanded him to initiate prayers five times each day. There is no traditional greeting for this holiday.

## IV · LIFE CYCLE EVENTS

### · Birth Ceremony ·

The ceremony is called an *akikah* ("ah-KEE-kah"). A ceremony unto itself, it usually lasts about 30 to 60 minutes. An *akikah* is very informal and is not universally practiced by Moslems. What transpires at it varies from culture to culture and, often, from home to home. Generally, it is simply a way to welcome a newborn infant.

#### BEFORE THE CEREMONY

**Are guests usually invited by a formal invitation?**

Non-Muslims will usually receive an oral invitation, either over the telephone or in person. For Muslims, the time and place of the event are usually posted in the mosque or announced after Friday prayers.

**If not stated explicitly, should one assume that children are invited?**

Yes.

**If one can't attend, what should one do?**

RSVP with regrets and send a gift. Usually cash is appropriate. While the range of the cash given as presents is wide, Muslims are taught to be generous.

## APPROPRIATE ATTIRE

**Men:** Casual shirt and slacks. Head covering is not required.

**Women:** A dress or skirt and blouse are recommended. Clothing should cover the arms and hems should reach below the knees. A scarf is required to cover the head. Women may wear open-toed shoes and/or modest jewelry.

For both men and women, there are no rules regarding colors of clothing, but openly wearing crosses, Stars of David, jewelry with the signs of the zodiac and pendants with faces or heads of animals or people is discouraged.

## GIFTS

### Is a gift customarily expected?
Yes. Usually cash is appropriate. While the range of the cash given as presents is wide, Muslims are taught to be generous.

### Should gifts be brought to the ceremony?
They can either be sent to the home of the parents or brought to the ceremony. If cash is given, it is usually presented in an envelope, along with a card.

## THE CEREMONY

### Where will the ceremony take place?
Either in the home of the parents of the child or in the general purpose room of their mosque.

### When should guests arrive and where should they sit?
Arrive at the time called for the ceremony to begin. Sit wherever you wish. Men and women will sit in different parts of the room. They should inquire about where women go and where men go. In the United States, Muslims and their guests sit on chairs.

### If arriving late, are there times when a guest should *not* enter the ceremony?
No.

### Are there times when a guest should *not* leave the ceremony?
No.

**Who are the major officiants, leaders or participants at the ceremony and what do they do?**

Possibly a family member, who may say some informal words about the newborn.

**What books are used?**

None.

**To indicate the order of the ceremony:**

An *akikah* is brief and informal. There is no need to indicate the order of the event.

**Will a guest who is not a Muslim be expected to do anything other than sit?**

No.

**Are there any parts of the ceremony in which a guest who is not a Muslim should *not* participate?**

No.

**If not disruptive to the ceremony, is it okay to:**
◙ **Take pictures?** No.
◙ **Use a flash?** No.
◙ **Use a video camera?** No.
◙ **Use a tape recorder?** Yes.

(Note: Different Islamic centers have different policies regarding such matters as cameras and tape recorders. If you wish to use such equipment during the ceremony, check in advance with an official of the mosque or center.)

**Will contributions to the mosque be collected at the ceremony?**

Some mosque leaders pass boxes to collect donations; others mount boxes in mosques for voluntary contributions. Non-Muslims are not expected to make a contribution since that would be perceived as having imposed an obligation upon guests and, thus, violate the traditional generosity shown toward guests in Islamic culture.

**How much is customary to contribute?**

This is entirely at the discretion of each person. Perhaps $1 to $5 maximum.

## AFTER THE CEREMONY

**Is there usually a reception after the ceremony?**

There may be a reception. Such traditions differ from culture to culture and from mosque to mosque. If so, light food and beverages will be served, but no alcoholic beverages. There may be dancing and/or music, again depending on the particular mosque and the culture in which it is set.

**Would it be considered impolite to neither eat nor drink?**
No.

**Is there a grace or benediction before eating or drinking?**
No.

**Is there a grace or benediction after eating or drinking?**
No.

**Is there a traditional greeting for the family?**
Yes. It is *"Mabrook"* ("MAH-brook"). This means "Congratulations."

**Is there a traditional form of address for clergy who may be at the reception?**
An imam may be directly addressed by the title of "imam" or by his name.

**Is it okay to leave early?**
Yes.

## · *Initiation Ceremony* ·

At the *"Shahada"* ("SHAH-hah-dah") or "witnessing," a Muslim repeats the Islamic declaration of faith: "There is no deity but God, and Muhammad is the messenger of God." "Taking *shahada*," as the ritual is called, is a ceremony unto itself. It is usually done at any age from the mid-teens upward. It must be witnessed by either two male Muslims or eight female Muslims. The *shahada* may last between 15 and 30 minutes.

### BEFORE THE CEREMONY

**Are guests usually invited by a formal invitation?**
The individual making the *shahada* will invite friends or family, either in person, by phone or by written invitation. Often, an announcement is made that certain individuals will make *shahada* at the end of a particular service.

**If not stated explicitly, should one assume that children are invited?**
Yes.

**If one can't attend, what should one do?**
RSVP with regrets. No gift is expected.

## APPROPRIATE ATTIRE

**Men:** Casual shirt and slacks. Head covering is not required.

**Women:** A dress or skirt and blouse are recommended. Clothing should cover the arms and hems should reach below the knees. A scarf is required to cover the head. Women may wear open-toed shoes and/or modest jewelry.

For both men and women, there are no rules regarding colors of clothing, but openly wearing crosses, jewelry with the signs of the zodiac and pendants with faces or heads of animals or people is discouraged.

## GIFTS

**Is a gift customarily expected?**
No.

**Should gifts be brought to the ceremony?**
See above.

## THE CEREMONY

**Where will the ceremony take place?**
Either in the main sanctuary or a special room of a mosque or at the home of the person making the *shahada*.

**When should guests arrive and where should they sit?**
Arrive early. Someone will advise guests where to sit.

**If arriving late, are there times when a guest should *not* enter the ceremony?**
No.

**Are there times when a guest should *not* leave the ceremony?**
No.

**Who are the major officiants, leaders or participants at the ceremony and what do they do?**
◙ *An imam*, who leads the prayers and delivers a sermon.
◙ *A muazzin*, who calls the faithful to prayer.

**What books are used?**
None, since prayers are memorized. (This means that praying individually means learning the proper rituals in advance. Newcomers to the faith pray in groups and follow the lead of the imam.)

**To indicate the order of the ceremony:**

A *shahada* is brief and informal. No need to indicate the order of the event.

**Will a guest who is not a Muslim be expected to do anything other than sit?**

No.

**Are there any parts of the ceremony in which a guest who is not a Muslim should *not* participate?**

No.

**If not disruptive to the ceremony, is it okay to:**
- **Take pictures?** Yes.
- **Use a flash?** No.
- **Use a video camera?** Yes.
- **Use a tape recorder?** Yes.

(Note: Different Islamic centers have different policies regarding such matters as cameras and tape recorders. If you wish to use such equipment during the ceremony, check in advance with an official of the mosque or center.)

**If the *shahada* is held in a mosque, will contributions to the mosque be collected at the service?**

There will not be a collection, but in some mosques, boxes are mounted on the wall for voluntary contributions. Non-Muslims are not expected to make a contribution since that would be perceived as having imposed an obligation upon guests and, thus, violate the traditional generosity shown toward guests in Islamic culture.

**How much is customary to contribute?**

This is entirely at the discretion of each person. Perhaps $1 to $5 maximum.

## AFTER THE CEREMONY

**Is there usually a reception after the ceremony?**

No.

**Is there a traditional greeting for the family?**

Yes. It is *"Mabrook"* ("MAH-brook"). This means "Congratulations."

**Is there a traditional form of address for clergy whom a guest may meet?**

An imam may be directly addressed by the title of "imam" or by his name.

# · *Marriage Ceremony* ·

Marriage is incumbent on every Muslim man and woman unless they are financially or physically unable to be married. It is regarded as the norm for all and essential to the growth and stability of the family, which is the basic unit of society. Marriage is regarded as a sacred contract or covenant, not a sacrament, that legalizes sexual intercourse and the procreation of children.

The marriage ceremony usually lasts about 30 minutes, but can last more than one hour. It is a ceremony unto itself.

## BEFORE THE CEREMONY

### Are guests usually invited by a formal invitation?

Non-Muslims are usually invited orally, either over the telephone or in person. For Muslims, invitations may be posted in a mosque or announced after the noon prayers on Friday.

### If not stated explicitly, should one assume that children are invited?

Yes.

### If one can't attend, what should one do?

RSVP with regrets and send a gift, either money or whatever items one deems appropriate for the needs of the newlyweds.

## APPROPRIATE ATTIRE

**Men:** Casual shirt and slacks. Head covering is not required.

**Women:** A dress or skirt and blouse are recommended. Clothing should cover the arms and hems should reach below the knees. A scarf is required to cover the head. Women may wear open-toed shoes and/or modest jewelry.

For both men and women, there are no rules regarding colors of clothing, but openly wearing crosses, Stars of David, jewelry with the signs of the zodiac and pendants with faces or heads of animals or people is discouraged.

## GIFTS

### Is a gift customarily expected?

Yes, either money or whatever items one deems appropriate for the needs of the newlyweds.

**Should gifts be brought to the ceremony?**

They can either be sent to the home of the newlyweds or brought to the ceremony.

## THE CEREMONY

**Where will the ceremony take place?**

In the main sanctuary of a mosque.

**When should guests arrive and where should they sit?**

Arrive at the time called for the wedding to start. Sit wherever you wish.

**If arriving late, are there times when a guest should *not* enter the ceremony?**

No.

**Are there times when a guest should *not* leave the ceremony?**

No.

**Who are the major officiants, leaders or participants at the ceremony and what do they do?**

- *An imam*, or Islamic prayer leader, who usually delivers a sermon about marriage. This may be in Arabic if the newlyweds are Arabic-speaking or in English if they are English-speaking. Or it may be a mixture of both languages.
- *Two witnesses*, who witness the oral and written contract entered into by the bride and groom.
- *The groom*, who offers marriage to the bride.
- *The bride*, who accepts the offer.

**What books are used?**

None.

**To indicate the order of the ceremony:**

Weddings are brief and informal. There is no need to indicate the order of the event.

**Will a guest who is not a Muslim be expected to do anything other than sit?**

No.

**Are there any parts of the ceremony in which a guest who is not a Muslim should *not* participate?**

No.

**If not disruptive to the ceremony, is it okay to:**
◙ **Take pictures?** Yes.
◙ **Use a flash?** Yes.
◙ **Use a video camera?** Yes.
◙ **Use a tape recorder?** Yes.

(Note: Different Islamic centers have different policies regarding such matters as cameras and tape recorders. If you wish to use such equipment during the ceremony, check in advance with an official of the mosque or center.)

**Will contributions to the mosque be collected at the ceremony?**
There will not be a collection, but in some mosques, boxes are mounted on the wall for voluntary contributions. Non-Muslims are not expected to make a contribution since that would be perceived as having imposed an obligation upon guests and, thus, violate the traditional generosity shown toward guests in Islamic culture.

**How much is customary to contribute?**
This is entirely at the discretion of each person. Perhaps $1 to $5 maximum.

### AFTER THE CEREMONY

**Is there usually a reception after the ceremony?**
Yes. This is called a *waleemah* ("wah-LEEH-mah"). It may last two hours or more and can be held anywhere: In the mosque, a home, a catering hall or any other site. Beverages and such food as meat, rice, fruit, and sweets will be served. There will be no alcoholic beverages. There may be dancing and/or music, but not if the *waleemah* is held in a mosque.

**Would it be considered impolite to neither eat nor drink?**
No.

**Is there a grace or benediction before eating or drinking?**
No.

**Is there a grace or benediction after eating or drinking?**
No.

**Is there a traditional greeting for the family?**
*"Mabrook alaik"* ("MAH-brook ah-LAYK"), "Congratulations," if addressing a male. *"Mabrook alaiki"* ("MAH-brook ah-LAYK-ee"), "Congratulations," if addressing a female.

**Is there a traditional form of address for clergy who may be at the reception?**

An imam may be directly addressed by the title of "imam" or by his name.

**Is it okay to leave early?**

Yes.

## · Funerals and Mourning ·

The vision in the Quran of afterlife is spiritual and physical. At a moment known only to God, all will be called to judgment. This is known as the Day of Decision or the Day of Reckoning. For the good and the bad, heaven and hell will be fully experienced. The Garden of Paradise is a heavenly mansion of perpetual peace and bliss with flowing rivers, fertile gardens, the enjoyment of one's spouse and of beautiful, dark-eyed female companions. The damned will be banished to hell, forever separated from God, and subjected to eternal torture and torment.

An Islamic funeral is a service unto itself and usually lasts about 30 to 60 minutes. In some cases, it may last more than an hour.

### BEFORE THE CEREMONY

**How soon after the death does the funeral usually take place?**

Two to three days.

**What should a non-Muslim do upon hearing of the death of a member of that faith?**

Call or visit the bereaved. If one visits, shake hands or hug and kiss the family members of the same gender, sit and talk quietly and offer some quiet prayer.

### APPROPRIATE ATTIRE

**Men:** Casual shirt and slacks. Head covering is not required.

**Women:** A dress is recommended. Clothing should cover the arms and hems should reach below the knees. A scarf is required to cover the head.

For both men and women, there are no rules regarding colors of clothing, but openly wearing crosses, Stars of David, jewelry with the signs of the zodiac and pendants with faces or heads of animals or people is discouraged.

Dark, somber colors are advised.

## GIFTS

**Is it appropriate to send flowers or make a contribution?**
Send flowers after the funeral to the home of the bereaved.

**Is it appropriate to send food?**
Yes.

## THE CEREMONY

**Where will the ceremony take place?**
At a funeral home or in the general purpose room of the mosque.

**When should guests arrive and where should they sit?**
Arrive at the time set for the funeral. An usher will advise guests on where to sit.

**If arriving late, are there times when a guest should *not* enter the ceremony?**
No.

**Will the bereaved family be present at the funeral home before the ceremony?**
No.

**Is there a traditional greeting for the family?**
No. Just offer your condolences.

**Will there be an open casket?**
Never.

**Who are the major officiants at the ceremony and what do they do?**
◗ *An imam*, who presides.

**What books are used?**
The Quran.

**To indicate the order of the ceremony:**
No directions are given during the service, which is intended to be as simple as possible.

**Will a guest who is not a Muslim be expected to do anything other than sit?**
No.

**Are there any parts of the ceremony in which a guest who is not a Muslim should *not* participate?**
No.

**If not disruptive to the ceremony, is it okay to:**
◘ **Take pictures?** No.
◘ **Use a flash?** No.
◘ **Use a video camera?** No.
◘ **Use a tape recorder?** No.

**Will contributions to the mosque be collected at the ceremony?**
No.

## THE INTERMENT

**Should guests attend the interment?**
Yes.

**Whom should one ask for directions?**
An imam.

**What happens at the graveside?**
The *Janazah* prayers ("jah-NAH-zah") for the dead are recited and the deceased is buried. Muslims are never cremated.

**Do guests who are not Muslims participate at the graveside ceremony?**
No, they are simply present.

## COMFORTING THE BEREAVED

**Is it appropriate to visit the home of the bereaved after the funeral?**
Yes. Visit any time during the days of mourning, which are religiously mandated not to exceed 40 days. The number of mourning days that one actually observes is individually set and can be determined by telephoning the home of the bereaved. When visiting the home of a mourner, talk quietly with the bereaved and other visitors. Often, visitors and mourners sit in silence while someone reads aloud from the Quran or a tape of a reading from the Quran is played.

**Will there be a religious service at the home of the bereaved?**
No.

**Will food be served?**

Possibly. Often, women in the local Muslim community prepare food for mourners and their guests.

**How soon after the funeral will a mourner usually return to a normal work schedule?**

Usually after a few days.

**How soon after the funeral will a mourner usually return to a normal social schedule?**

There are no prescriptions in Islam about such matters. This is more culturally determined than religiously determined. Usually, women do not engage in normal social activities until 40 days after the death of a member of their immediate family. There are no norms for men.

**Are there mourning customs to which a friend who is not a Muslim should be sensitive?**

Bereaved usually wear black, although this is a cultural norm and not a religious prescription.

**Are there rituals for observing the anniversary of the death?**

No.

## V · HOME CELEBRATIONS

Not applicable for Islam.

## Chapter 11 Contents

# Jehovah's Witnesses

## I · HISTORY AND BELIEFS

Jehovah's Witnesses is a worldwide faith known for assertive proselytizing and expectations of an imminent apocalypse. They have drawn attention because of their refusal to celebrate Christmas as the birthday of Jesus, by their dedicated missionary work and by using Jehovah as the sole name of God.

Jehovah's Witnesses derive their name from the 43rd chapter of the Book of Isaiah, in which the gods of the nations are invited to bring forth their witnesses to prove their claimed cases of righteousness or to hear the witnesses for Jehovah's side and acknowledge the truth: "Ye are My witnesses, saith Jehovah, and My servants whom I have chosen; that ye may know and believe Me, and understand that I am He; before Me there was no God formed, neither shall there be after Me. I, even I, am Jehovah; and besides Me there is no savior" (Isaiah 43:10, 11, American Standard Version of the Bible).

In the Bible, all faithful worshippers, such as Abel, Noah, Abraham and Jesus, were called "witnesses of God" (Hebrews 11:1-12:1; Revelation 3:14).

The faith was founded in western Pennsylvania in the early 1870s by Charles Taze Russell, who had organized a Bible study group to promote the basic teachings of the Bible. It was his desire to return to the teachings of first-century Christianity.

Jehovah's Witnesses believe that God demands unconditional obedience and that the infallible source of truth is the Bible, which is true in every detail. Jesus, who was the Son of God and was His first creation, was responsible for all the rest of God's creation on earth. While residing on earth, Jesus was entirely a man. After His death, He was raised by God to heaven and restored to a place second only to that of His Father, Jehovah.

The fulfillment of God's kingdom will occur through the battle of Armageddon, the appearance of the Lord in the air, the thousand-year rule on earth of Christ (during which resurrection and judgment take place). This process began in 1914 and its completion will soon occur.

Members of the Church are expected to devote their primary loyalty and time to the movement, and not participate in politics or interfaith movements. They believe that all human laws that do not conflict with God's law should be obeyed. They also do not vote in civic elections or serve in the military. They respect each country's flag (or other national symbols), but do not salute it, since they believe this would be idolatry.

**U.S. churches:** 11,000
**U.S. membership:** 985,000
*(data from the* 1998 Yearbook of Jehovah's Witnesses*)*

**For more information, contact:**
Jehovah's Witnesses
25 Columbia Heights
Brooklyn, NY 11201
(718) 625-3600

**Canadian churches:** 1,400
**Canadian membership:** 114,000
*(data from the* 1998 Yearbook of Jehovah's Witnesses*)*

**For more information, contact:**
Jehovah's Witnesses
P.O. Box 4100
Georgetown, ON  L7G 4Y4
(905) 873-4100

## II · THE BASIC SERVICE

Congregational meetings are highly instructional and primarily deal with Bible teachings, prophecy or counsel on Christian living. Some of these meetings are conducted as Bible studies with audience participation, usually using a magazine (such as *The Watchtower*) or a book published by the Jehovah's Witnesses' publishing house, the Watchtower Society. The person conducting the study may pose questions based on a paragraph that has been read aloud to the group.

Meetings last slightly more than one hour and are held on Sundays, with the times varying among congregations, and on two other days each week.

## APPROPRIATE ATTIRE

**Men:** Jacket and tie are usually worn, although they are not required. No head covering is required.

**Women:** A dress or a skirt and blouse. Dress "modestly" and "sensibly." Hems need not reach below the knees nor must clothing cover the arms. Open-toed shoes and modest jewelry are permissible. No head covering is required.

There are no rules regarding colors of clothing.

## THE SANCTUARY

**What are the major sections of the meeting hall?**
Kingdom Halls, the name of Jehovah's Witnesses' meeting halls, are usually plain structures, inside and out. They resemble auditoriums more than churches or synagogues.

## THE SERVICE

**When should guests arrive and where should they sit?**
Arrive early. Sit wherever you wish.

**If arriving late, are there times when a guest should *not* enter the service?**
No, but latecomers will be assisted by attendants to find an appropriate seat.

**Are there times when a guest should *not* leave the service?**
No.

**Who are the major officiants, leaders or participants and what do they do?**
▪ *The Congregation Elders,* who deliver talks on the Bible and lead Bible discussions with the congregants.

**What are the major ritual objects of the service?**
None.

**What books are used?**
The Old and New Testaments, primarily the New World Translation (New York: The Watchtower Bible and Tract Society of New York, 1961); *The Watchtower*, a semi-monthly journal published by Jehovah's Witnesses headquarters in Brooklyn, N.Y.; and a hymnal, *Sing Praises to Jehovah* (New York: The Watchtower Bible and Tract Society of New York, 1984).

**To indicate the order of the service:**

Periodic announcements will be made by an elder in the congregation.

## GUEST BEHAVIOR DURING THE SERVICE

**Will a guest who is not a Jehovah's Witness be expected to do anything other than sit?**

It is entirely optional for a guest of another faith to stand and sing with the congregation and to answer questions during a discussion of the Bible. During prayer, guests may bow their head reverently. Jehovah's Witnesses do not kneel during their congregational meetings.

**Are there any parts of the service in which a guest who is not a Jehovah's Witness should *not* participate?**

No.

**If not disruptive to the service, is it okay to:**

◼ **Take pictures?** Yes.

◼ **Use a flash?** Yes.

◼ **Use a video camera?** Yes.

◼ **Use a tape recorder?** Yes.

(Note: Do not use the above equipment during prayer. Using a flash camera during the Bible talk would also be inappropriate.)

**Will contributions to the church be collected at the service?**

No.

## AFTER THE SERVICE

**Is there usually a reception after the service?**

No.

**Is there a traditional form of address for clergy whom a guest may meet?**

Either "Brother" or "Mr.," followed by last name.

## GENERAL GUIDELINES AND ADVICE

None provided.

## SPECIAL VOCABULARY

**Key words or phrases which might be helpful for a visitor to know:**

◼ *Jehovah:* The personal name of the one true God. From the Book of Psalms (83:18) in the King James Version of the Bible: "That men may know that Thou, whose name alone is Jehovah, art the most high over all the earth." Also from the New World Translation of Isaiah (42:8): "I am Jehovah. That is My name."

▪ *Hebrew Scriptures* and *Christian Greek Scriptures:* The terms used, respectively, for the Old and New Testaments.

## DOGMA AND IDEOLOGY

**Jehovah's Witnesses believe:**

▪ The books of the Bible's Old and New Testament are divinely inspired and historically accurate.

▪ Jehovah created earth for humanity and settled the first human pair, Adam and Eve, in the Garden of Eden. If obedient to God, they had the prospect of living forever and expanding the paradise earthwide. With their sin, humanity lost this paradise. Yet, God's purpose for the earth will not fail. The means by which Jehovah will fulfill His purpose for earth is through the Kingdom of God with Jesus as King. This heavenly government will soon remove wickedness from the earth and convert it into a paradise wherein true worshippers will live forever. There will also be a resurrection of the dead into that Paradise.

▪ The Kingdom of God began to rule invisibly in heaven in 1914 and after the wicked are destroyed will usher in the 1,000 year Reign of Christ (the Millennium) during which the earth and humanity will be helped to reach perfection and to live endlessly on earth.

**Some basic pamphlets to which a guest can refer to learn more about Jehovah's Witnesses:**

"Jehovah's Witnesses in the Twentieth Century" (Brooklyn, N.Y.: The Watchtower Bible and Tract Society of New York, Inc., 1989).

"Jehovah's Witnesses Unitedly Doing God's Will Worldwide" (Brooklyn, N.Y.: The Watchtower Bible and Tract Society of New York, Inc., 1986).

"Does God Really Care About Us?" (Brooklyn, N.Y.: The Watchtower Bible and Tract Society of New York, Inc., 1992).

## III · HOLY DAYS AND FESTIVALS

▪ *The Memorial of Christ's Death*, also called the Lord's Evening Meal. This special congregational meeting is held in each Kingdom Hall after sundown of the first evening of the Jewish holiday of Passover, which occurs either in March or April. (The date varies because the Hebrew calendar is lunar-based.) There is no traditional greeting for this one holiday observed by Jehovah's Witnesses.

## IV · LIFE CYCLE EVENTS

### · *Birth Ceremony* ·

Not applicable to Jehovah's Witnesses.

### · *Initiation Ceremony* ·

Not applicable to Jehovah's Witnesses.

### · *Marriage Ceremony* ·

Jehovah's Witnesses view marriage as a sacred vow made before God. It seals a permanent union that can be broken only by infidelity or death. The marriage ceremony, which may last about 30 minutes, is a ceremony unto itself.

#### BEFORE THE CEREMONY

**Are guests usually invited by a formal invitation?**
Yes. An announcement is made in a Kingdom Hall issuing a general invitation to all members of the congregation. Guests who are not members of the congregation usually receive a written invitation.

**If not stated explicitly, should one assume that children are invited?**
Yes.

**If one can't attend, what should one do?**
Nothing is required if one is a member who has heard the invitation in a Kingdom Hall. If one has received a written invitation, RSVP with regrets.

#### APPROPRIATE ATTIRE

**Men:** A jacket and tie. No head covering is required.

**Women:** A dress or a skirt and blouse. Dress "modestly" and "sensibly." Hems need not reach below the knees nor must clothing cover the arms. Open-toed shoes and modest jewelry are permissible. No head covering is required.

There are no rules regarding colors of clothing.

#### GIFTS

**Is a gift customarily expected?**
While gifts are surely not required, they are certainly appropriate. Cash,

bonds or such household items as sheets, kitchenware or small appliances are customary.

**Should gifts be brought to the ceremony?**
Either to the ceremony or to the reception afterward.

## THE CEREMONY

**Where will the ceremony take place?**
In the main auditorium of a Kingdom Hall where Bible lectures are normally given.

**When should guests arrive and where should they sit?**
Arrive early to avoid causing a distraction. Attendants will seat guests. The front few rows are reserved for family.

**If arriving late, are there times when a guest should *not* enter the ceremony?**
No, but usually attendants will seat late-arriving guests in such a way as not to create a disturbance.

**Are there times when a guest should *not* leave the ceremony?**
No.

**Who are the major officiants, leaders or participants at the ceremony and what do they do?**
◙ *The Congregation Elder*, who gives a Bible talk to the bride and groom and solemnizes the marriage.

**What books are used?**
The Old and New Testaments, primarily the New World Translation (New York: The Watchtower Bible and Tract Society of New York, 1961).

**To indicate the order of the ceremony:**
The officiating elder will make periodic announcements.

**Will a guest who is not a Jehovah's Witness be expected to do anything other than sit?**
No.

**Are there any parts of the ceremony in which a guest who is not a Jehovah's Witness should *not* participate?**
No.

**If not disruptive to the ceremony, is it okay to:**
◙ **Take pictures?** Yes.
◙ **Use a flash?** Yes.
◙ **Use a video camera?** Yes.

◧ **Use a tape recorder?** Yes.

(Note: Do not use the above equipment during prayer. Flash pictures should not be taken during the Bible talk since this can be very distracting.)

**Will contributions to the church be collected at the ceremony?**
No.

## AFTER THE CEREMONY

**Is there usually a reception after the ceremony?**
Yes. It may be held in homes or a catering hall. It is never held in the Kingdom Hall where the wedding took place. Usually, refreshments are served. The reception may last more than two hours.

**Would it be considered impolite to neither eat nor drink?**
No.

**Is there a grace or benediction before eating or drinking?**
Yes.

**Is there a grace or benediction after eating or drinking?**
No.

**Is there a traditional greeting for the family?**
Just offer your congratulations.

**Is there a traditional form of address for clergy who may be at the reception?**
Either "Brother" or "Mr.," followed by last name.

**Is it okay to leave early?**
Yes.

## · *Funerals and Mourning* ·

Jehovah's Witnesses believe that the dead are "conscious of nothing at all" and are asleep in the grave awaiting resurrection to life. While the majority will be raised to life in an earthly paradise, a small number—144,000—will be raised as immortal spirit creatures to rule with Christ in the heavenly Kingdom of God.

The funeral service, which is a ceremony unto itself, may last about 15 to 30 minutes.

## BEFORE THE CEREMONY

**How soon after the death does the funeral usually take place?**
Usually within one week.

**What should a non-Jehovah's Witness do upon hearing of the death of a member of that faith?**

Telephone or visit the bereaved to offer your condolences.

## APPROPRIATE ATTIRE

**Men:** A jacket and tie. No head covering is required.

**Women:** A dress or a skirt and blouse. Dress "modestly" and "sensibly." Hems need not reach below the knees nor must clothing cover the arms. Open-toed shoes and modest jewelry are permissible. No head covering is required.

There are no rules regarding colors of clothing, but what is worn should respect the somberness of the occasion.

## GIFTS

**Is it appropriate to send flowers or make a contribution?**

Yes. Flowers may be sent to the home of the bereaved before or after the funeral or to the funeral home. Notice that contributions in memory of the deceased have been donated to a charity can be sent to the mourners' home before or after the funeral.

**Is it appropriate to send food?**

Yes. This can be sent to the home of the bereaved before or after the funeral.

## THE CEREMONY

**Where will the ceremony take place?**

Either at a Kingdom Hall or in a funeral home.

**When should guests arrive and where should they sit?**

Arrive early to avoid causing a distraction. Attendants will seat guests. The front few rows are reserved for family.

**If arriving late, are there times when a guest should *not* enter the ceremony?**

No, but attendants will direct latecomers to seats.

**Will the bereaved family be present at the Kingdom Hall or funeral home before the ceremony?**

Possibly.

**Is there a traditional greeting for the family?**

No. Just offer your condolences.

**Will there be an open casket?**

Possibly. This depends on the preference of the immediate family.

**Is a guest expected to view the body?**

There are no such expectations.

**What is appropriate behavior upon viewing the body?**

Look upon it somberly for a few moments.

**Who are the major officiants at the ceremony and what do they do?**

🔹 *The Congregation Elder,* who will deliver a talk from the Bible designed to comfort the bereaved.

**What books are used?**

Usually no books are used by the audience. Occasionally, a Bible, such as the New World Translation (New York: The Watchtower Bible and Tract Society of New York, 1961) or a songbook, such as *Sing Praises to Jehovah* (New York: The Watchtower Bible and Tract Society of New York, 1984) may be used.

**To indicate the order of the ceremony:**

Directions are not necessary because of the brevity of the service, which is led entirely by the Congregation Elder.

**Will a guest who is not a Jehovah's Witness be expected to do anything other than sit?**

No.

**Are there any parts of the ceremony in which a guest who is not a Jehovah's Witness should *not* participate?**

No.

**If not disruptive to the ceremony, is it okay to:**

🔹 **Take pictures?** No.
🔹 **Use a flash?** No.
🔹 **Use a video camera?** No.
🔹 **Use a tape recorder?** Yes.

**Will contributions to the church be collected at the ceremony?**

No.

## THE INTERMENT

**Should guests attend the interment?**

Such attendance is done at the discretion of the guest.

**Whom should one ask for directions?**

The funeral director or his or her assistants.

**What happens at the graveside?**

Brief comments on the Scriptures are followed by prayer.

**Do guests who are not Jehovah's Witnesses participate at the graveside ceremony?**

No, they are simply present.

## COMFORTING THE BEREAVED

**Is it appropriate to visit the home of the bereaved after the funeral?**

Yes. The length of the visit depends on the circumstances. Discussing with the bereaved what you appreciated about the deceased is helpful.

**Will there be a religious service at the home of the bereaved?**

No.

**Will food be served?**

Possibly. This depends on the preference of the mourners.

**How soon after the funeral will a mourner usually return to a normal work schedule?**

This depends on the preferences and the circumstances of the mourners. There is no set time for remaining away from work, although mourners are usually absent from work for at least a few days.

**How soon after the funeral will a mourner usually return to a normal social schedule?**

This is entirely an individual matter and depends on the preferences and the circumstances of the mourners. There is no set time for abstaining from social activities.

**Are there mourning customs to which a friend who is not a Jehovah's Witness should be sensitive?**

No.

**Are there rituals for observing the anniversary of the death?**

No.

## V · HOME CELEBRATIONS

Not applicable to Jehovah's Witnesses.

# Chapter 12 Contents

# 12

# Jewish

## I · HISTORY AND BELIEFS

The Jewish religion, Judaism, includes religious rituals and beliefs along with a code of ethical behavior. It also incorporates and reflects the ancient history of the Jews as a nation in its rituals, ceremonies and celebrations. Today, its adherents include people of every race and most nations.

The foundation of Judaism is the Torah, the first five books of the Bible (Genesis, Exodus, Leviticus, Numbers and Deuteronomy). According to the Torah, God made a covenant with the Jews, beginning with the three patriarchs: Abraham; his son, Isaac; and his grandson, Jacob, whose name God changed to "Israel." At a time when people worshipped many gods, the Jewish people, through this covenant, accepted the "One God" as the only God.

Central to this covenant is the concept of being "chosen" as a people, for as Moses tells his people in the Bible: "...The Lord has chosen you to be a people for His own possession, out of all the peoples that are on the face of the earth" (Deuteronomy 14:2). Being "chosen" does not confer special privilege. It means that the Jewish people are obliged to bring God's message to the world.

As part of God's covenant with Abraham, his descendants were promised the area now known as Israel—the Promised Land—as their homeland. They took possession of it in approximately 1200 B.C.E. (Before the Common Era, referred to as B.C. in the Christian calendar). In 70 C.E. (Common Era, referred to as A.D. in the Christian calendar), the conquering Romans destroyed Jerusalem and its Temple, which was the center of Jewish religious life, and drove the Jewish people from their land to end repeated rebellions. This began the period known as "The Diaspora," when the Jewish people were without a homeland. Many drifted to the northern and southern rim of the Mediterranean, while others emigrated eastward.

Jewish settlement in the American colonies began in 1654 in New Amsterdam (later called New York). Jewish immigration to Canada began in 1760, with the first synagogue being established in 1768. The modern Jewish state, Israel, was founded in 1948, three years after the end of the Holocaust in which six million Jews were killed.

Before the Diaspora, Judaism as a religion evolved under a hereditary priesthood that officiated at the Temple in Jerusalem, and through the ethical and moral teachings of a series of prophets. Following the Temple's destruction, religious leadership passed from priests to *rabbis*—teachers and scholars. Today, the rabbinate includes both men and women in all movements except the Orthodox.

There are now four major Jewish religious movements in the United States and Canada. In terms of theology, Reform Judaism is at the liberal end followed by Reconstructionist, Conservative, and Orthodox—both modern and traditional (which includes several fundamentalist groups, such as the Hasidim).

Hebrew, the traditional language of Jewish worship, is used to varying degrees in the services or celebrations of each movement. Each also has its own version of the prayerbook, and almost all include translations of the Hebrew material.

Reform Judaism, which began in the early 19th century in Germany, regards Judaism as an ongoing process resulting from the relationship between God and the Jewish people over its history. It considers Torah divinely inspired and subject to individual interpretation based on study, and emphasizes the ethical and moral messages of the prophets to help create a just society.

Reconstructionism, founded in the 1930s, is the most recent of the Jewish movements. Here the essence of Judaism is defined as embodying an entire civilization and not only a religion. At the core of this civilization is a people who have the authority and the responsibility to "reconstruct" its contents from generation to generation.

Conservative Judaism began in the mid-19th century as a reaction to what its founders perceived to be Reform's radicalism. It teaches that while the Torah as a whole is binding and that much of Jewish law remains authoritative, nonetheless new ideas and practices have always influenced Jewish beliefs and rituals and this should continue today, as well.

Orthodox Judaism teaches that Torah was divinely revealed to Moses at

Mount Sinai and that the *halachah* ("hah-lah-KHAH"), the interpretative process of that law, is both divinely guided and authoritative. Thus, no law stemming from the Torah can be tampered with even if it displeases modern sensibilities. Orthodoxy often rejects more modern forms of Judaism as deviations from divine truths and authentic modes of Jewish life.

Houses of worship in the Orthodox, Conservative and Reconstructionist movement are typically called "synagogues." Usually, only a Reform house of worship is called a "temple."

**U.S. synagogues/temples:** Over 2,000 total
*Reform:* 890
*Conservative:* 800
*Reconstructionist:* 80
*Orthodox:* Not available

**U.S. membership:** 4.1 million total
*Reform:* 2 million
*Conservative:* 1.6 million
*Reconstructionist:* 100,000
*Orthodox:* 375,000 (estimate)

*(1995 data from each denomination's central office, except Orthodox)*

**For more information, contact:**
Union of American Hebrew Congregations (Reform)
838 Fifth Avenue
New York, NY 10021
(212) 249-0100

United Synagogue of Conservative Judaism
155 Fifth Avenue
New York, NY 10010
(212) 533-7800

Jewish Reconstructionist Federation
1299 Church Road
Wyncote, PA 19095
(215) 887-1988

Union of Orthodox Jewish Congregations
45 West 36th Street
New York, NY 10018
(212) 563-4000

**Canadian synagogues/temples:** Over 248 total
*Reform:* 20
*Conservative:* 48
*Reconstructionist:* 2
*Orthodox:* 124

**Canadian membership:** Over 365,000 total
*Reform:* not available
*Conservative:* not available
*Reconstructionist:* not available
*Orthodox:* not available
*(data from the Canadian Jewish Congress and the*
1992 Corpus Almanac and Canadian Sourcebook*)*

**For more information, contact:**

Canadian Jewish Congress
1590, av. Docteur Penfield
Montreal, PQ  H3G 1C5
(514) 931-7531

Canadian Council for Conservative Judaism
c/o United Synagogue
1520 Steeles Avenue West
Thornhill, ON  L4K 3B9
(905) 738-1717

Canadian Council of Reform Rabbis
c/o Temple Israel
1301 Prince of Wales Drive
Ottawa, ON  K2C 1N2
(613) 224-1802

## II · THE BASIC SERVICE

According to Jewish tradition, communal prayer requires a *minyan* ("MIN-yahn"), a quorum of at least 10 persons over the age of 13. It takes place three times daily: In the early morning; at midday; and at sunset. Each communal prayer service takes about 15 to 30 minutes. If a Jewish person cannot join the communal prayer, they may pray alone, omitting from their service certain prayers that are said only when there is a *minyan*. Orthodox and some Conservative congregations only count males in the number of persons in the *minyan*.

Each service contains many common elements and some minor variations according to the time of day and the time of the month. The fullest Jewish service takes place on the Jewish Sabbath, or *Shabbat* ("shah-BAHT"), which begins at sunset on Friday and ends at nightfall on Saturday. All Orthodox and Conservative congregations have services on Friday evenings and Saturday mornings, as do most Reform and Reconstructionist congregations.

The major units of the service are the *Amidah* ("ah-mee-DAH"), a series of praises, thanks and petitions to God; and the *Sh'ma*, whose central phrase, "Hear O Israel, the Lord is our God, the Lord is One," is a declaration of faith, a pledge of allegiance and an affirmation of Judaism. Another key element is the public reading from the Torah, the first Five Books of the Bible.

The Friday evening service may last 30 to 90 minutes and the Saturday morning service may last from 90 minutes to over three hours, depending on the congregation. Services are usually longer in Orthodox and Conservative congregations than in Reform or Reconstructionist. The amount of Hebrew used during the service varies with each congregation, but Reform congregations will use the least and Orthodox the most. Prayerbooks normally include translations or interpretations of the Hebrew material.

## APPROPRIATE ATTIRE

**Men:** A jacket and tie are never inappropriate. In some Reform and Reconstructionist congregations more informal attire may be appropriate on occasion.

A small headcovering called a *yarmulke* ("YAHR-mihl-kah") or *kippah* ("keep-AH") is required in all Orthodox, Conservative and Reconstructionist congregations and in some Reform congregations. They will be available just before one enters the main sanctuary. If required in Reform congregations, a sign is usually posted to that effect.

**Women:** A dress, skirt and blouse, or a pants suit. In general, clothing should be modest, depending on the fashion and the locale.

In some Conservative synagogues, a hat or another headcovering may be required. Open-toed shoes and modest jewelry are appropriate. In Orthodox congregations, clothing should cover the arms, hems should reach below the knees and heads should be covered with a hat or veil. On the Sabbath, do not carry a purse or similar accessory since Jewish law prohibits labor, including carrying objects, on *Shabbat*.

Note: The *tallit* ("tah-LEET"), or prayer shawl, is worn by all Orthodox men, Conservative and Reconstructionist men and some women, and by some men and women in Reform congregations. Non-Jews should not wear the *tallit*.

Do not openly wear symbols of other faiths, such as a cross.

There are no rules regarding colors of clothing.

## THE SANCTUARY

### What are the major sections of the synagogue/temple?

▪ *The bimah* ("BEE-mah"): The part of the sanctuary from where the service is led and where the rabbi and cantor stand and sit. Also called the pulpit. It is usually raised above the level where congregants sit and is at the front or in the middle of the sanctuary.

◾ *The ark:* The cabinet on the pulpit where the Torah is kept.

◾ *The Torah reading table:* The table on which the Torah is opened and read.

◾ *The rabbi's pulpit:* Where the rabbi stands when delivering his or her sermon or when teaching and commenting on the service.

◾ *The eternal light:* A lamp, either gas or electric, which burns continuously above and in front of the ark where the Torah is kept.

◾ *The mehitsah* ("meh-HEET-sah"): A partition used in Orthodox congregations to separate the seating sections for men and women. In more traditional congregations, women are seated to the rear of the men or in a balcony above them. In others, they are seated in a section parallel to the men's. Some "modern" Orthodox congregations have eliminated the *mehitsah*, but men and women still sit separately.

## THE SERVICE

### When should guests arrive and where should they sit?

At events occuring on Saturday morning it is customary for guests who are not Jews to arrive at the scheduled time at Reform and Reconstructionist services. For Orthodox or Conservative services, which tend to be longer, unless you want to participate in the entire service, ask your host the time you should arrive so you can be present for the specific event within the service for which you have been invited.

Sit wherever you wish, while respecting any separation of men and women, which occurs in all Orthodox congregations.

### If arriving late, are there times when a guest should *not* enter the service?

Do not enter when the congregation is standing or during the rabbi's sermon. In most congregations, an usher will advise latecomers when to enter.

### Are there times when a guest should *not* leave the service?

Don't leave when the congregation is standing, when the Torah is being taken out or returned to the ark, when the rabbi is speaking or when the specific ceremony during the service for which you have been invited is taking place.

### Who are the major officiants, leaders or participants and what do they do?

◾ *The rabbi,* who directs the service and teaches and preaches. (Any Jewish person over the age of 13 may lead a service; in an Orthodox congregation, this can only be a male.) In larger congregations, there may be a senior rabbi and one or more rabbis who are his or her assistants.

- *The cantor*, who chants and sings parts of the service and leads the congregation in song.
- *The Torah reader*, who reads or chants from the Torah.
- *The gabbai* ("gab-BYE"), a lay person who oversees the honors of reading from the Torah and of saying blessings for the Torah reading.
- *The congregation's president*, or his or her representative, who may welcome congregants and visitors from the *bimah* and make announcements about upcoming events and programs.

Note: In smaller congregations, the same person may have more than one role. For instance, the rabbi may also be the cantor.

### What are the major ritual objects of the service?
- *The tallit*, or prayer shawl, which is worn by all Orthodox men, Conservative and Reconstructionist men and some women, and by some men and women in Reform congregations. Non-Jews should not wear the *tallit*.
- *The Torah* ("TOH-rah"), a scroll on which is handwritten the first five books of the Bible: Genesis, Exodus, Leviticus, Numbers and Deuteronomy.
- *The yad* ("yahd"), a metal pointer used when reading the Torah because one is not supposed to touch the handwritten letters.
- *The menorah* ("min-OHR-ah"), a seven-branched candelabra, which was part of the ancient Temple in Jerusalem and which is often placed on the *bimah* as an ornament.
- *The ark*, the place in which a Torah scroll(s) is kept on the *bimah*.
- *Torah ornaments*, such as a cover of fabric, a breastplate and crown of silver, which adorn the outside of the closed scroll.
- *Tefillin* ("teh-FILL-in"), or phylacteries, two small black leather boxes containing four biblical passages which a male Jew from the age of 13 wears on the left arm and the head during morning services on weekdays. They are held in place with leather straps. They are not worn for *Shabbat* services or festivals.

### What books are used?
The *siddur* ("SEE-door") or prayerbook, which varies among (and sometimes within) the various religious movements; and the *chumash* ("KOOH-mahsh"), which contains the first five books of the Bible (Genesis, Exodus, Leviticus, Numbers and Deuteronomy), and the traditional section from Prophets that is associated with each weekly Torah portion and which is

read after the public Torah reading (called the *Haftarah*, "hahf-TOH-rah"). It also may contain editorial commentaries on the text.

**To indicate the order of the service:**

In most congregations, the rabbi or another leader of the service will make periodic announcements. In some Orthodox congregations, it is generally assumed that those present know the order of the service and no announcements are made. In many Orthodox, Conservative and Reconstructionist congregations major portions of the service are read individually, often aloud, at the individual's own pace. As a result, the service may appear to be unorganized.

### GUEST BEHAVIOR DURING THE SERVICE

**Will a guest who is not Jewish be expected to do anything other than sit?**

They are expected to stand with the congregation. It is optional for them to read prayers aloud and sing with congregants if this would not violate their religious beliefs. Kneeling is not part of any Jewish service.

**Are there any parts of the service in which a guest who is not Jewish should *not* participate?**

In all Orthodox, Conservative and Reconstructionist and in most Reform congregations, non-Jews will not be called to read from the Torah or participate in any honors involving the Torah.

**If not disruptive to the service, is it okay to:**

◘ **Take pictures?** No.

◘ **Use a flash?** No.

◘ **Use a video camera?** No.

◘ **Use a tape recorder?** No.

**Will contributions to the synagogue/temple be collected at the service?**

No.

### AFTER THE SERVICE

**Is there usually a reception after the service?**

Yes. This is called a *kiddush* ("kee-DOOSH") or an *oneg Shabbat* ("OH-neg shah-BAHT"). It may last 30 to 60 minutes. Usually served is such light food as coffee, tea, fruit, pastries or punch. Sometimes appetizer-type foods are served. Wait for a blessing to be said before eating or drinking. Wine and grape juice are provided in almost all congregations for the ceremonial blessing before drinking the "fruit of the vine." A blessing called *ha'-motzi* ("hah-MOH-tsee") is recited before eating bread. In all Orthodox and some Conservative congregations, ritual handwashing is done before eating or drinking.

In most Reform congregations, no blessing is recited after meals. All Orthodox and many Conservative and Reconstructionist congregations have a grace after meals. This is called *birkat hamazon* ("beer-KAHT hah-mah-ZONE").

### Is there a traditional form of address for clergy who may be at the reception?
"Rabbi" or "Cantor."

### Is it okay to leave early?
Yes.

## GENERAL GUIDELINES AND ADVICE

In Orthodox congregations, decorum in synagogue calls for no public display of physical affection between the sexes. Often, Orthodox men and women do not even shake each other's hands. On *Shabbat*, most Orthodox Jews do not drive, smoke, write, use the telephone, turn electricity on or off, cook, handle money or do work of any kind. Many Conservative and Reconstructionist and some Reform Jews will abstain from some of these activities.

## SPECIAL VOCABULARY

### Key words or phrases which might be helpful for a visitor to know:

- *Torah* ("TOH-rah"): Most commonly used to refer to the scroll of the Five Books of Moses (Genesis, Exodus, Leviticus, Numbers and Deuteronomy).
- *Aliyah* ("ah-lee-YAH"): Literally "going up," it is the honor of being called to the *bimah* to participate in reading the Torah.
- *Sh'ma* ("shih-MAH"): A central prayer of the worship service. Essentially a statement of faith which is derived from Deuteronomy, Chapter 6: "Hear O Israel, the Lord is our God, the Lord is One."
- *Amidah* ("ah-mee-DAH"): A series of praises, thanks and petitions to God. Recited by the entire congregation while standing, they are the central part of the prayer service.
- *Simcha* ("SIHM-khah"): Means "to rejoice." May be used during a service to refer to a special happy event, such as a birth, a *bar* or *bat mitzvah* or a wedding.

◾ *Mazal Tov* ("MAH-zahl tohv"): Literally "Good luck," but used as "congratulations." Especially used at the occasion of a *simcha*.

## DOGMA AND IDEOLOGY

There is no single official creed that all Jews accept.

### Jews believe:

◾ There is only one God, to Whom prayer is directed, and with Whom each person has a personal and direct relationship.

◾ Congregational prayer and community are a cornerstone of faith.

◾ The Torah is a guide to righteous living, as a continual source of revelation, although not all accept it literally.

◾ Study of Torah is equivalent to prayer.

◾ God is supreme over all and possesses absolute sovereignty.

◾ People have free will and there is no original sin.

◾ Righteousness is not limited to members of the Jewish faith.

◾ They share a sense of community with and responsibility for Jews throughout the world.

### Some basic books to which a guest can refer to learn more about Judaism:

*What Is a Jew?* by Morris N. Kertzer, revised by Lawrence A. Hoffman (New York: Collier Books, 1993).

*The Jewish Home* by Daniel B. Syme (New York: UAHC Press, 1988).

*Exploring Judaism* by Jacob Staub and Rebecca Alpert (Philadelphia: Reconstructionist Press, 1994).

*Conservative Judaism: The New Century* by Neil Gillman (West Orange, N.J.: Behrman House, Inc. 1993).

*This Is My God: The Jewish Way of Life* by Herman Wouk (New York: Pocket Books, 1974).

## III · HOLY DAYS AND FESTIVALS

Jewish holy days and festivals celebrate historical events in the life of the Jewish people or are times that the Torah specifically sets aside for religious services. Noted below for each major holiday are those times when observant Jews are required to abstain from "work" on their days of observance. The definition of activities that constitute "work" varies, but all include transacting business.

A lunar-based religious calendar is used, so each new day starts at sunset. Sunday is the first day of the week. The Sabbath, the weekly seventh day of rest, begins at sunset on Friday and is observed until nightfall on Saturday. The coincidence of Jewish holidays with the solar-based Christian calendar varies as much as a month from year to year.

- *Rosh Hashanah* ("rohsh hah-SHAH-nah"): The Jewish religious New Year, which also commemorates the creation of the world, traditionally counted as being approximately 5800 years ago. Occurs on the first and second days of the Hebrew month of Tishrei and is observed on both days in Orthodox, Conservative and Reconstructionist congregations and on the first day only in Reform congregations. Usually occurs mid-September to mid-October. The greeting for Rosh Hashanah is "Happy New Year," in Hebrew *"Shana Tovah* ("shah-NAH toh-VAH"). Almost all Jews abstain from work on their days of observance.
- *Yom Kippur* ("yohm kee-POOR"): The Day of Atonement, on which one engages in reflection and prayer and formally repents for sins committed during the previous Hebrew year. Occurs on the 10th day of the Hebrew month of Tishrei, which usually falls in late September to mid-October. The greetings for Yom Kippur are "Have an easy fast" or "Happy New Year," in Hebrew *"Shana Tovah"* ("shah-NAH toh-VAH"). Jews 13 or older are required to abstain from work and fast (no liquids or food) from the sundown when Yom Kippur begins until nightfall of the following day.
- *Sukkot* ("soo-KOTE"): The Feast of Booths. An eight-day harvest holiday. This usually occurs in early or mid-October. A traditional greeting is "Happy holiday," or, in Hebrew, *"Chag samayach"* ("hahg sah-MAY-ahk"). Orthodox Jews in particular abstain from work during the first two days and last two days of the holiday, as do many Conservative Jews, while Reconstructionist and Reform Jews may abstain from work on the first and last days only.
- *Chanukah* ("HAH-noo-kah"): The Festival of Lights. Commemorates the victory in about 163 B.C.E. (Before the Common Era) of the Maccabees over the Syrians who tried to eradicate Judaism. It is observed for the eight days beginning with the 25th day of the Hebrew month of Kislev. This is usually in early to mid-December. The traditional greeting is "Happy Chanukah" or, in Hebrew, *"Chanukah samayach"* ("HAH-noo-kah sah-MAY-ahk"). There are no requirements to abstain from work during Chanukah.
- *Purim* ("POO-rim"): A celebration of deliverance from destruction. Marked by reading the Purim story from a *Megillah* ("m'gee-LAH"), a scroll of the Book of Esther, and merrymaking. Usually occurs in late February or early March. The traditional greeting is "Happy Holiday,"

in Hebrew, *"Chag samayach"* ("hahg sah-MAY-ack"); or "Happy Purim." There are no requirements to abstain from work on Purim.

■ *Pesach* ("PAY-sakh"): Passover. Celebrates the Jewish people's freedom from slavery in Egypt. Beginning with the 15th day of the Hebrew month of Nisan, it is observed for eight days by Orthodox, Conservative and Reconstructionist Jews and for seven days by Reform Jews. Almost all Jews abstain from eating bread and other foods made with yeast. Usually occurs in late March or early to mid-April. A traditional greeting is "Happy holiday," in Hebrew *"Chag samayach"* ("hahg sah-MAY-ack"); or "Happy Passover." Orthodox Jews in particular abstain from work during the first two days and the last two days of the holiday, as do many Conservative Jews. Reconstructionist and Reform Jews may abstain from work on the first and last days only.

■ *Shavuot* ("shah-voo-OTE"): The Festival of Weeks. Commemorates the giving of the Torah at Mount Sinai, as well as the first fruits of the spring harvest. Occurs on the sixth and seventh of the Hebrew month of Sivan, which usually occurs in May or June. A traditional greeting is "Happy holiday," or in Hebrew, *"Chag samayach"* ("hahg sah-MAY-ahk"). Orthodox Jews in particular abstain from work during both days of this holiday, as do many Conservative Jews, while Reconstructionist and Reform Jews observe it for only one day.

## IV · LIFE CYCLE EVENTS

### · Birth Ceremony ·

In Hebrew, the ceremony is called a *brit* ("breet"), which literally means "covenant," and can apply to newborn males and females.

For boys, the *brit milah* ("breet mee-LAH"), or the "covenant of circumcision," occurs on the eighth day of a male child's life. This is a sign of the covenant between God and the Jewish people. The biblical roots of circumcision are in Genesis, which states that God told Abraham, "Every male among you shall be circumcised..., and that shall be the sign of the covenant between Me and you throughout the generations" (Genesis 17:10).

The circumcision may be performed at home, in a synagogue/temple or in a hospital. It requires removing the entire foreskin of the penis, a simple surgical technique that takes only a few seconds. The entire ceremony, including giving the child his Hebrew name, may take 15 to 60 minutes.

For girls, the Naming ceremony is the *brit bat* ("breet baht"), the "covenant of the daughter," or the *brit hayyim* ("breet hy-YEEM") the "covenant of life." It is held at home or at the synagogue/temple, usually during the Torah reading portion of the Sabbath or weekday service.

If a more creative or non-traditional baby-naming ceremony is held at home, it may take about 20 minutes.

## BEFORE THE CEREMONY

### Are guests usually invited by a formal invitation?
They are usually invited by telephone or by written invitation.

### If not stated explicitly, should one assume that children are invited?
Yes.

### If one can't attend, what should one do?
RSVP with regrets and send a small gift appropriate for the child, such as clothing, a toy or baby equipment.

## APPROPRIATE ATTIRE

**Men:** If the ceremony is at home, dress casually, although a jacket and tie may be appropriate. If at a synagogue/temple, a jacket and tie is appropriate.

A small headcovering called a *yarmulke* ("YAHR-mihl-kah") or *kippah* ("keep-AH") is required in all Orthodox, Conservative and Reconstructionist congregations and in some Reform congregations, as well as in services in the homes of members of such congregations. They will be available just before one enters the main sanctuary or will be provided if the ceremony is at home. If required in a Reform congregation, a sign is usually posted to that effect.

**Women:** If the ceremony is at home, dress may be casual. If it is at a synagogue/temple, wear a dress, a skirt and blouse or a pants suit. Clothing should be modest, depending on the fashion and the locale. Open-toed shoes and jewelry are appropriate. In Orthodox congregations, clothing should cover the arms, hems should reach below the knees and heads should be covered with a hat or veil. On the Sabbath, do not carry a purse or similar accessory since Jewish law prohibits labor, including carrying objects, on *Shabbat*.

Note: A traditional prayer shawl, a *tallit* ("tah-LEET"), may also be available at the entrance to the sanctuary. The *tallit* is worn by all Orthodox men, Conservative and Reconstructionist men and some women, and by some men and women in Reform congregations. Non-Jews should not wear the *tallit*.

Do not openly wear symbols of other faiths, such as a cross.

There are no rules regarding colors of clothing, but this is a festive time.

## GIFTS

**Is a gift customarily expected?**
Yes, often cash, U.S. or Israeli savings bonds, toys or children's clothing or baby equipment.

**Should gifts be brought to the ceremony?**
Either to the synagogue/temple (if the ceremony is not on the Sabbath) or to the home.

## THE CEREMONY

**Where will the ceremony take place?**
At the child's home, or at a synagogue/temple.

**When should guests arrive and where should they sit?**
Arrive early. Sit anywhere, except in the front row, which is usually reserved for close family members.

**If arriving late, are there times when a guest should *not* enter the ceremony?**
Not for a *brit* at home. If the *brit* is at a synagogue/temple, ushers usually will tell latecomers when they can enter.

**Are there times when a guest should *not* leave the ceremony?**
Not if it is at home. If at a synagogue/temple, do not leave when the congregation is standing, when the Torah is being taken out or returned to the ark, when the rabbi is speaking, or when the specific ceremony during the service for which you have been invited is taking place.

**Who are the major officiants, leaders or participants at the ceremony and what do they do?**
For a male's *brit milah:*
- *A mohel* ("MOH-hail"), or specially trained ritual circumciser, who may also be a rabbi or physician.
- *A rabbi*, who may also be the *mohel*.
- *The child's parents*, who recite blessings and may hold the child during the ceremony.

- *The child's grandparents*, who bring the child into the room where the ceremony is held.
- *The child's godparents*, who hold the child during the actual circumcision and who must be members of the Jewish faith.

For a girl's naming ceremony:
- *A rabbi.*
- *The child's parents*, who recite blessings and may hold the child during the ceremony.
- *The child's grandparents*, who bring the child into the room where the ceremony is held.
- *The child's godparents.*
- *A cantor* (if the ceremony is in a synagogue), who leads the congregation in song.
- *The Torah reader* (if the ceremony is in a synagogue), who chants from the Torah.
- *The gabbai* ("gab-BYE") (if the ceremony is in a synagogue), who oversees the honors of reading from the Torah.

**What books are used?**
*The siddur* ("SEE-door"), or prayerbook, or a ceremony specially prepared by the parents.

**To indicate the order of the ceremony:**
The rabbi or another leader of the service will make periodic announcements.

**Will a guest who is not Jewish be expected to do anything other than sit?**
They are expected to stand with the congregation. It is optional for them to read prayers aloud and sing with other guests if this would not violate their religious beliefs.

**Are there any parts of the ceremony in which a guest who is not Jewish should *not* participate?**
In Orthodox, Conservative and Reconstructionist and in most Reform congregations, non-Jews will not be called to read from the Torah or participate in any honors involving the Torah.

**If not disruptive to the ceremony, is it okay to:**
- **Take pictures?** Ask the rabbi and ask permission of the host.
- **Use a flash?** Ask the rabbi and ask permission of the host.
- **Use a video camera?** Ask the rabbi and ask permission of the host.
- **Use a tape recorder?** Ask the rabbi and ask permission of the host.

**Will contributions to the synagogue/temple be collected at the ceremony?**

No.

## AFTER THE CEREMONY

**Is there usually a reception after the ceremony?**

There is almost always a reception called a *kiddush* ("kee-DOOSH"). Usually served is such light food as coffee, tea, fruit, pastries or punch. Sometimes appetizer-type foods are served. Wine and grape juice are provided in almost all congregations for the ceremonial blessing before drinking the "fruit of the vine." There is no music or dancing.

If in the home, the reception may last up to two hours. If in a synagogue/temple, it may last 30 to 60 minutes.

Among Orthodox Jews, the reception may include a meal and possibly a brief sermon or discourse by the father, or some distinguished family member, guest or the rabbi. At the home of the infant's parents, a catering hall or the site of the *brit*, the reception may last one hour.

**Would it be considered impolite to neither eat nor drink?**

No.

**Is there a grace or benediction before eating or drinking?**

Yes. Wait for a blessing to be said before eating or drinking. A blessing is said before drinking wine or grape juice. A blessing called *ha'motzi* ("hah-MOH-tsee") is recited before eating bread. In all Orthodox and some Conservative congregations, ritual handwashing is done before eating or drinking.

**Is there a grace or benediction after eating or drinking?**

In most Reform congregations, no blessing is recited after meals. All Orthodox and many Conservative and Reconstructionist congregations have a grace after meals. This is called *birkat hamazon* ("beer-KAHT hah-mah-ZONE").

**Is there a traditional greeting for the family?**

"Congratulations," or, in Hebrew, *"Mazal tov"* ("MAH-zahl tohv").

**Is there a traditional form of address for clergy who may be at the reception?**

"Rabbi" or "Cantor." There is no special form of address for the *mohel*.

**Is it okay to leave early?**

Yes.

## · Initiation Ceremony ·

These ceremonies mark an adolescent's entry into religious adulthood and responsibility, after which they are included in the *minyan* ("MIN-yahn") or quorum of 10 Jewish people (men or women in Reform, Reconstructionist and Conservative congregations; only men in Orthodox) needed to hold congregational prayers.

For a boy, *bar mitzvah* ("bahr MITS-vah"), or "son of the commandment," occurs upon reaching the age of 13, when, according to Jewish tradition, males are liable for their own transgressions and their fathers no longer bear this responsibility.

A *bat mitzvah* ("baht MITS-vah"), or "daughter of the commandment," is held at the age of 12 or 13. According to Jewish law, females attain religious adulthood and responsibility upon reaching 12 years and one day. There are no specific legal requirements in Judaism for a girl to participate in a ceremony marking this occasion, and *bat mitzvah* ceremonies began only in the 20th century.

In Orthodox, Conservative and Reconstructionist congregations, a boy publicly reads from the Torah for the first time at a *bar mitzvah* and a girl reads from the *Haftarah* (a reading from Prophets) at a *bat mitzvah*. In a Reform congregation, both boys and girls publicly read from the Torah. In those Reform congregations where the *Haftarah* is read, boys and girls also read from this text. He or she may also lead other parts of the service, and usually deliver a speech to the congregation on the significance of attaining religious adulthood.

A *bar* or *bat mitzvah* service is always part of a larger, basic service and is almost always on a Saturday morning.

*Bar* or *bat mitzvah* services usually last about one hour in Reform congregations and about two hours in Orthodox, Conservative and Reconstructionist congregations. The balance of the basic Sabbath service will add about an hour (or more) to the entire service.

### BEFORE THE CEREMONY

**Are guests usually invited by a formal invitation?**
Yes.

**If not stated explicitly, should one assume that children are invited?**
No.

## If one can't attend, what should one do?

RSVP with your regrets and send a small gift or check ($25-$75) for the *bar/bat mitzvah* boy or girl.

### APPROPRIATE ATTIRE

**Men:** A jacket and tie are never inappropriate. At some times, more informal attire may be appropriate in some Reform and Reconstructionist congregations.

A small headcovering called a *yarmulke* ("YAHR-mihl-kah") or *kippah* ("keep-AH") is required in all Orthodox, Conservative and Reconstructionist congregations and in some Reform congregations. They will be available just before one enters the main sanctuary. If required in Reform congregations, a sign is usually posted to that effect.

**Women:** A dress, a skirt and blouse or a pants suit. In general, clothing should be modest, depending on the fashion and the locale. Open-toed shoes and modest jewelry are appropriate. In some Conservative synagogues, a hat or another form of head covering may be required, especially if a woman ascends to the ark where the Torah is kept or to the pulpit. In Orthodox congregations, clothing should cover the arms, hems should reach below the knees and heads should be covered with a hat or veil. On the Sabbath, do not carry a purse or similar accessory since Jewish law prohibits labor, including carrying objects, on *Shabbat*.

Note: A traditional prayer shawl, a *tallit* ("tah-LEET"), may also be available at the entrance to the sanctuary. The *tallit* is worn by all Orthodox men, Conservative and Reconstructionist men and some women, and by some men and women in Reform congregations. Non-Jews should not wear the *tallit*.

Do not openly wear symbols of other faiths, such as a cross.

There are no rules regarding colors of clothing, but this is a festive occasion.

### GIFTS

#### Is a gift customarily expected?

Yes. Customary gifts are cash or U.S. or Israeli savings bonds valued at $50 to $250, or books or ritual items of Judaica.

#### Should gifts be brought to the ceremony?

Gifts should be sent to the child's home.

## THE CEREMONY

### Where will the ceremony take place?

In the sanctuary of the synagogue/temple.

### When should guests arrive and where should they sit?

It is more customary for guests who are not Jews to arrive at the time called at Reform and Reconstructionist Saturday morning services than at Conservative and Orthodox services, which tend to be longer. Unless you want to participate in the entire sevice, ask your host the time you should arrive so you can be present for the specific event within the service for which you have been invited. Sit wherever you wish, while respecting any separation of men and women, which occurs in all Orthodox congregations.

### If arriving late, are there times when a guest should *not* enter the ceremony?

Do not enter when the congregation is standing or during the rabbi's sermon. In most congregations, an usher will advise latecomers when they can enter.

### Are there times when a guest should *not* leave the ceremony?

Yes, when the congregation is standing, when the Torah is being taken out or returned to the ark, when the rabbi is speaking, or when the specific ceremony during the service for which you have been invited is taking place.

### Who are the major officiants, leaders or participants at the ceremony and what do they do?

- *The bar or bat mitzvah boy or girl.*
- *The child's parents.*
- *The rabbi,* who directs the service and teaches and preaches. (Any Jewish person over the age of 13 may lead a service; in an Orthodox congregation, this can only be a male.) In larger congregations, there may be a senior rabbi and one or more rabbis who are his or her assistants.
- *The cantor,* who chants and sings parts of the service and leads the congregation in song.
- *The Torah reader,* who chants from the Torah.
- *The gabbai* ("gab-BYE"), a lay person who oversees the honors of reading from the Torah and of saying blessings for the Torah reading.
- *The congregation's president,* or his or her representative, who may welcome congregants and visitors from the *bimah* ("BEE-mah") and make announcements about upcoming events and programs.

Note: In smaller congregations, the same person may have more than one role. For instance, the rabbi may also be the cantor.

### What books are used?

The *siddur* ("SEE-door"), or prayerbook, which varies among (and sometimes within) the various religious movements; and the *chumash* ("KOOH-mahsh"), which contains the first five books of the Torah, also known as the Five Books of Moses: Genesis, Exodus, Leviticus, Numbers and Deuteronomy. It also contains a traditional section from Prophets which is associated with each Torah section and which is read after the Torah reading (which is called the *Haftarah*, pronounced "hahf-TOH-rah") and may contain editorial commentaries on the text.

### To indicate the order of the ceremony:

In most congregations, the rabbi or another leader of the service will make periodic announcements. In some Orthodox congregations, it is generally assumed that those present know the order of the service and no announcements are made. In many Orthodox congregations major portions of the service are read individually, often aloud, at the individual's own pace. As a result, the service may appear to be unorganized.

### Will a guest who is not Jewish be expected to do anything other than sit?

They are expected to stand with the congregation. It is optional for them to read prayers aloud and to sing with congregants, if this would not violate their religious beliefs.

### Are there any parts of the ceremony in which a guest who is not Jewish should *not* participate?

In Orthodox, Conservative and Reconstructionist and in most Reform congregations, non-Jews are not called to read from the Torah or participate in any honors involving the Torah.

### If not disruptive to the ceremony, is it okay to:

▪ **Take pictures?** Not on Saturdays; possibly on other days. Ask your host.
▪ **Use a flash?** Not on Saturdays; possibly on other days. Ask your host.
▪ **Use a video camera?** Not on Saturdays; possibly on other days. Ask your host.
▪ **Use a tape recorder?** Not on Saturdays; possibly on other days. Ask your host.

### Will contributions to the synagogue/temple be collected at the ceremony?

No.

## AFTER THE CEREMONY

### Is there usually a reception after the ceremony?

There is usually a small, relatively brief (15-30 minutes) reception for the entire congregation and invited guests. This is called a *kiddush* ("kee-DOOSH") and almost always is held in a reception area of the synagogue/temple. Usually served is coffee, tea, fruit, pastries or punch. Sometimes appetizer-type foods are served. There may be wine and, in some congregations, whiskey.

For invited guests only, there may be a larger reception and celebration after the *kiddush* at which a full meal is served and at which there is music and dancing. This may be held in a reception room of the synagogue/temple, in a separate catering hall/hotel or at the home of the *bar* or *bat mitzvah* child. This meal and celebration may last three hours or more.

### Would it be considered impolite to neither eat nor drink?

No. In general, guests should not expect non-kosher food, such as pork or shellfish, or expect to mix dairy and meat products at the reception if it is kosher (observes the traditional Jewish dietary laws). All Orthodox receptions, most Conservative and Reconstructionist and some Reform receptions are kosher.

### Is there a grace or benediction before eating or drinking?

Yes. Wait for a blessing to be said before eating or drinking. A blessing is said before drinking wine or grape juice. A blessing called *ha'motzi* ("hah-MOH-tsee") is recited before eating. It might be led by a rabbi, cantor or layperson who is an honored guest. In all Orthodox and some Conservative congregations, ritual handwashing is done before eating or drinking.

### Is there a grace or benediction after eating or drinking?

Not in most Reform congregations or households. All Orthodox and many Conservative and Reconstructionist congregations or households have a grace after meals called *birkat hamazon* ("beer-KAHT hah-mah-ZONE").

### Is there a traditional greeting for the family?

"Congratulations" or, in Hebrew, "*Mazal tov*" ("MAH-zahl tohv").

### Is there a traditional form of address for clergy who may be at the reception?

"Rabbi" or "Cantor."

### Is it okay to leave early?

Yes, but usually only after the main course has been served.

# · *Marriage Ceremony* ·

Judaism considers marriage a divine command, a sacred bond and a means of personal fulfillment. Marriage is deemed the natural and desirable state of every adult. The Hebrew word for marriage is *kiddushin* ("kee-doo-SHEEN"), which means "sanctification."

The *huppah* ("hoo-PAH") or wedding canopy, under which the ceremony takes place, symbolizes the canopy of the heavens under which all life transpires. A glass, which the groom breaks underfoot after he and the bride have said their wedding vows, is an ancient tradition that has been interpreted in many ways, including commemorating at this time of great joy, a moment of great sadness: The destruction of the Temple in Jerusalem in 70 C.E. (Common Era).

The wedding ceremony is always a ceremony unto itself. Not part of a larger service, it may take about 15 to 30 minutes.

## BEFORE THE CEREMONY

**Are guests usually invited by a formal invitation?**
Yes.

**If not stated explicitly, should one assume that children are invited?**
No.

**If one can't attend, what should one do?**
RSVP with regrets and send a gift.

## APPROPRIATE ATTIRE

**Men:** Attire depends on the social formality of the event. A small head-covering called a *yarmulke* ("YAHR-mil-kah") or *kippah* ("keep-AH") is required in all Orthodox, Conservative and Reconstructionist ceremonies and in some Reform ceremonies. They will be provided to guests.

**Women:** Attire depends on the social formality of the event. For most Orthodox ceremonies, clothing, such as a dress or skirt and blouse, should be modest and cover the arms and hems should reach below the knees. Open-toed shoes and modest jewelry are appropriate. In some Orthodox and Conservative ceremonies, a head covering may be required.

Do not openly wear symbols of other faiths, such as a cross.

There are no rules regarding colors of clothing, but this is a very festive event.

## GIFTS

### Is a gift customarily expected?

Yes. Appropriate are such household items as small appliances or sheets or towels. Money is also appropriate, with amounts between $50 and $200 recommended. The bride often is listed in the bridal registry at a local department store.

### Should gifts be brought to the ceremony?

No. Send them to the bride's home or to the reception.

## THE CEREMONY

### Where will the ceremony take place?

Depending on the desires of the couple, it may be at a synagogue/temple, a catering hall, at home or any other location chosen by them.

### When should guests arrive and where should they sit?

It is customary to arrive at the time called. Ushers usually will be present to seat you. Otherwise, sit wherever you wish.

### If arriving late, are there times when a guest should *not* enter the ceremony?

Do not enter during the processional or recessional.

### Are there times when a guest should *not* leave the ceremony?

Not during the processional or recessional or while the officiant is blessing or addressing the couple.

### Who are the major officiants, leaders or participants at the ceremony and what do they do?

- *The rabbi*, who leads the ceremony.
- *The cantor*, who sings during the ceremony or who may lead it instead of a rabbi.
- *The bride and groom.*
- *Parents of the bride and groom* and other members of the wedding party.

### What books are used?

None. There may be special material prepared by the bridal couple.

### To indicate the order of the ceremony:

There may be a program.

### Will a guest who is not Jewish be expected to do anything other than sit?

No.

**Are there any parts of the ceremony in which a guest who is not Jewish should *not* participate?**

No.

**If not disruptive to the ceremony, is it okay to:**
- **Take pictures?** Possibly. Ask your host.
- **Use a flash?** Possibly. Ask your host.
- **Use a video camera?** Possibly. Ask your host.
- **Use a tape recorder?** Possibly. Ask your host.

**Will contributions to the synagogue/temple be collected at the ceremony?**

No.

### AFTER THE CEREMONY

**Is there usually a reception after the ceremony?**

Weddings are times of great celebration. Often, a full meal is served at which there is music and dancing. This may be held in a reception room of the synagogue/temple, in a separate catering hall, at a hotel, or at another site. There may also be a light smorgasbord before the ceremony itself.

Guests should not expect to mix dairy and meat products at the reception if it is kosher (observes the traditional Jewish dietary laws). All Orthodox receptions, most Conservative and Reconstructionist and some Reform receptions are kosher.

**Would it be considered impolite to neither eat nor drink?**

No.

**Is there a grace or benediction before eating or drinking?**

Yes. Wait for a blessing to be said before eating or drinking. A benediction called *ha'motzi* ("hah-MOH-tsee") is recited before eating bread. It might be said by a rabbi, cantor or a lay person who is an honored guest.

**Is there a grace or benediction after eating or drinking?**

All Orthodox and many Conservative and Reconstructionist ceremonies have a grace after meals called *birkat hamazon*. This is increasingly common in Reform ceremonies.

**Is there a traditional greeting for the family?**

"Congratulations," or, in Hebrew, "*Mazal tov*" ("MAH-zal tohv").

**Is there a traditional form of address for clergy who may be at the reception?**

"Rabbi" or "cantor."

**Is it okay to leave early?**

Yes, but usually only after the main course has been served.

## · Funerals and Mourning ·

A Jewish funeral will last between 15 and 60 minutes. It is a time of intense mourning and public grieving. It is a service unto itself and is not part of a larger service.

The Reform movement rejects all notions of bodily resurrection and of a physical life after death. Instead, it believes in the immortality of every soul, which will eventually return to God. True immortality resides in memories treasured in this world by those who knew and loved the deceased.

The Reconstructionist movement does not believe in bodily resurrection. It believes that, upon death, the soul rejoins the universe.

The Conservative movement talks about the resurrection of the dead, but does not specify whether this will be a physical or a spiritual resurrection. The former would occur upon the coming of the Messiah; the latter would occur by those remaining on earth sensing and remembering the deceased.

Orthodox Jews believe in bodily resurrection and a physical life after death. This would occur upon the coming of the Messiah. In the meantime, there are rough equivalents to heaven and hell, with righteous souls enjoying the pleasures of *olam ha'bah* ("oh-LAHM hah-BAH"), "the world to come," which has a Garden of Eden-like quality; and the wicked suffering in the fiery pits of *Gehenna* ("geh-HEN-ah").

Traditional Jewish law forbids cremation, but cremation is allowed among Reform Jews.

### BEFORE THE CEREMONY

**How soon after the death does the funeral usually take place?**

The day after the death, unless there are extraordinary circumstances. In some Reform families, within two to three days after the death.

**What should a non-Jew do upon hearing of the death of a member of that faith?**

Telephone or visit the bereaved at home and offer condolences and to help out in any way. Possibly bring food to their home. Especially for Orthodox families, make certain the food is kosher (conforms with traditional Jewish dietary laws). If particularly close with the bereaved, offer to take them to the funeral home to arrange details for the funeral.

## APPROPRIATE ATTIRE

**Men:** A jacket and tie. A small headcovering called a *yarmulke* ("YAHR-mil-kah") or *kippah* ("keep-AH") is required at Orthodox, Conservative and Reconstructionist funerals and at some Reform funerals. They will be available at the funeral home or synagogue/temple.

**Women:** A dress or a skirt and blouse. Clothing should be modest.

At some Conservative funerals, a hat or another form of headcovering may be required. Open-toed shoes and modest jewelry are appropriate. For Orthodox funerals, clothing should cover the arms, hems should reach below the knees and heads should be covered with a hat or veil.

Do not openly wear symbols of other faiths, such as a cross.

Somber colors for clothing are recommended.

## GIFTS

### Is it appropriate to send flowers or make a contribution?

Flowers are never appropriate for Orthodox, Conservative and Reconstructionist funerals, but are sometimes appropriate for Reform funerals. Contributions in memory of the deceased are customary. Small contributions are often given to a charity or cause favored by the deceased and which may be listed in an obituary in a local newspaper; to a special fund established by the bereaved family; or to a Jewish organization, particularly the Jewish National Fund (42 East 69th Street, New York, N.Y. 10021; telephone (800) 345-8565) that plants trees in Israel and which will send the bereaved family a letter informing them that you have "planted a tree in Israel" in memory of the deceased.

### Is it appropriate to send food?

Yes, to the home of the bereaved after the funeral. Even if the family is not ritually observant, it is best if the food is kosher (conforms with traditional Jewish dietary laws) to avoid even the possibility of offending them.

## THE CEREMONY

### Where will the ceremony take place?

Either at a synagogue/temple or a funeral home.

### When should guests arrive and where should they sit?

Arrive on time. Ushers may be available to direct guests to seating.

**If arriving late, are there times when a guest should *not* enter the ceremony?**

Do not enter during the processional or recessional, if they take place, or while eulogies are being delivered.

**Will the bereaved family be present at the synagogue/temple or the funeral home before the ceremony?**

Yes, usually for no longer than one hour.

**Is there a traditional greeting for the family?**

Offer condolences, such as "I'm sorry for your loss."

**Will there be an open casket?**

Never.

**Who are the major officiants at the ceremony and what do they do?**

- *A rabbi,* who officiates and delivers a eulogy.
- *A cantor,* who sings.
- *Family member(s) or friend(s),* who may also deliver a eulogy or memorial.

**What books are used?**

None. The service is led entirely by the rabbi, with no lay participation other than eulogies or memorials by relative(s) or friend(s).

**To indicate the order of the ceremony:**

The officiating rabbi will make occasional announcements.

**Will a guest who is not Jewish be expected to do anything other than sit?**

Guests are expected to stand with the other mourners.

**Are there any parts of the ceremony in which a guest who is not Jewish should *not* participate?**

No.

**If not disruptive to the ceremony, is it okay to:**

- **Take pictures?** No.
- **Use a flash?** No.
- **Use a video camera?** No.
- **Use a tape recorder?** Possibly. Ask permission from a member of the deceased's immediate family.

**Will contributions to the synagogue/temple be collected at the ceremony?**

No.

## THE INTERMENT

### Should guests attend the interment?

It is expected only of family and close friends, not acquaintances.

### Whom should one ask for directions?

The funeral director.

### What happens at the graveside?

The service will vary, depending as much on the family's background as on its religious affiliation. At the simplest graveside service, the rabbi recites prayers and leads the family in the mourner's *kaddish* ("KAH-dish"), the prayer for the deceased. At a traditional service, once the mourners have arrived at the cemetery, there is a slow procession to the grave itself, with several pauses along the way. After prayers and *kaddish* have been recited, all present participate in filling in the grave by each putting one spadeful of earth into it. As the closest family members leave the gravesite, they pass between two rows of relatives and friends.

### Do guests who are not Jews participate at the graveside ceremony?

They participate in filling in the grave, if this custom is followed. Otherwise, they are simply present.

## COMFORTING THE BEREAVED

### Is it appropriate to visit the home of the bereaved after the funeral?

Yes. The family sits in mourning for seven days after the funeral. This is called the *shiva* period ("SHIH-vah"). Visits should last about 30 minutes. They are usually made during the daytime or early evening hours. After expressing your condolences, it is customary to sit quietly or talk to other callers, and wait to be spoken to by the principal mourners.

There are no ritual objects at the home of the bereaved, but some home traditions during the mourning period may include:

- Covering mirrors in the home to concentrate on mourning and not on vanity.
- Burning a special memorial candle for seven days in memory of the deceased.
- Immediate members of the family sitting on small chairs or boxes; wearing a black ribbon that has been cut and slippers or just socks rather than shoes; and, for men, not shaving.

All these symbolize mourners' lack of interest in their comfort or how they appear to others.

## Will there be a religious service at the home of the bereaved?

Yes. Twice a day, morning and evening. These usually last about 10 to 20 minutes. Non-Jews should take a prayerbook when these are offered and may silently read the English, if this does not violate their religious beliefs. They should stand when those present stand during the brief service.

## Will food be served?

Probably. Guests should not wait for a grace or benediction before eating. Guests will eat as they arrive, after expressing their condolences to the breaved.

## How soon after the funeral will a mourner usually return to a normal work schedule?

One week.

## How soon after the funeral will a mourner usually return to a normal social schedule?

One month to one year, depending on the deceased's relation to the person as well as personal inclination.

## Are there mourning customs to which a friend who is not Jewish should be sensitive?

For eleven months after the death of their parent or child, 30 days for other relatives, mourners who follow traditional practice will attend daily morning and/or evening services at synagogue/temple, where he (or she, too, in a more "modern" Orthodox household) participates in the service and, in particular, recites the mourners' *kaddish* ("KAH-dish"), the special prayer for the deceased.

## Are there rituals for observing the anniversary of the death?

The anniversary of the death is called a *yahrzeit* ("YAHR-tzite"), upon which the bereaved attends service at a synagogue/temple and lights at home a *yahrzeit* candle that burns for 24 hours. An "unveiling" of the tombstone usually takes place on approximately the first anniversary of the death and involves a simple ceremony at the gravesite. Attendance is by specific invitation only.

# V · HOME CELEBRATIONS

## · Passover Seder ·

### When does it occur?

In the springtime.

**What is its significance?**
Passover commemorates the Jewish people's liberation from slavery in Egypt.

**What is the proper greeting to the celebrants?**
"Happy Passover" or "Happy holiday," which in Hebrew is "*Chag samayach*" ("hahg sah-MAY-ahk").

## BEFORE THE CEREMONY

**Are guests usually invited by a formal invitation?**
Yes. They may receive a phone call, or be invited face-to-face.

**If not stated explicitly, should one assume children are invited?**
No. Clarify this with your host.

**If one can't attend, what should one do?**
Express regrets. Send flowers or special Passover candy.

## APPROPRIATE ATTIRE

**Men:** Ask your host about attire. Some may prefer jacket and tie; others may request more informal attire. A small headcovering called a *yarmulke* ("YAHR-mil-kah") or *kippah* ("keep-AH") is required at all Orthodox and most Conservative and Reconstructionist *seders* and at some Reform *seders*. If required, your host will provide them for you.

**Women:** Ask your host about attire. Some may prefer a dress or a skirt and blouse or a pants suit. Open-toed shoes and modest jewelry are appropriate.

Do not openly wear symbols of other faiths, such as a cross.

There are no rules regarding colors of clothing, but this is a festive occasion.

## GIFTS

**Is a gift customarily expected?**
This is entirely optional.

**If one decides to give a gift, is a certain type of gift appropriate?**
Flowers for the *seder* table or special Passover candy are welcome.

## THE CEREMONY

The Passover *seder* ("SAY-dihr") is a festive dinner at home at which the story of the Jewish people's liberation from slavery in Egypt, the Exodus, is told. Rituals precede and follow the meal. A *seder* is usually led by the head of the household, although everyone present participates.

*Seders* (including the meal) may take from 90 minutes to more than three hours, depending upon the detail in which the story is told and family customs. It is customary to arrive at the time called; this is a dinner, as well as a religious celebration.

## What are the major ritual objects of the ceremony?

- *A seder plate*, on which are symbols of various aspects of the Passover story.
- *Matzah* ("MAH-tzah"), or flat, unleavened bread, similar to the bread made by the Jewish people as they fled Egypt.

## What books are used?

A *haggadah* ("hah-GAH-dah"), a text in Hebrew and English which tells the Passover story and its meaning for each generation. There are hundreds of different versions of the *haggadah*. Many focus on different elements of the holiday or interpret it from their own particular perspective, such as feminism or ecology, but all tell the basic story of the Exodus.

## Will a guest who is not Jewish be expected to do anything other than sit?

If asked to do so by the leader, they should read aloud English portions of the *haggadah*.

## Are there any parts of the ceremony in which a non-Jewish guest should *not* participate?

No.

## If not disruptive to the ceremony, is it okay to:

- **Take pictures?** Probably; ask your host.
- **Use a flash?** Probably; ask your host.
- **Use a video camera?** Probably; ask your host.
- **Use a tape recorder?** Probably; ask your host.

### EATING AND DRINKING

## Is a meal part of the celebration?

Yes. It is usually served after the first part of the ritual portion of the *seder*.

## Will there be alcoholic beverages?

Wine is an integral part of the *seder*. Other alcoholic beverages may be served prior to or after the *seder*, depending upon the family's customs.

**Would it be considered impolite not to eat?**
Yes, since the meal is central to the celebration.

**Is there a grace or benediction before eating or drinking?**
Yes. Wait for a blessing before eating or drinking. There are usually several blessings over wine and different types of food. There is also a ritual washing of the hands.

**Is there a grace or benediction after eating or drinking?**
Yes. This is called *birkat hamazon* ("beer-KAHT hah-mah-ZONE").

**At the meal, will a guest be asked to say or do anything?**
If asked to do so by the leader, they should read aloud English portions of the *haggadah*.

**Will there be:**
▪ **Dancing?** No.
▪ **Music?** Usually there is just singing. Guitar or piano may accompany the singing.

### GENERAL GUIDELINES AND ADVICE

Listen to the *seder* leader for instructions about the meaning and the order of the *seder* and for what to do.

## · *Shabbat Dinner* ·

**When does it occur?**
Friday evenings.

**What is its significance?**
*Shabbat* ("shah-BAHT"), or the Sabbath, commemorates the day on which God rested after creating the world during the previous six days. The Jewish Sabbath begins at sunset on Friday and ends at nightfall on Saturday. The *Shabbat* dinner, which is held at home on Friday evening, is a family-oriented celebration of the Sabbath.

**What is the proper greeting to the celebrants?**
"*Shabbat shalom*" ("shah-BAHT shah-LOME"), Hebrew for "Peaceful Sabbath."

### BEFORE THE CEREMONY

**Are guests usually invited by a formal invitation?**
Yes. They may receive a phone call or be invited face-to-face.

**If not stated explicitly, should one assume that children are invited?**
Yes.

**If one can't attend, what should one do?**
Express regrets.

## APPROPRIATE ATTIRE

**Men:** Ask your host about attire. Some may prefer jacket and tie; others may prefer more informal attire. A small headcovering called a *yarmulke* ("YAHR-mil-kah") or *kippah* ("keep-AH") is required during all Orthodox and most Conservative and Reconstructionist *Shabbat* dinners and at some Reform *Shabbat* dinners. If required, they will be provided.

**Women:** Ask your hosts about attire. Some may prefer a dress or a skirt and blouse or a pants suit. Open-toed shoes and modest jewelry are appropriate. In Orthodox homes, clothing should cover the arms, hems should reach below the knees. Do not carry a purse or similar accessory since Jewish law prohibits labor, including carrying objects, on *Shabbat*.

Do not openly wear symbols of other faiths, such as a cross.

There are no rules regarding colors of clothing, but in Orthodox homes, such bright colors as red or hot pink are not appropriate.

## GIFTS

**Is a gift customarily expected?**
This is entirely optional.

**If one decides to give a gift, is a certain type of gift appropriate?**
Flowers or candy would be welcome.

## THE CEREMONY
Welcoming the Sabbath is a joyous event and may include the following, although some may be done before guests arrive: Lighting the Sabbath candles and reciting the blessing over them; reciting *kiddush* ("kee-DOOSH"), a prayer accompanied by wine or grape juice before dinner; reciting *ha'motzi* ("hah-MOH-tsee"), the blessing over bread; parents blessing their children; songs to celebrate and welcome the sabbath.

Depending on how many rituals are observed, they may take about five to 15 minutes.

The ceremony is usually led by the head of the household, although everyone present may participate. The sabbath dinner is a celebration unto itself and is not part of a larger service. Its duration will be that of a social dinner. Arrive at the time called, since this is a social dinner, as well as a religious celebration.

### What are the major ritual objects of the ceremony?

- *A kippah* ("keep-AH"), or small headcovering.
- *Sabbath Candlesticks* (two), for the ceremonial lighting of candles to welcome *Shabbat* and mark its beginning.
- *A kiddush* ("kee-DOOSH") *cup*, for the ritual blessing over wine.
- *A loaf of challah* ("HAH-lah"), specially prepared, braided Sabbath bread.

### What books are used?

A *siddur* ("SEE-door"), or prayerbook, or an abbreviated version of it that is just for this purpose.

### Will a guest who is not Jewish be expected to do anything other than sit?

Stand when other participants stand. If asked to do so by the leader, guests should read aloud English portions of the prayerbook if these do not violate their religious beliefs.

### Are there any parts of the ceremony in which a non-Jewish guest should *not* participate?

No.

### If not disruptive to the ceremony, is it okay to:

- **Take pictures?** Not in Orthodox homes; possibly in others. Ask your host.
- **Use a flash?** Not in Orthodox homes; possibly in others. Ask your host.
- **Use a video camera?** Not in Orthodox homes; possibly in others. Ask your host.
- **Use a tape recorder?** Not in Orthodox homes; possibly in others. Ask your host.

### EATING AND DRINKING

### Is a meal part of the celebration?

Yes, an integral part.

### Will there be alcoholic beverages?

Wine is part of the *Shabbat* ritual. Other alcoholic beverages may be served, depending on the family's social customs.

**Would it be considered impolite to neither eat nor drink?**
Yes, since the meal is central to the celebration.

**Is there a grace or benediction before eating or drinking?**
Yes. Wait for a blessing to be said before eating or drinking. The blessing over bread is called *ha'motzi* ("hah-MOH-tsee"). In some homes, there is also a ritual washing of the hands.

**Is there a grace or benediction after eating or drinking?**
Yes. This is called *birkat hamazon* ("beer-KAHT hah-mah-ZONE"). It will be said in all Orthodox homes and in some other Jewish homes.

**At the meal, will a guest be asked to say or do anything?**
Stand when other participants stand. If asked to do so by the leader, guests should read aloud English portions of the prayerbook and join in any singing, if these do not violate their religious beliefs.

**Will there be:**
▪ **Dancing?** No.
▪ **Music?** Usually there is just singing. Guitar or piano may accompany the singing.

## GENERAL GUIDELINES AND ADVICE

On *Shabbat*, most Orthodox Jews do not drive, smoke, write, use the telephone, turn electricity on or off, cook or handle money. It is expected that guests observe the same customs while visiting an Orthodox home.

Do not expect such foods as pork or shellfish or expect to mix dairy and meat products since Orthodox and many other Jewish households "keep kosher" (observe the traditional Jewish dietary laws).

Orthodox men ordinarily do not shake the hands of women to whom they are not married, and Orthodox women ordinarily do not shake the hands of men to whom they are not married; nor is there public display of physical affection (such as kissing or hugging) between men and women who are not married to each other.

# Chapter 13 Contents

# 13

# Lutheran

## I · HISTORY AND BELIEFS

Lutherans trace their faith back to the German reformer, Martin Luther (1483-1546), who sought to reform doctrines and practices of the Roman Catholic Church. Objecting to the Church's teachings that one is saved by faith and by doing good works, he maintained that, according to the Bible, one is made just in God's eyes only by trusting in Jesus's accomplishments for humanity. This is distinct from any good that one does.

Luther also objected to corruption among the clergy and advocated worship in the language of the people rather than in Latin. He favored a married, rather than a celibate, clergy.

Although the Church of Rome considered Luther disloyal and drove him out, later, many priests and laity, especially in northern Germany, eventually agreed with Luther's teachings and revamped already existing churches around them.

German and Scandinavian immigrants brought the Lutheran faith to North America. By 1900, scores of small Lutheran church bodies were divided from one another by language, theology and the extent of their assimilation into North American society. Although still somewhat divided along ethnic lines, the main divisions today are between those who are theologically liberal and theologically conservative.

In the United States, the two main Lutheran denominations are the Evangelical Lutheran Church in America and the Lutheran Church—Missouri Synod. The former was created by uniting many earlier churches; the latter, which is a national Church despite its name, is more conservative theologically.

In Canada, the Evangelical Lutheran Church in Canada is comparable to the Evangelical Lutheran Church in America; while the Lutheran Church–Canada, is the Canadian counterpart to the Lutheran Church–Missouri Synod, and relates closely to that body.

*The Evangelical Lutheran Church in America:*
**U.S. churches:** 11,000
**U.S. membership:** 5.2 million

*The Lutheran Church–Missouri Synod:*
**U.S. churches:** 6,100
**U.S. membership:** 2.6 million

*(data from the* 1998 Yearbook of American and Canadian Churches)

---

**For more information, contact:**
The Evangelical Lutheran Church in America
8765 West Higgins Road
Chicago, IL 60631
(773) 380-2700
info@elca.org
www.elca.org

The Lutheran Church–Missouri Synod
International Center
1333 South Kirkwood Road
St. Louis, MO 63122-7295
(314) 965-9917
infocenter@lcms.org
www.lcms.org

*The Evangelical Lutheran Church in Canada:*
**Canadian churches:** 864
**Canadian membership:** 198,683

*Lutheran Church–Canada:*
**Canadian churches:** 387
**Canadian membership:** 84,763

*(data from* Directory, Lutheran Churches in Canada, *1997)*

---

**For more information contact:**
The Evangelical Lutheran Church in Canada
302–393 Portage Avenue
Winnipeg, MB  R2B 3H6
(204) 284-9150

Lutheran Church–Canada
3074 Portage Avenue
Winnipeg, MB  R3K 0Y2
(204) 895-3433

## II · THE BASIC SERVICE

The basic worship service is a relatively simple formal liturgy that retains the traditional form of the mass with an emphasis on the preaching of God's word and celebration of the Lord's Supper. (The ritual commemorating the Supper is known as Holy Communion). The service includes hymns, psalms, responsive readings, Bible readings, a sermon and, often, the communion liturgy.

Lutherans believe that the Lord's Supper is a direct encounter with God, and that Jesus Christ's body and blood are present through the bread and wine of the Eucharist.

The service usually lasts less than one hour.

### APPROPRIATE ATTIRE

**Men:** Jacket and tie or slightly more casual clothing. Varies from congregation to congregation. No head covering is required.

**Women:** Dress, skirt and blouse, or pants suit are acceptable. Open-toed shoes and modest jewelry are fine. Hems need not reach below the knees. No head covering is required.

In some congregations, "dressy" leisure clothes are acceptable for men and women, especially in summer. Shorts should never be worn.

There are no rules regarding colors of clothing.

### THE SANCTUARY

#### What are the major sections of the church?

The architecture of Lutheran churches varies from the most traditional gothic to avant-garde modern styles. These are the key areas in every church:

- *The narthex:* The vestibule or entrance hall. This is at the end of the nave (see below) and opposite the altar area. Usually, the main outside door enters into the narthex.
- *The nave:* Where congregants sit.
- *The choir loft:* Where the choir sits.
- *The chancel:* Includes the altar and pulpit and seating for clergy. The pastor conducts the worship from this area.

## THE SERVICE

### When should guests arrive and where should they sit?

Although this standard varies by culture and community, it is generally appropriate to arrive a few minutes early to be seated since services typically begin at the hour called. Usually, ushers will be available to assist you in finding a seat.

### If arriving late, are there times when a guest should *not* enter the service?

Do not enter during the spoken part of the service. Entry during songs is fine.

### Are there times when a guest should *not* leave the service?

Do not exit while any prayers are being recited or the sermon is being delivered. Leaving during songs is fine. Almost everyone remains until the end. If you plan to leave by a certain time, sit near the rear of the church and leave quietly.

### Who are the major officiants, leaders or participants and what do they do?

- *The pastor*, who preaches, oversees others and administers sacraments.
- *Assisting ministers*, who aid with prayers and administering certain sacraments.
- *The lector*, who reads the scripture lessons.
- *An acolyte*, who lights candles and assists with communion and other tasks. This is usually a teenager.
- *The choir*, which leads singing.
- *Ushers and greeters*, who welcome guests, seat them and distribute books.
- *The music leader*, who plays an organ and directs the choir.

### What are the major ritual objects of the service?

- *The altar*, which symbolizes the presence of God.
- *The pulpit*, which the pastor uses for preaching.
- *The lectern*, where scripture is read.
- *The baptismal font*, which is used for baptizing. It is usually near the front of the church.
- *A cross or a crucifix* (a cross with a representation of the body of Jesus Christ on it).

### What books are used?

A Bible and a hymnal, usually the *Lutheran Book of Worship* (Minneapolis, Minn.: Augsburg Fortress, 1978) and/or *The Lutheran Hymnal* (St. Louis, Mo.: Concordia Publishing House, 1941) and/or *Lutheran Worship* (St.

Louis, Mo.: Concordia Publishing House, 1982). Books will be found in the pews or chair racks, or will be handed out by the ushers.

**To indicate the order of the service:**
There will be a program and/or the pastor or assisting minister will make periodic announcements.

## GUEST BEHAVIOR DURING THE SERVICE

**Will a guest who is not a Lutheran be expected to do anything other than sit?**
The level of participation depends on whether or not the guest is Christian. Christians will generally be expected to stand, kneel and sing with the congregation and read prayers aloud. Non-Christians are expected to stand with congregants, but not necessarily to kneel, sing or pray with them. Remaining seated when others are kneeling is fine.

**Are there any parts of the service in which a non-Lutheran guest should *not* participate?**
Who is welcome to receive Holy Communion varies among Lutheran churches. The worship bulletin will usually state the policy for visitors.

**If not disruptive to the service, is it okay to:**
◘ **Take pictures?** Only with prior permission from the pastor.
◘ **Use a flash?** Only with prior permission from the pastor.
◘ **Use a video camera?** Only with prior permission from the pastor.
◘ **Use a tape recorder?** Only with prior permission from the pastor.

**Will contributions to the church be collected at the service?**
Generally, contributions are collected by ushers passing an offering plate or basket among the seated congregation. It is the guest's choice whether or not to contribute.

**How much is customary to contribute?**
A donation (cash or check) of $1 to $5 is appropriate.

## AFTER THE SERVICE

**Is there usually a reception after the service?**
This will vary by location. Coffee and cookies may be served in a reception area or in the church basement. The reception may last about half an hour.

**Is there a traditional form of address for clergy who may be at the reception?**
"Pastor" followed by last name.

**Is it okay to leave early?**
Yes.

## GENERAL GUIDELINES AND ADVICE

Guests have a special place of honor in the thinking of most congregations. You may be invited to sign a guest book or "friendship pad" or to introduce yourself.

Respect the dignity of the service. Although you need not stand when the congregation does, you may feel more comfortable doing so.

Do not hesitate to ask an usher or a "greeter" (who is often identified by a nametag) any questions about the service. Also, feel free to ask a worshipper in your pew for assistance in following the liturgy, should you have any difficulty.

A typical mistake guests sometimes make is to automatically stand and follow other worshippers who are in the same pew when they go to the altar to receive Holy Communion. Guests should remain in the pew and not go forward to receive Communion. Do not fear you will stand out: Others will be staying in the pews, also.

## SPECIAL VOCABULARY

**Key words or phrases which might be helpful for a visitor to know:**

- *Holy Communion:* A rite through which Lutherans believe they receive Christ's body and blood as assurance that God has forgiven their sins.
- *Grace:* The loving mercy that God shows us in Jesus Christ.
- *Alleluia (Hallelujah):* From the Hebrew, "Praise ye the Lord!"
- *Lessons:* Readings from the Bible (or "Scripture"), including the Old Testament, the Epistles (generally from one of the letters of St. Paul or another New Testament writer) and the Gospel (a reading from Matthew, Mark, Luke or John, the "biographers" of Jesus).
- *Creed:* Statement of belief. Generally, one of the early Christian creeds is used, either the Apostles' Creed or the Nicene Creed.

## DOGMA AND IDEOLOGY

**Lutherans believe:**

- The Law of God, as found, for example, in the Ten Commandments, tells what God expects of us and how we are to live. The Law also shows us that we fall short of God's expectations and that we are disobedient to God.

▪ The Gospel is the good news of how God remains faithful to His justice, which demands punishment for our disobedience (our sin); and to His love and mercy, which does not want to see any of us punished or separated from Him because of our sin.

▪ The good news (which is what "Gospel" means) is that the eternal Son of God, who is Himself fully God, became a man in the person of Jesus of Nazareth, lived a life of perfect obedience that we cannot live, and suffered God's own punishment for our sin so we don't have to. Instead, we are freely forgiven through Jesus Christ and given eternal life with God as a free gift.

**Some books to which a guest can refer to learn more about the Lutheran faith:**

*The Small Catechism* by Martin Luther (St. Louis, Mo.: Concordia Publishing House).

*The Lutherans in North America*, edited by E. Clifford Nelson (Philadelphia: Fortress Press, 1980).

*Lutheran Worship: History and Practice*, edited by Fred L. Precht (St. Louis, Mo.: Concordia Publishing House, 1993).

*These Evangelical Lutheran Churches of Ours* by Kenn Ward (Winfield, B.C.: Wood Lake Books, 1994).

## III · HOLY DAYS AND FESTIVALS

▪ *Advent*. Occurs four weeks before Christmas. The purpose is to begin preparing for Christmas and to focus on Christ. There is no traditional greeting to Lutherans for this holiday. Additional services are sometimes added to the church schedule.

▪ *Christmas*. Occurs on the evening of December 24 and the day of December 25. Marks the birth and the incarnation of God as a man. The traditional greeting to Lutherans is "Merry Christmas" or "Blessed Christmas."

▪ *Lent*. Begins on Ash Wednesday, which occurs six weeks before Easter. The purpose is to prepare for Easter. There is no traditional greeting to Lutherans for Lent. Between Lent and Easter, abstention from entertainment is encouraged, as is increased giving to the poor. Often, there are midweek worship services. Some churches sponsor a light soup supper once a week, with proceeds going toward combatting world hunger and encouraging global peace. While traditionally among many Christian denominations, Lent is a time of fasting or abstaining from certain foods, relatively few contemporary Lutherans now do this and such fasting is given little prominence by the Church.

- *Easter.* Always falls on the Sunday after the first full moon that occurs on or after March 21. Celebrates the Resurrection of Jesus Christ. The traditional greeting to Lutherans is "Happy Easter!" In worship services, the pastor may greet congregants with, "He is risen!" Congregants respond with "He is risen, indeed!"
- *Pentecost Sunday.* The seventh Sunday after Easter. Celebrates the coming of the Holy Spirit, which is the empowering spirit of God in human life. This is often considered the birth of the Christian Church. There is no traditional greeting for this holiday.
- *Reformation Day.* Occurs on October 31. Reformation Sunday, the day on which Reformation Day is celebrated, is the Sunday before Reformation Day. Commemorates October 31, 1517, the day on which Martin Luther is said to have nailed 95 statements of belief (called the "95 Theses") on the door of the Castle Church in Wittenberg, Germany. This was then the practice for inviting scholarly debate. There is no traditional greeting for this holiday.

---

## IV · LIFE CYCLE EVENTS

### · *Birth Ceremony* ·

Baptism is the one-time sacrament of initiation into the family of God, the Holy Christian Church. In the Lutheran Church, infants are baptized. (Also baptized are previously unbaptized youths or adults when they confess faith in Jesus Christ and ask to join the church.)

As a sacrament, baptism is a means by which God creates and strengthens faith and through which He assures the forgiveness of sins and the promise of eternal life with Him. Baptism is done with water applied to the head of the person being initiated and in the Name of the Father, the Son and the Holy Spirit (the three persons of God). It marks entry into Christian faith, not simply the birth of a child.

Typically, the baptism is part of a Sunday service. When this occurs, the service will be slightly longer than the "Basic Service" described above, which usually lasts less than an hour, and will focus on the baptism.

#### BEFORE THE CEREMONY

**Are guests usually invited by a formal invitation?**
Guests are usually invited by a note or phone call.

**If not stated explicitly, should one assume that children are invited?**
Yes.

**If one can't attend, what should one do?**

Call the family to express congratulations or send a baptism card. These are available at most card shops.

## APPROPRIATE ATTIRE

**Men:** Jacket and tie or slightly more casual clothing. Varies from congregation to congregation. No head covering is required.

**Women:** Dress, skirt and blouse, or pants suit are acceptable. Open-toed shoes and modest jewelry are fine. Hems need not reach below the knees. No head covering is required.

In some congregations, "dressy" leisure clothes are acceptable for men and women, especially in summer. Shorts should never be worn.

There are no rules regarding colors of clothing.

## GIFTS

**Is a gift customarily expected?**

Yes, clothing or toys for a newborn are most frequently given. Money is not appropriate.

**Should gifts be brought to the ceremony?**

It is customary to bring a gift to the home following the ceremony.

## THE CEREMONY

**Where will the ceremony take place?**

Partly at the baptismal font in the main sanctuary of the church; partly near the altar.

**When should guests arrive and where should they sit?**

Arrive a few minutes early to be seated since services typically begin at the hour called. Ushers will help you find a seat.

**If arriving late, are there times when a guest should *not* enter the ceremony?**

Do not enter during the spoken part of the service. Entry during songs is fine.

**Are there times when a guest should *not* leave the ceremony?**

Almost everyone remains until the end. If you plan to leave by a certain time, sit near the rear of the church and leave quietly. Do not leave while any prayers are being recited or the sermon is being delivered. Departure during songs is advised.

**Who are the major officiants, leaders or participants at the ceremony and what do they do?**

◾ *The pastor*, who presides and baptizes.

◾ *An assisting minister*, who leads prayers and assists the pastor.

◾ *Ushers*, who greet congregants and guests and assist in seating.

◾ *The sponsors*, who answer questions and confess to the Christian faith on behalf of the infant being baptized. (Parents also may serve this function.) Sponsors are not used at youth or adult baptisms since those being baptized can speak for themselves.

**What books are used?**

A Bible and a hymnal, usually the *Lutheran Book of Worship* (Minneapolis, Minn.: Augsburg Fortress, 1978) and/or *The Lutheran Hymnal* (St. Louis, Mo.: Concordia Publishing House, 1941) and/or *Lutheran Worship* (St. Louis, Mo.: Concordia Publishing House, 1982). Books will be found in the pews or chair racks, or will be handed out by the ushers.

**To indicate the order of the ceremony:**

There will be a program and/or the pastor or assisting minister will make periodic announcements.

**Will a guest who is not a Lutheran be expected to do anything other than sit?**

The level of participation depends on whether or not the guest is Christian. Christians will generally be expected to stand, kneel and sing with congregation and read prayers aloud. Non-Christians are expected to stand with congregants, but not necessarily to kneel, sing or pray with them. Remaining seated when others are kneeling is fine.

**Are there any parts of the ceremony in which a guest who is not a Lutheran should *not* participate?**

Who is welcome to receive Holy Communion varies among Lutheran churches. The worship bulletin will usually state the policy for visitors.

**If not disruptive to the ceremony, is it okay to:**

◾ **Take pictures?** Only with prior permission from the pastor.

◾ **Use a flash?** Only with prior permission from the pastor.

◾ **Use a video camera?** Only with prior permission from the pastor.

◾ **Use a tape recorder?** Only with prior permission from the pastor.

**Will contributions to the church be collected at the ceremony?**

Generally, contributions are collected by ushers passing an offering plate or basket among the seated congregation. It is the guest's choice whether or not to contribute.

**How much is customary to contribute?**

A donation (cash or check) of $1 to $5 is appropriate.

### AFTER THE CEREMONY

**Is there usually a reception after the ceremony?**

There may be a reception after the ceremony at the home of the infant's parents. This may include a meal or refreshments and presenting of gifts to the baptized. Since this is generally a family affair, you should behave as you would as a guest in someone's home.

**Would it be considered impolite to neither eat nor drink?**

No.

**Is there a grace or benediction before eating or drinking?**

No.

**Is there a grace or benediction after eating or drinking?**

No.

**Is there a traditional greeting for the family?**

Offer your congratulations.

**Is there a traditional form of address for clergy who may be at the reception?**

"Pastor" followed by last name.

**Is it okay to leave early?**

Yes.

## · Initiation Ceremony ·

Confirmation is a church rite in which one who was previously baptized expresses his or her faith in Jesus Christ. The ceremony is an additional liturgy added to the "Basic Service." In it, confirmands come forward individually as their names are called and the pastor places his or her hands on the confirmand's head and prays God's blessing on that person. (Women are ordained as priests only in the Evangelical Lutheran Church in America, not in the Lutheran Church-Missouri Synod.) Generally, a special verse of scripture, selected especially for that confirmand, is read.

Confirmation usually takes place in early adolescence and often in a group.

## BEFORE THE CEREMONY

**Are guests usually invited by a formal invitation?**
Yes.

**If not stated explicitly, should one assume that children are invited?**
Yes.

**If one can't attend, what should one do?**
Send a gift or call the family to express congratulations.

## APPROPRIATE ATTIRE

**Men:** Jacket and tie or slightly more casual clothing. Varies from congregation to congregation. No head covering is required.

**Women:** Dress, skirt and blouse, or pants suit are acceptable. Open-toed shoes and modest jewelry are fine. Hems need not reach below the knees. No head covering is required.

In some congregations, "dressy" leisure clothes are acceptable for men and women, especially in summer. Shorts should never be worn.

There are no rules regarding colors of clothing.

## GIFTS

**Is a gift customarily expected?**
It is customary to present a gift at the confirmation of youths. It is appropriate to give money (between $20 and $40) or religious books and objects.

**Should gifts be brought to the ceremony?**
The gift should be brought to the home after the service.

## THE CEREMONY

**Where will the ceremony take place?**
In the main sanctuary of the church.

**When should guests arrive and where should they sit?**
Although this standard varies by culture and community, it is generally appropriate to arrive a few minutes early to be seated since services typically begin at the hour called.

**If arriving late, are there times when a guest should *not* enter the ceremony?**

Do not enter during prayers. Usually, ushers will help you find a seat.

**Are there times when a guest should *not* leave the ceremony?**

Almost everyone remains until the end. If you plan to leave by a certain time, sit near the rear of the church and leave quietly. Do not leave while any prayers are being recited or the sermon is being delivered. Departure during songs is advised.

**Who are the major officiants, leaders or participants at the ceremony and what do they do?**

- *The pastor*, who preaches, oversees others and administers sacraments.
- *The assisting ministers*, who aid with prayers and certain sacraments.
- *Ushers and greeters*, who welcome guests, seat them and distribute books.
- *The music leader*, who plays an organ, directs the choir and leads singing.
- *The readers*, who read lessons from scripture.

**What books are used?**

A Bible and a hymnal, usually the *Lutheran Book of Worship* (Minneapolis, Minn.: Augsburg Fortress, 1978) and/or *The Lutheran Hymnal* (St. Louis, Mo.: Concordia Publishing House, 1941) and/or *Lutheran Worship* (St. Louis, Mo.: Concordia Publishing House, 1982). Books will be found in the pews or chair racks, or will be handed out by the ushers.

**To indicate the order of the ceremony:**

There will be a program and/or the pastor or assisting minister will make periodic announcements.

**Will a guest who is not a Lutheran be expected to do anything other than sit?**

The level of participation depends on whether or not the guest is Christian. Christians will generally be expected to stand, kneel and sing with the congregation and read prayers aloud. Non-Christians are expected to stand with congregants, but not necessarily to kneel, sing or pray with them. Remaining seated when others are kneeling is fine.

**Are there any parts of the ceremony in which a non-Lutheran should *not* participate?**

Who is welcome to receive Holy Communion varies among Lutheran churches. The worship bulletin will usually state the policy for visitors.

**If not disruptive to the ceremony, is it okay to:**

- **Take pictures?** Only with prior permission from the pastor.

▣ **Use a flash?** Only with prior permission from the pastor.
▣ **Use a video camera?** Only with prior permission from the pastor.
▣ **Use a tape recorder?** Only with prier permission from the pastor.

**Will contributions to the church be collected at the ceremony?**
Generally, contributions are collected by ushers passing an offering plate or basket among the seated congregation. It is the guest's choice whether or not to contribute.

**How much is customary to contribute?**
A donation (cash or check) of $1 to $5 is appropriate.

### AFTER THE CEREMONY

**Is there usually a reception after the ceremony?**
There may be a reception at the church in the fellowship hall. Generally, individual families plan receptions in their homes for invited guests. There will probably be light refreshments or a meal. If at home, alcoholic beverages may be served.

If it is held at the church, the reception may last about 30 minutes. If in a home or restaurant, it usually lasts at least two hours.

**Would it be considered impolite to neither eat nor drink?**
No.

**Is there a grace or benediction before eating or drinking?**
Guests should wait for the saying of grace or an invocation before eating.

**Is there a grace or benediction after eating or drinking?**
There may be a benediction after the meal.

**Is there a traditional greeting for the family?**
It is proper to congratulate the confirmand and his or her family.

**Is there a traditional form of address for clergy who may be at the reception?**
"Pastor" followed by last name.

**Is it okay to leave early?**
Yes.

## · *Marriage Ceremony* ·

A church wedding is an act of worship, not a civil service. In the service, the couple profess their love for and their commitment to each other before God and ask His blessing on their marriage. The same decorum exercised in any worship service should be exercised in the wedding service.

The ceremony may either be a service unto itself or be part of the Holy Communion service. The bridal party will proceed in, then the pastor will read appropriate lessons from the Bible and ask the bride and groom about their lifelong commitment to one another. The pastor will deliver a brief homily, wedding vows and rings will be exchanged, and the pastor will pronounce the couple husband and wife.

If the ceremony is a service by itself, it will last 15 to 30 minutes. If part of the celebration of Holy Communion and also depending on the music selected, it will last around half an hour.

## BEFORE THE CEREMONY

### Are guests usually invited by a formal invitation?
Yes.

### If not stated explicitly, should one assume that children are invited?
Yes.

### If one can't attend, what should one do?
Reply in writing or call and send a gift.

## APPROPRIATE ATTIRE

Local social norms prevail, although weddings tend to be somewhat formal.

**Men:** Jacket and tie. No head covering required.

**Women:** Dress, skirt and blouse, or pants suit are acceptable. Open-toed shoes and modest jewelry are fine. Hems need not reach the knees. No head covering required.

There are no rules regarding colors of clothing.

## GIFTS

### Is a gift customarily expected?
Yes. Appropriate gifts are such household items as appliances, dishes, towels or blankets. The bride often is listed in the bridal registry at a local department store.

### Should gifts be brought to the ceremony?
If you are also invited to the reception afterwards, gifts are more often brought to the reception and placed on the gift table there.

## THE CEREMONY

**Where will the ceremony take place?**

In the main sanctuary of the House of Worship. The bridal party will stand near the altar in the chancel, the area in front of the sanctuary which includes the altar and pulpit and seating for clergy.

**When should guests arrive and where should they sit?**

It is appropriate to arrive before the time called for the ceremony. An usher will tell you where to sit.

**If arriving late, are there times when a guest should *not* enter the ceremony?**

Do not enter during the processional, recessional or during prayer.

**Are there times when a guest should *not* leave the ceremony?**

Do not leave during the processional, recessional or during prayer.

**Who are the major officiants, leaders or participants at the ceremony and what do they do?**

◘ *The pastor*, who presides.

**What books are used?**

A hymnal may be used.

**To indicate the order of the ceremony:**

There will be a program.

**Will a guest who is not a Lutheran be expected to do anything other than sit?**

Guests are not expected to do anything other than sit and enjoy.

**Are there any parts of the ceremony in which a guest who is not a Lutheran should *not* participate?**

Who is welcome to receive Holy Communion varies among Lutheran churches. The worship bulletin will usually state the policy for visitors.

**If not disruptive to the ceremony, is it okay to:**

◘ **Take pictures?** Only with prior permission from the pastor.

◘ **Use a flash?** Only with prior permission from the pastor.

◘ **Use a video camera?** Only with prior permission from the pastor.

◘ **Use a tape recorder?** Only with prior permission from the pastor.

**Will contributions to the church be collected at the ceremony?**

No.

## AFTER THE CEREMONY

**Is there usually a reception after the ceremony?**

Customs vary locally and by individual preference. However, there will generally be a reception in the church, at home or in a catering hall. Depending on local custom, there may be music and dancing. The menu will vary from light refreshments and cake to a full meal. Alcoholic beverages may be served if the reception is held outside the church.

If the reception is held at a church, it will be less than 30 minutes. If at a home or restaurant, it will usually last at least two hours.

**Would it be considered impolite to neither eat nor drink?**

Yes. If you have dietary restrictions, inform your host or hostess in advance.

**Is there a grace or benediction before eating or drinking?**

Guests should wait for the saying of grace or an invocation before eating.

**Is there a grace or benediction after eating or drinking?**

No.

**Is there a traditional greeting for the family?**

Congratulate the new couple and their parents.

**Is there a traditional form of address for clergy who may be at the reception?**

"Pastor" followed by last name.

**Is it okay to leave early?**

Yes.

## · Funerals and Mourning ·

For Lutherans, death is not the end of life, but the beginning of new life. While Lutherans will grieve, they do not mourn as do those who have no hope of ever seeing the deceased again or without the sure hope that those who die in faith in Jesus Christ are assured eternal life with God.

The funeral is usually a service unto itself. The pastor presides. Pall bearers carry or push the casket on rollers into the funeral home or church sanctuary. The service will rarely last more than 30 minutes. All attending are expected to remain to the end.

## BEFORE THE CEREMONY

### How soon after the death does the funeral usually take place?

There is no set period by which the funeral should occur, but it usually takes place within three days after death.

### What should a non-Lutheran do upon hearing of the death of a member of that faith?

Call the bereaved, visit or send a note to express your sympathy at their loss. Express your care and love for the bereaved.

## APPROPRIATE ATTIRE

**Men:** Jacket and tie. No head covering is required.

**Women:** A dress or skirt and blouse are acceptable. Open-toed shoes and modest jewelry are fine. Hems need not reach the knees. No head covering is required.

Local social customs govern, but conservative clothing and dark, somber colors are recommended.

## GIFTS

### Is it appropriate to send flowers or make a contribution?

It is appropriate to send flowers unless the family expresses otherwise. Send them to the deceased's home or to the funeral home where the funeral will be held.

It is also appropriate to make a donation in the form of a "memorial" in memory of the deceased. The family will often announce, either through the funeral home or in the funeral worship folder, the preferred charity or church for memorial contributions. Memorials are often mailed or hand-delivered to the funeral home or church office. There is no standard amount to be donated.

### Is it appropriate to send food?

You may want to send food to the home of the bereaved for the family and their guests.

## THE CEREMONY

### Where will the ceremony take place?

Typically, in the church of the deceased, although it may be at a funeral home.

## When should guests arrive and where should they sit?

It is customary to arrive early enough to be seated when the service begins. Someone will tell you where and when to sit.

## If arriving late, are there times when a guest should *not* enter the ceremony?

Do not enter during the procession or prayer.

## Will the bereaved family be present at the church or funeral home before the ceremony?

If there is a visitation at the funeral home the night before the funeral, you can attend and express your sorrow and regret.

## Is there a traditional greeting for the family?

Just offer your condolences.

## Will there be an open casket?

Possibly.

## Is a guest expected to view the body?

This is optional.

## What is appropriate behavior upon viewing the body?

Stand quietly and then move on.

## Who are the major officiants at the ceremony and what do they do?

◾ *The pastor*, who presides.

## What books are used?

A hymnal, usually the *Lutheran Book of Worship* (Minneapolis, Minn.: Augsburg Fortress, 1978) or *The Lutheran Hymnal* (St. Louis, Mo.: Concordia Publishing House, 1941) and/or *Lutheran Worship* (St. Louis, Mo.: Concordia Publishing House, 1982).

## To indicate the order of the ceremony:

There will be a program or the pastor will make periodic announcements.

## Will a guest who is not a Lutheran be expected to do anything other than sit?

The level of participation depends on whether or not the guest is Christian. Christians will generally be expected to stand, kneel and sing with the congregation and read prayers aloud. Non-Christians are expected to stand with congregants, but not necessarily to kneel, sing or pray with them. Remaining seated when others are kneeling is fine.

**Are there any parts of the ceremony in which a guest who is not a Lutheran should *not* participate?**

Who is welcome to receive Holy Communion varies among Lutheran churches. The worship bulletin will usually state the policy for visitors.

**If not disruptive to the ceremony, it is okay to:**

◘ **Take pictures?** Only with prior permission from the pastor.

◘ **Use a flash?** Only with prior permission from the pastor.

◘ **Use a video camera?** Only with prior permission from the pastor.

◘ **Use a tape recorder?** Only with prior permission from the pastor.

**Will contributions to the church be collected at the ceremony?**
No.

## THE INTERMENT

**Should guests attend the interment?**
Yes.

**Whom should one ask for directions?**
Either join the funeral procession or ask the funeral director for directions.

**What happens at the graveside?**
The casket is carried to the grave. Prayers and readings are offered. The pastor blesses the earth placed on the casket and blesses those gathered at the graveside.

**Do guests who are not Lutherans participate at the graveside service?**
If this does not conflict with their own religious beliefs, they recite the Lord's Prayer and join in these responses to other prayers: "The Lord be with you" and "And also with you."

## COMFORTING THE BEREAVED

**Is it appropriate to visit the home of the bereaved after the funeral?**
Yes, more than once is appropriate. Share in the conversation and refreshments.

**Will there be a religious service at the home of the bereaved?**
No.

**Will food be served?**
Possibly. If food is served, wait for the saying of grace before eating. It

would be impolite not to eat, unless you have dietary restrictions. (If so, mention these to your host or hostess.) There may be alcoholic beverages, depending on the family's custom.

### How soon after the funeral will a mourner usually return to a normal work schedule?

Bereaved often stay home from work for several days.

### How soon after the funeral will a mourner usually return to a normal social schedule?

Not for several weeks after the funeral.

### Are there mourning customs to which a friend who is not a Lutheran should be sensitive?

No.

### Are there rituals for observing the anniversary of the death?

While there are no specific such rituals, some congregations remember the first year anniversary in prayers in church.

## V · HOME CELEBRATIONS

Not applicable to Lutherans.

# Chapter 14 Contents

# 14

## Methodist

### I · HISTORY AND BELIEFS

The Methodist movement began in 18th-century England under the preaching of John Wesley, an Anglican priest who was a prodigious evangelical preacher, writer and organizer. While a student at Oxford University, he and his brother, Charles, led the Holy Club of devout students, whom scoffers called the "Methodists."

Wesley's teachings affirmed the freedom of human will as promoted by grace. He saw each person's depth of sin matched by the height of sanctification to which the Holy Spirit, the empowering spirit of God, can lead persons of faith.

Although Wesley remained an Anglican and disavowed attempts to form a new church, Methodism eventually became another church body. During a conference in Baltimore, Maryland, in 1784, the Methodist Church was founded as an ecclesiastical organization and the first Methodist bishop in the United States was elected.

The Methodist movement was first represented in Canada by Laurence Coughlan, who began to preach in Newfoundland in 1766. It wasn't until 1884, however, that the Methodist Church was formed in Canada from the merger of the Methodist Episcopal Church and smaller Methodist bodies, with the Wesleyan Methodist Church, the Conference of Eastern British America and the New Connexion Church, which had united in 1874. The Free Methodists, entering from the U.S. in 1876, were few in number and have remained separate.

In the nineteenth century, strong missionary programs helped plant Methodism abroad. Methodist missionaries from America followed their

British colleagues to India and Africa, where they founded new churches. Americans and Canadians also founded churches in East Asia, Latin America and continental Europe.

Local Methodist churches are called "charges." Their ministers are appointed by the bishop at an annual conference, and each church elects its own administrative board, which initiates planning and sets local goals and policies.

There are about 125 Methodist denominations around the globe and 23 separate Methodist bodies in the United States. Of these, the United Methodist Church is numerically the largest.

In Canada, the Methodist Church ceased to exist as a separate denomination in 1925, when it joined with Congregationalists and the majority of Presbyterian churches to form the United Church of Canada. The Free Methodist Church in Canada, which was incorporated in 1927 and which gained full autonomy from the U.S. parent denomination in 1990, remains intact.

**U.S. churches:** 36,361
**U.S. membership:** 8.5 million
*(data from the* 1998 Yearbook of American and Canadian Churches*)*

**For more information, contact:**
The United Methodist Church
204 North Newlin Street
Veedersburg, IN 47987
(800) 251-8140
infoserv@umcom.umc.org
www.umc.org

**Canadian churches:** 129
**Canadian membership:** 5,360
*(data from the* 1998 Yearbook of American and Canadian Churches*)*

**For more information, contact:**
Free Methodist Church in Canada
4315 Village Centre Ct.
Mississauga, ON  L4Z 1S2
(905) 848-2603

## II · THE BASIC SERVICE

To Methodists, worship is a congregation's encounter and communion with God and with one another in God's name. It includes praise and prayer, scripture readings, a sermon and sometimes Holy Communion. Most Methodist services last about one hour.

## APPROPRIATE ATTIRE

**Men:** Jacket and tie. No head covering is required.

**Women:** A dress. The arms do not necessarily have to be covered nor do hems have to be below the knees. Open-toed shoes and modest jewelry are permissible. No head covering is required.

There are no rules regarding colors of clothing.

## THE SANCTUARY

### What are the major sections of the church?

- *The platform or chancel:* A raised section at the front of the church. This is where the leaders and the choir function.
- *The nave:* Where congregants sit on pews.

## THE SERVICE

### When should guests arrive and where should they sit?

Arrive at the time for which the service has been called.

An usher will indicate where to sit. There are usually no restrictions on where to sit.

### If arriving late, are there times when a guest should *not* enter the service?

Yes. Ushers will seat you when appropriate.

### Are there times when a guest should *not* leave the service?

No.

### Who are the major officiants, leaders or participants and what do they do?

- *The pastor*, who presides, preaches and celebrates communion.
- *The associate pastor or the assisting lay person*, who aids the senior pastor in leading the service.
- *The choir or soloists*, who sing hymns and psalms.

### What are the major ritual objects of the service?

- *Bread*, which is eaten during Holy Communion and signifies the body of Jesus Christ.
- *Grape juice*, which the pastor presents to congregants to drink during Holy Communion and which signifies the blood of Jesus Christ.

### What books are used?

*The United Methodist Hymnal* (Nashville, Tenn.: United Methodist Publishing

House, 1989) and a Bible. Methodists have no official Bible translation, although the New Revised Standard Version (which is printed by several publishers) is the most commonly used translation.

**To indicate the order of the service:**
A program will be provided and periodic announcements will be made by the Pastor or another leader.

## GUEST BEHAVIOR DURING THE SERVICE

**Will a guest who is not a Methodist be expected to do anything other than sit?**
Standing and kneeling with the congregation and reading prayers aloud and singing with congregants are all optional. Guests are welcome to participate if this does not compromise their personal beliefs.

**Are there any parts of the service in which a guest who is not a Methodist should *not* participate?**
Yes. Methodists invite all to receive Holy Communion, but guests should be aware that partaking of communion is regarded as an act of identification with Christianity. Feel free to remain seated as others go forward for communion. Likewise, if communion bread and cups are passed among the pews, feel free to pass them along without partaking.

**If not disruptive to the service, is it okay to:**
◙ **Take pictures?** Possibly. Ask ushers.
◙ **Use a flash?** Possibly. Ask ushers.
◙ **Use a video camera?** Possibly. Ask ushers.
◙ **Use a tape recorder?** Possibly. Ask ushers.

**Will contributions to the church be collected at the service?**
Yes. The offering plate will be passed through the congregation during the service. This usually occurs immediately before or after the sermon.

**How much is customary to contribute?**
The customary offering is from $1 to $4.

## AFTER THE SERVICE

**Is there usually a reception after the service?**
Yes, in the church's reception area. It usually lasts less than 30 minutes, and pastry, coffee and tea are ordinarily served.

It is not considered impolite to neither eat nor drink. There is no grace or benediction before or after eating or drinking.

**Is there a traditional form of address for clergy who may be at the reception?**
"Reverend" or "Pastor."

**Is it okay to leave early?**
Yes.

## GENERAL GUIDELINES AND ADVICE

The chief potential for mistake occurs during Holy Communion. Feel free not to partake if you cannot in good conscience do so. But Christian guests should also be aware that the Methodist church never refuses communion to anyone.

The cups at Holy Communion always contain grape juice, not wine. Children, as well as adults, are welcome to partake.

## SPECIAL VOCABULARY

None provided.

## DOGMA AND IDEOLOGY

**Methodists believe:**
- The doctrine of the Trinity: God is the Father; the Son (embodied by Jesus Christ); and the Holy Spirit (the empowering spirit of God).
- In the natural sinfulness of humanity.
- In humanity's fall from grace and the need for individual repentance.
- In freedom of will.

In practice, Methodists are highly diverse in their beliefs and tend to emphasize right living more than orthodoxy of belief.

**A basic book to which a guest can refer to learn more about the Methodist Church:**
*United Methodist Worship* by Hoyt Hickman (Nashville, Tenn.: Abingdon Press, 1991).

## III · HOLY DAYS AND FESTIVALS

- *Advent.* Occurs four weeks before Christmas. The purpose is to begin preparing for Christmas and to focus on Christ. There is no traditional greeting for this holiday.
- *Christmas.* Occurs on the evening of December 24 and the day of Decem-

ber 25. Marks the birth and the incarnation of God as a man. The traditional greeting is "Merry Christmas."

■ *Lent.* Begins on Ash Wednesday, which occurs six weeks before Easter. The purpose is to prepare for Easter. Between Lent and Easter, fasting and abstention from entertainment are encouraged, as is increased giving to the poor. Often, there are midweek worship services. There are no traditional greetings for this holiday.

■ *Easter.* Always falls on the Sunday after the first full moon that occurs on or after March 21. Celebrates the resurrection of Jesus Christ. The traditional greeting to Methodists is "Happy Easter!"

■ *Pentecost Sunday.* The seventh Sunday after Easter. Celebrates the coming of the Holy Spirit, which is the empowering spirit of God in human life. This is often considered the birth of the Christian church. There are no traditional greetings for this holiday.

## IV · LIFE CYCLE EVENTS

### · *Birth Ceremony* ·

Baptism initiates an infant into Christianity. It is administered once to each person, usually when they are an infant. The major ritual object used during the ceremony is a baptismal font, which holds the baptismal water. The pastor sprinkles or pours water on the person's head or immerses the person in water. This signifies the washing away of sins. God is invoked to strengthen this new Christian, and the congregation, as well as the parent(s) and godparent(s), pledge to nurture him or her in the Christian faith and life.

Baptism is part of the larger weekly congregational Sunday morning service, which usually lasts about an hour.

### BEFORE THE CEREMONY

**Are guests usually invited by a formal invitation?**
Yes.

**If not stated explicitly, should one assume that children are invited?**
Yes.

**If one can't attend, what should one do?**
Any one of these is appropriate: Send flowers or a gift; or telephone the parents with your congratulations and your regrets that you can't attend.

## APPROPRIATE ATTIRE

**Men:** Jacket and tie. No head covering is required.

**Women:** A dress. The arms do not necessarily have to be covered nor do hems have to be below the knees. Open-toed shoes and modest jewelry are permissible. No head covering is required.

There are no rules regarding colors of clothing.

## GIFTS

### Is a gift customarily expected?
No, but it is appropriate. Gifts such as savings bonds or baby clothes or toys are commonly given.

### Should gifts be brought to the ceremony?
Usually gifts can be brought to the reception.

## THE CEREMONY

### Where will the ceremony take place?
In the parents' church.

### When should guests arrive and where should they sit?
Arrive at the time for which the service has been called. Ushers will indicate where to sit. There are usually no restrictions on where to sit.

### If arriving late, are there times when a guest should *not* enter the ceremony?
Yes. Ushers will seat you when appropriate.

### Are there times when a guest should *not* leave the ceremony?
No.

### Who are the major officiants, leaders or participants in the ceremony and what do they do?
▪ *The pastor*, who will baptize the child.

### What books are used?
*The United Methodist Hymnal* (Nashville, Tenn.: United Methodist Publishing House, 1989) and a Bible. Methodists have no official Bible translation, although the New Revised Standard Version (which is printed by several publishers) is the most commonly used translation.

### To indicate the order of the ceremony:
A program will be provided and periodic announcements will be made by the pastor or his or her assistant.

**Will a guest who is not a Methodist be expected to do anything other than sit?**

Standing and kneeling with the congregation and reading prayers aloud and singing with congregants are all optional. Guests are welcome to participate if this does not compromise their personal beliefs.

**Are there any parts of the ceremony in which a guest who is not a Methodist should *not* participate?**

Yes. Methodists invite all to receive Holy Communion, but guests should be aware that partaking of communion is regarded as an act of identification with Christianity. Feel free to remain seated as others go forward for communion. Likewise, if communion bread and cups are passed among the pews, feel free to pass them along without partaking. Christian guests should be aware that the Methodist church never refuses communion to anyone. The cups at Holy Communion always contain grape juice, not wine. Children, as well as adults, are welcome to partake.

**If not disruptive to the ceremony, is it okay to:**
- **Take pictures?** Possibly. Ask ushers.
- **Use a flash?** Possibly. Ask ushers.
- **Use a video camera?** Possibly. Ask ushers.
- **Use a tape recorder?** Possibly. Ask ushers.

**Will contributions to the church be collected at the ceremony?**

Yes. The offering plate will be passed through the congregation during the service. This usually occurs immediately before or after the sermon.

**How much is customary to contribute?**

The customary offering is from $1 to $4.

## AFTER THE CEREMONY

**Is there usually a reception after the ceremony?**

There is often a reception lasting about 30 minutes in the church's reception area. Pastry, coffee and tea are ordinarily served.

**Would it be considered impolite to neither eat nor drink?**

No.

**Is there a grace or benediction before eating or drinking?**

No.

**Is there a grace or benediction after eating or drinking?**

No.

**Is there a traditional greeting for the family?**
No. Just offer your congratulations.

**Is there a traditional form of address for clergy who may be at the reception?**
"Reverend" or "Pastor."

**Is it okay to leave early?**
Yes.

## · Initiation Ceremony ·

Confirmation is conferred on an early adolescent. It is a Methodist's first profession of faith. The candidates affirm for themselves the Christian faith and church into which they were baptized (usually as infants).

Teens participate in the ceremony with members of their confirmation class. The 15-minute ceremony is part of a larger Sunday morning service, which lasts about an hour.

### BEFORE THE CEREMONY

**Are guests usually invited by a formal invitation?**
No.

**If not stated explicitly, should one assume that children are invited?**
Yes.

**If one can't attend, what should one do?**
Either of these is appropriate: Send flowers or a gift or telephone the parents with your congratulations and your regrets that you can't attend.

### APPROPRIATE ATTIRE

**Men:** Jacket and tie. No head covering is required.

**Women:** A dress. The arms do not necessarily have to be covered nor do hems have to be below the knees. Open-toed shoes and modest jewelry are permissible. No head covering is required.

There are no rules regarding colors of clothing.

### GIFTS

**Is a gift customarily expected?**
No.

**Should gifts be brought to the ceremony?**
See above.

## THE CEREMONY

**Where will the ceremony take place?**
Usually at the front of the main sanctuary of the church.

**When should guests arrive and where should they sit?**
Arrive at the time for which the service has been called.

An usher will indicate where to sit. There are usually no restrictions on where to sit.

**If arriving late, are there times when a guest should *not* enter the ceremony?**
Yes. Ushers will seat you when appropriate.

**Are there times when a guest should *not* leave the ceremony?**
No.

**Who are the major officiants, leaders or participants at the ceremony and what do they do?**
▪ *The pastor*, who confirms the teen.

**What books are used?**
*The United Methodist Hymnal* (Nashville, Tenn.: United Methodist Publishing House, 1989) and a Bible. Methodists have no official Bible translation, although the New Revised Standard Version (which is printed by several publishers) is the most commonly used translation.

**To indicate the order of the ceremony:**
A program will be provided, and periodic announcements will be made by the pastor or his assistant.

**Will a guest who is not a Methodist be expected to do anything other than sit?**
Standing and kneeling with the congregation and reading prayers aloud and singing with congregants are all optional. Guests are welcome to participate if this does not compromise their personal beliefs.

**Are there any parts of the ceremony in which a guest who is not a Methodist should *not* participate?**
Yes. Methodists invite all to receive Holy Communion, but guests should be aware that partaking of communion is regarded as an act of identification with Christianity. Feel free to remain seated as others go forward for communion. Likewise, if communion bread and cups are passed among the pews, feel free to pass them along without partaking. Christian guests

should be aware that the Methodist church never refuses communion to anyone. The cups at Holy Communion always contain grape juice, not wine. Children, as well as adults, are welcome to partake.

**If not disruptive to the ceremony, is it okay to:**
◘ **Take pictures?** Possibly. Ask ushers.
◘ **Use a flash?** Possibly. Ask ushers.
◘ **Use a video camera?** Possibly. Ask ushers.
◘ **Use a tape recorder?** Possibly. Ask ushers.

**Will contributions to the church be collected at the ceremony?**
Yes. The offering plate will be passed through the congregation during the service. This usually occurs immediately before or after the sermon.

**How much is customary to contribute?**
The customary offering is from $1 to $4.

### AFTER THE CEREMONY

**Is there usually a reception after the ceremony?**
There is often a reception lasting about 30 minutes in the church's reception area. Pastry, coffee and tea are ordinarily served.

**Would it be considered impolite to neither eat nor drink?**
No.

**Is there a grace or benediction before eating or drinking?**
No.

**Is there a grace or benediction after eating or drinking?**
No.

**Is there a traditional greeting for the family?**
No. Just offer your congratulations.

**Is there a traditional form of address for clergy who may be at the reception?**
"Reverend" or "Pastor."

**Is it okay to leave early?**
Yes.

## · *Marriage Ceremony* ·

Marriage is the uniting of a man and a woman in a union that is intended—and which is pledged—to be lifelong. The marriage ceremony is a service unto itself. It may last between 15 and 30 minutes.

## BEFORE THE CEREMONY

**Are guests usually invited by a formal invitation?**
Yes.

**If not stated explicitly, should one assume that children are invited?**
No.

**If one can't attend, what should one do?**
RSVP with your regrets and send a gift.

## APPROPRIATE ATTIRE

**Men:** Jacket and tie. No head covering is required.

**Women:** A dress. The arms do not necessarily have to be covered nor do hems have to be below the knees. Open-toed shoes and modest jewelry are permissible. No head covering is required.

There are no rules regarding colors of clothing.

## GIFTS

**Is a gift ordinarily expected?**
Yes. Such gifts as small appliances, sheets, towels or other household gifts are appropriate.

**Should gifts be brought to the ceremony?**
No, send them to the home of the newlyweds.

## THE CEREMONY

**Where will the ceremony take place?**
Usually in the main sanctuary of a church.

**When should guests arrive and where should they sit?**
Arrive early. Depending on the setting, ushers may show guests where to sit.

**If arriving late, are there times when a guest should *not* enter the ceremony?**
Ushers will assist latecomers.

**Are there times when a guest should *not* leave the ceremony?**
No.

**Who are the major officiants, leaders or participants at the ceremony and what do they do?**

◾ *The pastor*, who officiates.

◾ *The bride and groom.*

◾ *The wedding party.*

**What books are used?**

Possibly a hymnal.

**To indicate the order of the ceremony:**

A program will be provided.

**Will a guest who is not a Methodist be expected to do anything other than sit?**

Standing and kneeling with the congregation and reading prayers aloud and singing with congregants are all optional. Guests are welcome to participate if this does not compromise their personal beliefs.

**Are there any parts of the ceremony in which a guest who is not a Methodist should *not* participate?**

Yes. Holy Communion may be offered at the service. Methodists invite all to receive Holy Communion, but guests should be aware that partaking of communion is regarded as an act of identification with Christianity. Feel free to remain seated as others go forward for communion. Likewise, if communion bread and cups are passed among the pews, feel free to pass them along without partaking.

**If not disruptive to the ceremony, is it okay to:**

◾ **Take pictures?** Possibly. Ask ushers.

◾ **Use a flash?** Possibly. Ask ushers.

◾ **Use a video camera?** Possibly. Ask ushers.

◾ **Use a tape recorder?** Possibly. Ask ushers.

**Will contributions to the church be collected at the ceremony?**

No.

### AFTER THE CEREMONY

**Is there usually a reception after the ceremony?**

There is often a reception that may last one to two hours. It may be at a home, a catering facility or in the same building as the ceremony. Ordinarily, food and beverages are served and there is dancing and music. Alcoholic beverages may be served.

**Would it be considered impolite to neither eat nor drink?**
No.

**Is there a grace or benediction before eating or drinking?**
No.

**Is there a grace or benediction after eating or drinking?**
No.

**Is there a traditional greeting for the family?**
No. Just offer your congratulations.

**Is there a traditional form of address for clergy who may be at the reception?**
"Reverend" or "Pastor."

**Is it okay to leave early?**
Yes, but usually only after toasts have been made and the wedding cake has been served.

## · *Funerals and Mourning* ·

The United Methodist Church affirms that life is eternal and that, in faith, one can look forward to life with God after death.

United Methodists have diverse beliefs about afterlife and are generally content to look forward to it as a glorious mystery. Funerals have as their purposes: 1) expressing grief and comforting one another in our bereavement; 2) celebrating the life of the deceased; and 3) affirming faith in life with God after death. Which of these is most emphasized at the funeral depends on the circumstances of the death and the extent of the faith of the deceased.

### BEFORE THE CEREMONY

**How soon after the death will the funeral usually take place?**
Usually within two to three days.

**What should a non-Methodist do upon hearing of the death of a member of that faith?**
Telephone or visit the bereaved.

### APPROPRIATE ATTIRE

**Men:** Jacket and tie. No head covering is required.

**Women:** A dress. Open-toed shoes and modest jewelry are permissible. No head covering is required.

There are no rules regarding colors of clothing, but somber, dark colors are recommended for men and women.

## GIFTS

**Is it appropriate to send flowers or make a contribution?**
Yes. Send flowers to the home of the bereaved. Contributions are also optional. The recommended charity may be mentioned in the deceased's obituary.

**Is it appropriate to send food?**
Yes. Send it to the home of the bereaved.

## THE CEREMONY

**Where will the ceremony take place?**
At a church or funeral home.

**When should guests arrive and where should they sit?**
Arrive early. Ushers will advise where to sit.

**If arriving late, are there times when a guest should *not* enter the ceremony?**
No.

**Will the bereaved family be present at the church or funeral home before the ceremony?**
Possibly.

**Is there a traditional greeting for the family?**
Simply express your condolences.

**Will there be an open casket?**
Usually.

**Is a guest expected to view the body?**
This is entirely optional.

**What is appropriate behavior upon viewing the body?**
Silent prayer.

**Who are the major officiants at the ceremony and what do they do?**
▪ *A pastor*, who officiates.

**To indicate the order of the ceremony:**
A program will be provided.

**Will a guest who is not a Methodist be expected to do anything other than sit?**
No.

**Are there any parts of the service in which a guest who is not a Methodist should *not* participate?**
No.

**If not disruptive to the ceremony, is it okay to:**
◙ **Take pictures?** No.
◙ **Use a flash?** No.
◙ **Use a video camera?** No.
◙ **Use a tape recorder?** No.

**Will contributions to the church be collected at the ceremony?**
No.

### THE INTERMENT

**Should guests attend the interment?**
Yes.

**Whom should one ask for directions?**
The funeral director.

**What happens at the graveside?**
Prayers are recited by the pastor and the body is committed to the ground. If there has been a cremation, which is done privately before the service, the ashes are either buried or put in a vault. Military or fraternal rites may be part of the graveside service.

**Do guests who are not Methodists participate at the graveside ceremony?**
No. They are simply present.

### COMFORTING THE BEREAVED

**Is it appropriate to visit the home of the bereaved after the funeral?**
Yes, at any mutually convenient time. How long one stays depends on your closeness to the bereaved. Typically, one stays about 30 to 45 minutes.

**Will there be a religious service at the home of the bereaved?**
No.

**Will food be served?**

No.

**How soon after the funeral will a mourner usually return to a normal work schedule?**

This is entirely at the discretion of the bereaved.

**How soon after the funeral will a mourner usually return to a normal social schedule?**

This is entirely at the discretion of the bereaved.

**Are there mourning customs to which a friend who is not a Methodist should be sensitive?**

No.

**Are there rituals for observing the anniversary of the death?**

There may be a service commemorating the deceased.

## V · HOME CELEBRATIONS

Not applicable to Methodists.

# Chapter 15 Contents

# 15

# Mormon (Church of Jesus Christ of Latter-day Saints)

## I · HISTORY AND BELIEFS

The Church of Jesus Christ of Latter-day Saints, the largest indigenous American religious group, was founded by Joseph Smith in the early 19th century. Living in upstate New York, Smith had a vision in 1820 in which God and Jesus Christ appeared to him. Three years later, the angel Moroni told him of the location of gold tablets containing God's revelations. In 1830, Smith published a translation of these revelations entitled *The Book of Mormon*. He soon became the "seer, translator, prophet and apostle" of a group committed to restoring the church established centuries before by Christ.

Latter-day Saints stressed the coming of Christ's Kingdom to earth and encouraged others to adhere to the teachings of the Savior.

Smith's group moved first to Ohio, and then to Missouri, where violence ensued prompted by their polygamy and their anti-slavery stance. Persecution forced the group to move to Illinois, where they built their own city and named it Nauvoo. In 1844, while imprisoned for destroying an opposition printing press, Smith was killed by a mob that attacked the jail.

Schisms erupted amid the subsequent leadership vacuum and concern over polygamy, a practice that Smith had said in 1843 had come to him in a vision and which became Church doctrine in 1852. Most Latter-day Saints followed the leadership of Brigham Young, who led them into the Great Salt Lake area of what is now Utah. Latter-day Saints are headquartered there to this day.

While many Latter-day Saints' beliefs are similar to orthodox Christian ideas, Smith uniquely taught that God, although omniscient, has a material body. He taught that through repentance and baptism by immersion, anyone can gain entrance to Christ's earthly kingdom. Through "proxies" who receive baptism in a Latter-day Saints' temple, the dead may also share in the highest of post-mortal rewards or blessings.

The Church teaches that men and women are equal in the eyes of the Lord and that they cannot achieve the highest eternal rewards without each other.

The charge given by Jesus to Matthew, "Go ye unto all the world" to share the teachings of His gospel, motivates the Church's 57,000 full-time missionaries around the world. Most are college-age males who serve for two years at their own expense. Their success has led to the church currently having more than 25,000 congregations in 160 nations and territories around the world.

In addition to churches, where worship services are conducted, temples are located around the world. These are closed on Sundays, but open every other day of the week for marriages and other sacred ordinances. Only faithful members of the Church may enter a temple.

**U.S. churches and temples:** 10,000+
**U.S. membership:** 4.3 million
*(1995 data from The Church of Jesus Christ of Latter-day Saints)*

**For more information, contact:**
The Church of Jesus Christ of Latter-day Saints
50 East North Temple St.
Salt Lake City, UT 84150
(801) 240-1000

**Canadian churches and temples:** 450+
**Canadian membership:** 150,000
*(1997 data from The Church of Jesus Christ of Latter-day Saints)*

**For more information, contact:**
The Church of Jesus Christ of Latter-day Saints
1185 Eglinton Avenue East
P.O. Box 116
North York, ON  M3C 3C6
(416) 424-2485

## II · THE BASIC SERVICE

The basic service is called a "sacrament meeting." It includes: An opening song sung by the congregation; an opening prayer assigned in advance and offered from the pulpit by a lay member of the congregation; a "sacramental song" sung by the congregation; "sacramental prayers" recited by a young (usually 16- to 18-year-old) lay priest on the bread and the water of communion and upon their distribution among congregants by teenagers on trays and in individual cups; brief talks by one or more youths of the congregation on a subject of their choice related to the Gospels; a sermon, often delivered by a lay member of the congregation; a closing song by the congregation; and a benediction or closing prayer offered by a congregant.

The sacrament represents a reminder of the crucifixion and the atonement of Jesus for the sins of humanity. It also renews the covenants congregants made when they were baptized into the Church.

The service usually lasts slightly over an hour.

## APPROPRIATE ATTIRE

**Men:** A suit or sport jacket and tie. No head covering required.

**Women:** A dress or a skirt and blouse. No head covering required, but the overall fashion statement should be conservative and dignified. Hems should be near the knees. Open-toed shoes and modest jewelry are permissible.

Modest and dignified clothing is appreciated.

## THE SANCTUARY

### What are the major sections of the church?
- *The chapel:* Where the worship service is held.
- *The choir loft:* From which the choir sings.
- *The pulpit:* Where the lay priests officiate.
- *The pews:* Where congregants sit.

## THE SERVICE

### When should guests arrive and where should they sit?
Arrive early and sit where you wish.

### If arriving late, are there times when a guest should *not* enter the service?
Do not enter during communion.

### Are there times when a guest should *not* leave the service?
Do not leave during communion unless absolutely necessary.

**Who are the major officiants, leaders or participants and what do they do?**

◼ *A bishop*, who presides over the service.

◼ *Two bishop's counselors*, assistants to the bishop. The bishop and his two counselors take weekly turns conducting the worship service.

**What are the major ritual objects of the service?**

The bread and water of the Sacrament (the communion), which are passed among congregants in trays and individual cups.

**What books are used?**

The King James Version of the Bible and *The Book of Mormon, The Doctrine of Covenants, The Hymns of the Church of Jesus Christ of Latter-day Saints*, and *The Pearl of Great Price* (Salt Lake City, Utah: Published by the Church of Jesus Christ of Latter-day Saints). The Bible and other scriptures are used only by those conducting the service, but congregants may refer to their personal copies of the scriptures to follow along, if they wish.

**To indicate the order of the service:**

A program may be distributed.

## GUEST BEHAVIOR DURING THE SERVICE

**Will a guest who is not a Latter-day Saint be expected to do anything other than sit?**

Guests of other faiths are invited to sing and pray with the congregation, but they are not expected to do so, especially if participating would violate their own religious beliefs. One of the few times the congregation stands during the service is midway through the service during the singing of the "Rest Hymn." Again, guests are invited to stand, but are not obligated to do so.

**Are there any parts of the service in which a guest who is not a Latter-day Saint should *not* participate?**

No, although it is one's personal choice whether to receive the sacrament.

**If not disruptive to the service, is it okay to:**

◼ **Take pictures?** No.

◼ **Use a flash?** No.

◼ **Use a video camera?** No.

◼ **Use a tape recorder?** No.

**Will contributions to the church be collected at the service?**

No.

## AFTER THE SERVICE

**Is there usually a reception after the service?**
No.

**Is there a traditional form of address for clergy whom a guest may meet?**
The chief officiant is referred to as "Bishop," followed by his last name. His counselors are addressed as "Brother," followed by their last names.

## GENERAL GUIDELINES AND ADVICE

There is no kneeling at Latter-day Saint services.

## SPECIAL VOCABULARY

**Key words or phrases which might be helpful for a visitor to know:**

- *Sacrament,* the communion of bread and water.
- *"Brother"* and *"Sister,"* terms for fellow members of the Church.

## DOGMA AND IDEOLOGY

**Mormons believe:**

- The Godhead is composed of God the Father; His son, Jesus Christ; and the Holy Ghost. They are considered one in purpose, but are separate in being.
- Revelation from God did not cease nearly 2,000 years ago with the crucifixion of Jesus Christ. Rather, it has continued through the centuries through various living prophets. The presidents of the church are considered to be prophets in the same sense that Moses and other biblical leaders were also prophets.
- *The Book of Mormon* is divinely inspired scripture, as is the Holy Bible. They are used side-by-side in Church curriculum.
- *The Word of Wisdom,* a health code divinely revealed in 1833, forbids the use of tobacco, alcoholic beverages, tea and coffee, and emphasizes a healthy diet and physical and spiritual fitness.
- The biblical principle of tithing, or donating ten percent of one's income to the church, is adhered to by faithful members.
- A professional clergy is not needed. Instead, churches are led and staffed by lay members without financial compensation.

**Some basic books to which a guest can refer to learn more about the Church of Jesus Christ of Latter-day Saints:**

*The Book of Mormon* (Salt Lake City, Utah: Published by the Church of Jesus Christ of Latter-day Saints).

*The Doctrine of Covenants* (Salt Lake City, Utah: Published by the Church of Jesus Christ of Latter-day Saints).

*The Pearl of Great Price* (Salt Lake City, Utah: Published by the Church of Jesus Christ of Latter-day Saints).

*Our Search for Happiness* by M. Russell Ballard (Salt Lake City, Utah: Deseret Books, 1993).

## III · HOLY DAYS AND FESTIVALS

▪ *Christmas*, which always falls on December 25, celebrates the birth of Christ. A traditional greeting for this holiday is "Merry Christmas."

▪ *Easter*, occurs in April. Commemorates the death and resurrection of Jesus. Always falls on the Sunday after the full moon that occurs on or after the spring equinox of March 21. There is no traditional greeting for this holiday.

## IV · LIFE CYCLE EVENTS

### · *Birth Ceremony* ·

The ceremony for the blessing and naming of a newborn infant is part of a regular worship service on the first Sunday of the month. The ceremony, which is the same for males and females, consists of a brief blessing. The worship service of which the blessing is a part lasts slightly more than one hour.

#### BEFORE THE CEREMONY

**Are guests usually invited by a formal invitation?**

Invitations are usually fairly informal and often given verbally.

**If not stated explicitly, should one assume that children are invited?**

Yes.

**If one can't attend, what should one do?**

RSVP with regrets.

## APPROPRIATE ATTIRE

**Men:** A suit or sport jacket and tie. No head covering required.

**Women:** A dress or a skirt and blouse. No head covering required, but the overall fashion statement should be conservative and dignified. Hems should be near the knees. Open-toed shoes and modest jewelry are permissible.

Modest and dignified clothing is appreciated.

## GIFTS

**Is a gift customarily expected?**
No.

**Should gifts be brought to the ceremony?**
See above.

## THE CEREMONY

**Where will the ceremony take place?**
In the parents' church.

**When should guests arrive and where should they sit?**
Arrive early and sit wherever you wish.

**If arriving late, are there times when a guest should *not* enter the ceremony?**
Do not enter during communion.

**Are there times when a guest should *not* leave the ceremony?**
Do not leave during communion.

**Who are the major officiants, leaders or participants at the ceremony and what do they do?**
- *The child's father, a lay leader or another designated holder of the Priesthood,* who blesses the child.
- *A bishop,* who presides over the service.
- *Two bishop's counselors,* assistants to the bishop.

**What books are used?**
No books are used for the blessing itself. Used for the rest of the worship service, of which the blessing is a part, are The King James Version of the Bible and *The Hymns of the Church of Jesus Christ of Latter-day Saints, The Book of Mormon, The Doctrine of Covenants* and *The Pearl of Great Price* (Salt Lake

290 · *How to Be a Perfect Stranger*

City, Utah: Published by the Church of Jesus Christ of Latter-day Saints). The Bible and other scriptures are used only by those conducting the service, but congregants may refer to their personal copies of the scriptures to follow along, if they wish.

**To indicate the order of the ceremony:**
A program may be distributed.

**Will a guest who is not a Latter-day Saint be expected to do anything other than sit?**
Guests of other faiths are invited to sing and pray with the congregation, but they are not expected to do so, especially if participating would violate their own religious beliefs. One of the few times the congregation stands during the service is midway through the service during the singing of the "Rest Hymn." Again, guests are invited to stand, but are not obligated to do so.

**Are there any parts of the ceremony in which a guest who is not a Latter-day Saint should *not* participate?**
No, although it is one's personal choice whether to receive the sacrament.

**If not disruptive to the ceremony, is it okay to:**
◘ **Take pictures?** No.
◘ **Use a flash?** No.
◘ **Use a video camera?** No.
◘ **Use a tape recorder?** No.

**Will contributions to the church be collected at the ceremony?**
No.

## AFTER THE CEREMONY

**Is there usually a reception after the ceremony?**
No.

**Is there a traditional form of address for clergy whom a guest may meet?**
The chief officiant is referred to as "Bishop," followed by his last name. His counselors are addressed as "Brother," followed by their last names.

## · *Initiation Ceremony* ·

Baptism follows the biblical example of immersion and is for the remission of one's sins. Since young children are incapable of sin, they are not baptized until the age of eight, which is considered the age of moral accountability.

The baptismal ceremony may be for an individual child or for a group of children or for an adult convert. The ceremony lasts about 15 to 30 minutes.

At the first worship service after the baptism, the individual is "confirmed" as a member of the Church by the laying on of hands by a member of the lay priesthood.

## BEFORE THE CEREMONY

**Are guests usually invited by a formal invitation?**
Invitations are usually issued verbally.

**If not stated explicitly, should one assume that children are invited?**
Yes.

**If one can't attend, what should one do?**
RSVP with regrets.

## APPROPRIATE ATTIRE

**Men:** A suit or sport jacket and tie. No head covering required.

**Women:** A dress or a skirt and blouse. No head covering required, but the overall fashion statement should be conservative and dignified. Open-toed shoes and modest jewelry are permissible.

Modest and dignified clothing is appreciated.

## GIFTS

**Is a gift customarily expected?**
No.

**Should gifts be brought to the ceremony?**
See above.

## THE CEREMONY

**Where will the ceremony take place?**
There is a service in the chapel or in the baptismal font room of the church, then guests, family and the child proceed to the baptistry for the baptism itself.

**When should guests arrive and where should they sit?**
Arrive at the time for which the ceremony has been called and sit wherever you wish.

**If arriving late, are there times when a guest should *not* enter the ceremony?**

No.

**Are there times when a guest should *not* leave the ceremony?**

No, but since the service is relatively brief, all present are expected for its duration.

**Who are the major officiants, leaders or participants at the ceremony and what do they do?**

- *A presiding officer,* usually (but not necessarily) a bishop, who presides over the service.
- *The father or a lay priest,* who performs the baptismal immersion.
- *Other lay members,* who deliver the invocation and benediction and deliver a brief talk.

**What books are used?**

No texts are distributed, although speakers may refer to the Scriptures.

**To indicate the order of the ceremony:**

A program may be distributed.

**Will a guest who is not a Latter-day Saint be expected to do anything other than sit?**

No.

**Are there any parts of the ceremony in which a guest who is not a Latter-day Saint should *not* participate?**

No.

**If not disruptive to the ceremony, is it okay to:**

- **Take pictures?** No.
- **Use a flash?** No.
- **Use a video camera?** No.
- **Use a tape recorder?** No.

**Will contributions to the church be collected at the ceremony?**

No.

## AFTER THE CEREMONY

**Is there usually a reception after the ceremony?**

Depending on the family, there may be a reception at their home or elsewhere. If so, light food may be served, but no alcoholic beverages.

**Would it be considered impolite to neither eat nor drink?**
No.

**Is there a grace or benediction before eating or drinking?**
Possibly. Tradition calls for a prayer of thanks for the food.

**Is there a grace or benediction after eating or drinking?**
No.

**Is there a traditional greeting for the family?**
Just offer your "congratulations."

**Is there a traditional form of address for clergy who may be at the reception?**
A bishop is referred to as "Bishop," followed by his last name. Other officiants are addressed as "Brother," followed by their last names.

**Is it okay to leave early?**
Yes.

## · Marriage Ceremony ·

Reflecting the Church's emphasis on strong family solidarity and the potential for eternal family relationships, Latter-day Saints believe that marriage performed in a Church temple need not end at death, but, instead, has the potential of continuing forever. Also reflecting Church interpretations of the "strict morality" taught by Jesus are proscriptions against adultery and prescriptions for absolute fidelity during marriage.

### BEFORE THE CEREMONY

**Are guests usually invited by a formal invitation?**
Yes.

**If not stated explicitly, should one assume that children are invited?**
Children do not attend a marriage ceremony performed in the temples, but they may be invited to a ceremony performed in a church or a civil ceremony performed elsewhere.

**If one can't attend, what should one do?**
RSVP with regrets.

### APPROPRIATE ATTIRE

**Men:** A suit or sport jacket and tie. No head covering required.

**Women:** A dress or a skirt and blouse. No head covering required, but the overall fashion statement should be conservative and dignified. Hems should be near the knees. Open-toed shoes and modest jewelry are permissible.

Modest and dignified clothing is appreciated.

### GIFTS

**Is a gift customarily expected?**
The option to present a gift (and the nature of the gift) is left to the invited individual.

**Should gifts be brought to the ceremony?**
Gifts are traditionally presented at postnuptial receptions.

### THE CEREMONY

**Where will the ceremony take place?**
Members of the Church are encouraged to be married in one of its temples, which are located around the world. A temple, which is different from a local church building where worship services are conducted, is closed on Sundays, but open every other day of the week for marriages and other sacred ordinances.

Only faithful members of the Church may enter a temple. Guests invited to the temple marriage ceremony must present a "temple recommend" issued by their bishop to indicate that they are, indeed, faithful members.

A couple may also choose to be married in a local church meetinghouse, a home or another location.

**When should guests arrive and where should they sit?**
Arrive at the time for which the service is called and sit wherever you wish.

**If arriving late, are there times when a guest should *not* enter the ceremony?**
No.

**Are there times when a guest should *not* leave the ceremony?**
Leaving early is discouraged.

**Who are the major officiants, leaders or participants at the ceremony and what do they do?**
Authorized clergy perform the ceremony.

**What books are used?**
Possibly Scriptures.

**Will a guest who is not a Latter-day Saint be expected to do anything other than sit?**
No.

**Are there any parts of the ceremony in which a guest who is not a Latter-day Saint should *not* participate?**
All guests only observe the ceremony.

**If not disruptive to the ceremony, is it okay to:**
- **Take pictures?** No.
- **Use a flash?** No.
- **Use a video camera?** No.
- **Use a tape recorder?** No.

**Will contributions to the church be collected at the ceremony?**
No.

## AFTER THE CEREMONY

**Is there usually a reception after the ceremony?**
There is usually a reception, but where it is held and what is done there is the personal choice of the bride and groom. Traditionally, it is an open-house type of affair.

**Would it be considered impolite to neither eat nor drink?**
No.

**Is there a grace or benediction before eating or drinking?**
Possibly. This is the choice of the hosts.

**Is there a grace or benediction after eating or drinking?**
No.

**Is there a traditional greeting for the family?**
No. Just offer your congratulations.

**Is there a traditional form of address for clergy who may be at the reception?**
A bishop is referred to as "Bishop," followed by his last name. His counselors are addressed as "Brother," followed by their last names.

**Is it okay to leave early?**
Yes, since at the traditional open-house type of reception guests stay as long as they feel is appropriate.

## · *Funerals and Mourning* ·

Latter-day Saints believe that all who have ever lived on earth are literally the spiritual children of God and resided with him in a pre-mortal existence. The same with those who ever will live on earth. Through the resurrection of Jesus, all will be resurrected and through atonement and obedience to His gospel, all have the opportunity for salvation.

A Latter-day Saint funeral is a service unto itself. The length of the service varies according to the program outlined by the family, but it usually lasts about 60 to 90 minutes.

### BEFORE THE CEREMONY

**How soon after the death does the funeral usually take place?**
There is no set limit, although typically it occurs within one week after the death. The timing of the funeral is solely the choice of the immediate family and depends on circumstances.

**What should someone who is not a Latter-day Saint do upon hearing of the death of a member of that faith?**
Visit, telephone or write to the family, expressing your condolences and offering your assistance, if needed.

### APPROPRIATE ATTIRE:

**Men:** A suit or sport jacket and tie. No head covering required.

**Women:** A dress, suit or a skirt and blouse. No head covering required, but the overall fashion statement should be conservative and dignified. Hems should be near the knees. Open-toed shoes and modest jewelry are permissible.

Modest and dignified clothing is appreciated.

### GIFTS

**Is it appropriate to send flowers or make a contribution?**
It is appropriate, but not expected to do either. These may be sent, before or after the funeral, to the funeral itself (which may be held in a church or a funeral home) or to the home of the bereaved.

**Is it appropriate to send food?**
Food for the bereaved family members is usually prepared and organized by the woman's organization of the local congregation.

## THE CEREMONY

**Where will the ceremony take place?**

Either in a church or a funeral home or at the graveside.

**When should guests arrive and where should they sit?**

Arrive at the time for which the service has been called. Sit wherever you wish.

**If arriving late, are there times when a guest should *not* enter the ceremony?**

No.

**Will the bereaved family be present at the church or the funeral home before the ceremony?**

Usually.

**Is there a traditional greeting for the family?**

No. Just offer your condolences.

**Will there be an open casket?**

Sometimes. This is done at the choice of the family.

**Is a guest expected to view the body?**

Viewing is entirely optional.

**What is appropriate behavior upon viewing the body?**

Observe it with dignity and reverence.

**Who are the major officiants at the ceremony and what do they do?**

- *The officer of the church* who conducts the service. This person is chosen by the family, but is typically the bishop of the congregation to which the deceased belonged.
- *Speakers* who deliver eulogies.

**What books are used?**

Speakers will use Scriptures. Hymn books may be used by the congregation.

**To indicate the order of the ceremony:**

A program may be distributed.

**Will a guest who is not a Latter-day Saint be expected to do anything other than sit?**

No.

**Are there any parts of the ceremony in which a guest who is not a Latter-day Saint should *not* participate?**
No.

**If not disruptive to the ceremony, is it okay to:**
◙ **Take pictures?** No.
◙ **Use a flash?** No.
◙ **Use a video camera?** No.
◙ **Use a tape recorder?** Possibly, if it can be done with discretion.

**Will contributions to the church be collected at the ceremony?**
No.

## THE INTERMENT

**Should guests attend the interment?**
Yes, unless it is a private interment, which is rare. If the burial is private, attendance is only by invitation.

**Whom should one ask for directions?**
The director of the funeral home or the person who officiated at the service may give directions from the pulpit. Also, the printed program may have directions.

**What happens at the graveside?**
The grave is dedicated in a prayer offered by a lay priest, who is usually (but not necessarily) a member of the family of the deceased. Then the deceased is buried.

**Do guests who are not Latter-day Saints participate at the graveside ceremony?**
No, they are simply present.

## COMFORTING THE BEREAVED

**Is it appropriate to visit the home of the bereaved after the funeral?**
Yes, if one wishes to do so.

**Will there be a religious service at the home of the bereaved?**
No.

**Will food be served?**
There may be light food, but no alcoholic beverages. At the choice of the hosts, a grace or benediction may be said before eating.

**How soon after the funeral will a mourner usually return to a normal work schedule?**

There is no set time. Absence from work is at the discretion of the mourner.

**How soon after the funeral will a mourner usually return to a normal social schedule?**

There is no set time. Absence from social events is at the discretion of the mourner.

**Are there mourning customs to which a friend who is not a Latter-day Saint should be sensitive?**

No.

**Are there rituals for observing the anniversary of the death?**

No.

## V · HOME CELEBRATIONS

Latter-day Saints observe a Family Home Evening one night each week. This is usually held on Mondays, but may be held on any other day. The intention is to cement family ties and cohesion. Usually attending are family members, but occasionally guests may be invited.

While there are no set activities, a Family Home Evening may include conversation, reading and singing together, taking walks or engaging in other recreational pursuits, playing games or praying together.

## Chapter 16 Contents

# 16

# Presbyterian

## I · HISTORY AND BELIEFS

The Presbyterian church was founded on the ideals of the Protestant Reformation and based on the concept of democratic rule under the authority of God. John Calvin (1509-1564) is the father of Presbyterianism.

All Presbyterians are required to trust in Christ as their forgiving savior, promise to follow Christ and His example for living, and commit themselves to attend church and to become involved in its work. They believe in the Holy Spirit (the empowering presence of God) speaking through the Bible, and in the sanctity of life.

Presbyterian theology emphasizes the majesty of God, who is conceived not just as truth or beauty, but also as intention, purpose, energy and will. The human counterpart of this is understanding the Christian life as the embodiment of the purposes of God and the working out of these purposes in one's life. Because of this, Presbyterians include many social activists, and those who try to shape and influence culture and history.

The Presbyterian Church (USA) was formed when the Presbyterian Church in the United States merged in 1983 with the United Presbyterian Church in the United States of America. The consolidation ended a schism that occurred during the Civil War when Southern Presbyterians broke away from the Presbyterian Church in the United States of America to create the Presbyterian Church in the Confederate States. Today's Presbyterian Church is the result of at least 10 different denominational mergers over the last 250 years and is strongly ecumenical in outlook.

The Presbyterian Church in Canada was formed in 1875 by the union of four branches of Presbyterianism that had been established as Europeans

301

settled the country. The church experienced remarkable growth during the next 50 years, reaching almost 1.5 million members, the largest church in the country of 8.7 million people. Presbyterians had initiated discussions with the Methodist and Congregationalist churches, leading to the formation of the United Church of Canada in 1925. But a third of Presbyterians were not satisfied with the final plans and stayed out of the new denomination.

**U. S. churches:** 11,328
**U. S. membership:** 3.6 million
*(data from the* 1998 Yearbook of American and Canadian Churches*)*

**For more information, contact:**
The Presbyterian Church (USA)
100 Witherspoon Street
Louisville, KY 40202
(502) 569-5000

**Canadian churches:** 1,010
**Canadian membership:** 145,328
*(data from the* 1998 Yearbook of American and Canadian Churches*)*

**For more information, contact:**
The Presbyterian Church in Canada
50 Wynford Drive
North York, ON  M3C 1J7
(416) 441-1111 or (800) 619-7301

## II · THE BASIC SERVICE

There are four main components to a basic worship service:
- *The Gathering*, which includes the call to worship, the opening prayer, hymns of praise and confession and pardons.
- *The Word*, which includes readings from the Bible (either the Old or New Testament, or both), psalms and hymns, a sermon and a baptism if one is scheduled for that day.
- *The Response* (in Canada), which usually includes prayers and the gathering of people's offerings.
- *The Eucharist*, or communion, which represents the Last Supper of Jesus Christ and His subsequent resurrection.
- *The Sending*, which includes hymns, psalms and a blessing.

The service usually lasts about one hour.

## APPROPRIATE ATTIRE

**Men:** Jacket and tie or, at the discretion of the individual, more casual clothing. No head covering is required.

**Women:** Dress or a skirt and blouse or, at the discretion of the individual, more casual clothing. Open-toed shoes and modest jewelry permitted. Hems need not reach the knees nor must arms be covered. No head covering is required.

There are no rules regarding colors of clothing.

## THE SANCTUARY

### What are the major sections of the church?

- *The narthex:* The vestibule or entrance hall. This is at the end of the nave (see below) and opposite the altar area. Usually, the main outside door enters into the narthex.
- *The nave:* Where congregants sit.
- *The chancel:* Includes the altar and pulpit and seating for clergy. The pastor conducts the worship from this area.

## THE SERVICE

### When should guests arrive and where should they sit?
It is customary to arrive at the time called. Sit wherever you like.

### If arriving late, are there times when a guest should *not* enter the service?
If you arrive late, take your cues from an usher, who will seat you.

### Are there times when a guest should *not* leave the service?
Unless it's an emergency, do not leave the service until it is over.

### Who are the major officiants, leaders or participants and what do they do?

- *The pastor, or minister (in Canada),* who preaches and leads the service.
- *A lay leader or worship leader,* who is present in some churches to assist the pastor.

### What are the major ritual objects of the service?

- *Bread and wine,* which are consecrated into the body and blood of Jesus Christ.
- *The chalice and paten,* which, respectively, hold the consecrated bread and wine.

◙ *The communion table*, where the chalice and paten are placed.

◙ *A cross* without the body of Christ resting on it. The absence of Christ represents His resurrection.

◙ *An open Bible* on a lectern. Its openness symbolizes that the Old and New Testaments are the primary source of scripture and of faith for Presbyterians.

**What books are used?**

In the U.S., the two main books in the service are a hymnal and a Bible. Since there are no prescribed editions of either, hymnals and the version of the Bible may differ from one congregation to another. The most recent edition of the Old and New Testaments recommended for Presbyterians is the New Revised Standard Version, which is printed by several publishers. The most recent hymnal is the *Presbyterian Hymnal* (Louisville, Ky.: Westminster/John Knox Press, 1990). No individual Presbyterian or individual Presbyterian church is required to use these.

In Canada, the two main books in worship are *The Book of Praise* and the Bible. *The Book of Praise* contains the hymns sung by the congregation. There is also growing use of a Psalter (1997) that allows for the Psalms to be read or (in very few churches) chanted.

**To indicate the order of the service:**

A program or bulletin will be distributed and the pastor or minister will announce the service.

## GUEST BEHAVIOR DURING THE SERVICE

**Will a guest who is not a Presbyterian be expected to do anything other than sit?**

Nothing is "expected" of guests. If they wish, they may stand, sing and pray with the congregation if this does not compromise their own religious beliefs.

**Are there any parts of the service in which a guest who is not a Presbyterian should *not* participate?**

No.

**If not disruptive to the service, is it okay to:**

◙ **Take pictures?** No.

◙ **Use a flash?** No.

◙ **Use a video camera?** No.

◙ **Use a tape recorder?** No.

**Will contributions to the church be collected at the service?**
Yes, but guests are not expected to contribute.

**How much is customary to contribute?**
Between $1 and $5.

## AFTER THE SERVICE

**Is there usually a reception after the service?**
Often, there is a reception in the reception area which may last 30 minutes. Coffee is sometimes served. More substantial fare should not be expected. Alcohol will not be served. There is no benediction or grace before beginning.

**Is there a traditional form of address for clergy who may be at the reception?**
"Reverend," followed by the pastor's last name. In Canada, simply "Mr." or "Ms." followed by the minister's last name. Not "Reverend."

**Is it okay to leave early?**
Yes.

## GENERAL GUIDELINES AND ADVICE

Nothing is "expected" of guests. They may stand, sing and pray with the congregation if this does not compromise their own religious beliefs. This is their choice.

## SPECIAL VOCABULARY

None provided.

## DOGMA AND IDEOLOGY

**Presbyterians believe:**
- God alone is the Lord of conscience. This fundamental tenet of Presbyterianism refers to the belief that no temporal religious authority—no clergy—intercedes between each person and God; that the primary relationship is between each person and God.
- God is revealed in Jesus Christ.
- The Bible (both the Old and New Testaments) is the authoritative witness to God in Christ; that God is incarnate in Jesus and the Bible is the authoritative account of His life.
- Clergy and laypersons are peers in the church.

◙ The Church is guided by a constitution and doctrinal statements that have the force of church law. The constitution, which was the model for the constitution of the United States, addresses religious practice; the doctrinal statements address belief.

**Some basic books to which a guest can refer to learn more about Presbyterianism:**

*A Brief History of the Presbyterians*, by Lefferts A. Loetscher (Louisville, Ky.: Westminster/John Knox Press, 1983).

*This Presbyterian Church of Ours*, by John Congram (Winfield, B.C.: Wood Lake Books, 1995).

## III · HOLY DAYS AND FESTIVALS

◙ *Advent*. Occurs four weeks before Christmas. The purpose is to begin preparing for Christmas and to focus on Christ. There is no traditional greeting for this holiday.

◙ *Christmas*. Occurs on the evening of December 24 and the day of December 25. Marks the birth and the incarnation of God as a man. The traditional greeting is "Merry Christmas."

◙ *Lent*. Begins on Ash Wednesday, which occurs six weeks before Easter. The purpose is to prepare for Easter. There is no traditional greeting for Lent. Between Lent and Easter, abstention from entertainment is encouraged, as is increased giving to the poor. Often, there are midweek worship services. Very few Presbyterians fast during Lent.

◙ *Easter*. Always the Sunday after the first full moon falling on or after March 21. Celebrates the Resurrection of Jesus Christ. The traditional greeting is "Happy Easter!" In worship services, the Pastor may greet congregants with, "He is risen!" Congregants respond with "He is risen, indeed!"

◙ *Pentecost Sunday*. The seventh Sunday after Easter. Celebrates the coming of the Holy Spirit, which is the empowering spirit of God in human life. This is often considered the birth of the Christian church. There is no traditional greeting for this holiday.

## IV · LIFE CYCLE EVENTS

### · *Birth Ceremony* ·

Baptism is usually the celebration of the birth of an infant into the church, although it can occur anytime from birth onward through adulthood.

The ceremony is usually integrated into a regular church service and may last about 15 minutes.

In the Presbyterian Church, baptism is administered only once.

The Church teaches that baptism "initiates us into the Church, bestows the promise of God's grace upon us, assures us that God forgives our sins, calls us to a life of Christian service and fulfillment."

A Presbyterian baptism has five parts:

- "Presentation" in which the parents or guardian of the child bring their child forward for baptism. This happens immediately after the sermon.
- "Profession of Faith and Promise," in which parents and the entire congregation promise to love and care for the newly baptized.
- "Thanksgiving and Prayer" in which the congregation stands and offers God a prayer of praise and thanks.
- The actual "Washing with Water" in which the minister addresses the infant by his or her new official name and says, "I baptize you in the name of the Father, and of the Son, and of the Holy Spirit." He or she then pours or sprinkles water over the child's head, or dips or immerses him or her in water.
- The newly baptized infant is welcomed into the congregation and proclaimed a member of God's family.

## BEFORE THE CEREMONY

**Are guests usually invited by a formal invitation?**

Guests of other faiths are usually invited by a phone call.

**If not stated explicitly, should one assume that children are invited?**

Yes.

**If one can't attend, what should one do?**

RSVP with regrets. No present is expected.

## APPROPRIATE ATTIRE

**Men:** Jacket and tie or, at the discretion of the individual, more casual clothing. No head covering is required.

**Women:** Dress or a skirt and blouse or, at the discretion of the individual, more casual clothing. Open-toed shoes and modest jewelry permitted. Hems need not reach the knees nor must arms be covered. No head covering is required.

There are no rules regarding colors of clothing.

## GIFTS

**Is a gift customarily expected?**
No.

**Should gifts be brought to the ceremony?**
See above.

## THE CEREMONY

**Where will the ceremony take place?**
In the main sanctuary of the church.

**When should guests arrive and where should they sit?**
It is customary to arrive at the time called. Sit wherever you like.

**If arriving late, are there times when a guest should *not* enter the ceremony?**
If you arrive late, take your cues from an usher, who will seat you.

**Are there times when a guest should *not* leave the ceremony?**
Unless it's an emergency, do not leave the service until it is over.

**Who are the major officiants, leaders or participants at the ceremony and what do they do?**

- *The pastor or minister*, who leads the service and performs the actual baptism.
- *An elder*, who is a layperson elected and ordained by church members to exercise leadership of the church. He or she presents the child to the pastor for baptism and asks the parents and the congregation a series of questions that address their commitment to nurture the person being baptized and to help them follow Christ.
- *The parents*, who present the child to the elder and answer his or her questions.

**What books are used?**
In the U.S., the two main books in the service are a hymnal and a Bible. Since there are no prescribed editions of either, hymnals and the version of the Bible may differ from one congregation to another. The most recent edition of the Old and New Testaments recommended for Presbyterians is the New Revised Standard Version, which is printed by several publishers. The most recent hymnal is the *Presbyterian Hymnal* (Louisville, Ky.: Westminster/John Knox Press, 1990). No individual Presbyterian or individual Presbyterian church is required to use these.

In Canada, the two main books in worship are *The Book of Praise* and the Bible. *The Book of Praise* contains the hymns sung by the congregation. There is also growing use of a Psalter (1997) that allows for the Psalms to be read or (in very few churches) chanted.

**To indicate the order of the ceremony:**
A program or bulletin will be distributed and the pastor or minister will announce the service.

**Will a guest who is not a Presbyterian be expected to do anything other than sit?**
Nothing is "expected" of guests. If they wish, they may stand, sing and pray with the congregation, if this does not compromise their own religious beliefs.

Guests who are Christian may take communion with the congregation, if their faith permits it.

**Are there any parts of the ceremony in which a guest who is not a Presbyterian should *not* participate?**
Guests need not participate in the "Profession of Faith and Promise," in which the entire congregation promises to love and care for the newly baptized; and the "Thanksgiving and Prayer," in which the congregation stands and offers God a prayer of praise and thanks.

**If not disruptive to the ceremony, is it okay to:**
- **Take pictures?** No.
- **Use a flash?** No.
- **Use a video camera?** No.
- **Use a tape recorder?** No.

**Will contributions to the church be collected at the ceremony?**
Yes, but guests are not expected to contribute.

**How much is customary to contribute?**
Between $1 and $5.

## AFTER THE CEREMONY

**Is there usually a reception after the ceremony?**
No.

**Is there a traditional form of address for clergy whom a guest may meet?**
"Reverend," followed by the pastor's last name.

## · *Initiation Ceremony* ·

The confirmation ceremony initiates one into the Church and may last 15 to 30 minutes. The participant is usually a pre-adolescent or early adolescent. The ceremony may be performed with an individual or with a class or others who are also being confirmed.

During the ceremony, there are a series of questions and answers between the pastor and the confirmands. These are formulaic. If the participants have not been baptized, this is done at the confirmation.

### BEFORE THE CEREMONY

**Are guests usually invited by a formal invitation?**
Guests of other faiths are usually invited by a phone call.

**If not stated explicitly, should one assume that children are invited?**
Yes.

**If one can't attend, what should one do?**
RSVP with regrets. A present is not expected.

### APPROPRIATE ATTIRE

**Men:** Jacket and tie or, at the discretion of the individual, more casual clothing. No head covering is required.

**Women:** Dress or a skirt and blouse or, at the discretion of the individual, more casual clothing. Open-toed shoes and modest jewelry permitted. Hems need not reach the knees nor must arms be covered. No head covering is required.

There are no rules regarding colors of clothing.

### GIFTS

**Is a gift customarily expected?**
No.

**Should gifts be brought to the ceremony?**
See above.

### THE CEREMONY

**Where will the ceremony take place?**
In the main sanctuary of the church.

**When should guests arrive and where should they sit?**

It is customary to arrive at the time called. Sit wherever you like.

**If arriving late, are there times when a guest should *not* enter the ceremony?**

If you arrive late, take your cues from an usher, who will seat you.

**Are there times when a guest should *not* leave the ceremony?**

Unless it's an emergency, do not leave the service until it is over.

**Who are the major officiants, leaders or participants at the ceremony and what do they do?**

- *The pastor*, who leads the service.
- *An elder*, who is a layperson elected and ordained by church members to exercise leadership of the church.

**What books are used?**

In the U.S., the two main books in the service are a hymnal and a Bible. Since there are no prescribed editions of either, hymnals and the version of the Bible may differ from one congregation to another. The most recent edition of the Old and New Testaments recommended for Presbyterians is the New Revised Standard Version, which is printed by several publishers. The most recent hymnal is the *Presbyterian Hymnal* (Louisville, Ky.: Westminster/John Knox Press, 1990). No individual Presbyterian or individual Presbyterian church is required to use these.

In Canada, the two main books in worship are *The Book of Praise* and the Bible. *The Book of Praise* contains the hymns sung by the congregation. There is also growing use of a Psalter (1997) that allows for the Psalms to be read or (in very few churches) chanted.

**To indicate the order of the ceremony:**

A program or bulletin will be distributed and the pastor or minister will announce the service.

**Will a guest who is not a Presbyterian be expected to do anything other than sit?**

Nothing is "expected" of guests. If they wish, they may stand, sing and pray with the congregation, if this does not compromise their own religious beliefs.

**Are there any parts of the ceremony in which a guest who is not a Presbyterian should *not* participate?**

No.

**If not disruptive to the ceremony, is it okay to:**

◼ **Take pictures?** No.
◼ **Use a flash?** No.
◼ **Use a video camera?** No.
◼ **Use a tape recorder?** No.

**Will contributions to the church be collected at the ceremony?**
Yes, but guests are not expected to contribute.

**How much is customary to contribute?**
Between $1 and $5.

### AFTER THE CEREMONY

**Is there usually a reception after the ceremony?**
Often, there is a reception in the reception area that may last 30 minutes.
Coffee is sometimes served. More substantial fare should not be expected.
Alcohol will not be served.

**Would it be considered impolite to neither eat nor drink?**
No.

**Is there a grace or benediction before eating or drinking?**
No.

**Is there a grace or benediction after eating or drinking?**
No.

**Is there a traditional greeting for the family?**
No. Just offer your congratulations.

**Is there a traditional form of address for clergy who may be at
the reception?**
"Reverend," followed by the pastor's last name. In Canada, simply "Mr." or
"Ms." followed by the minister's last name. Not "Reverend."

**Is it okay to leave early?**
Yes.

## · *Marriage Ceremony* ·

Presbyterians consider the marital relationship as sacred, but the wedding
ceremony is not a sacrament. For Presbyterians, there are only two sacraments: Baptism and communion.

The wedding ceremony varies widely, but generally follows the order of
worship used by the church during Sunday services, with the addition of
exchanging rings and vows. The wedding ceremony takes 30 to 60 minutes.

## BEFORE THE CEREMONY

**Are guests usually invited by a formal invitation?**
Yes.

**If not stated explicitly, should one assume that children are invited?**
No.

**If one can't attend, what should one do?**
RSVP with regrets and send a gift or card.

## APPROPRIATE ATTIRE

**Men:** Jacket and tie or, at the discretion of the individual, more casual clothing. No head covering is required.

**Women:** Dress or a skirt and blouse or, at the discretion of the individual, more casual clothing. Open-toed shoes and modest jewelry permitted. Hems need not reach the knees nor must arms be covered. No head covering is required.

There are no rules regarding colors of clothing.

## GIFTS

**Is a gift customarily expected?**
Yes, usually such gifts as household items (towels, sheets, small appliances) are appropriate.

**Should gifts be brought to the ceremony?**
Gifts should be sent to the home of the newlyweds or brought to the reception.

## THE CEREMONY

**Where will the ceremony take place?**
In the church.

**When should guests arrive and where should they sit?**
Arrive on time. An usher will show guests where to sit.

**If arriving late, are there times when a guest should *not* enter the ceremony?**
Follow the usher's cues for entering the service. Do not enter during the procession or recession of the wedding party.

**Are there times when a guest should *not* leave the ceremony?**
Do not leave during the procession or recession of the wedding party.

**Who are the major officiants, leaders or participants at the ceremony and what do they do?**
◘ *The pastor or minister*, who leads the service.
◘ *The bride and groom* and the members of the wedding party.

**What books are used?**
In the U.S., the two main books in the service are a hymnal and a Bible. Since there are no prescribed editions of either, hymnals and the version of the Bible may differ from one congregation to another. The most recent edition of the Old and New Testaments recommended for Presbyterians is the New Revised Standard Version, which is printed by several publishers. The most recent hymnal is the *Presbyterian Hymnal* (Louisville, Ky.: Westminster/John Knox Press, 1990). No individual Presbyterian or individual Presbyterian church is required to use these.

In Canada, the two main books in worship are *The Book of Praise* and the Bible. *The Book of Praise* contains the hymns sung by the congregation. There is also growing use of a Psalter (1997) that allows for the Psalms to be read or (in very few churches) chanted.

**To indicate the order of the ceremony:**
The pastor or minister will make announcements as the service proceeds. A printed program or bulletin for the service may be distributed.

**Will a guest who is not a Presbyterian be expected to do anything other than sit?**
Nothing is "expected" of guests. If they wish, they may stand, sing and pray with the congregation, if this does not compromise their own religious beliefs.

**Are there any parts of the ceremony in which a guest who is not a Presbyterian should *not* participate?**
No.

**If not disruptive to the ceremony, is it okay to:**
◘ **Take pictures?** Yes.
◘ **Use a flash?** No.
◘ **Use a video camera?** Yes.
◘ **Use a tape recorder?** Yes.

**Will contributions to the church be collected at the ceremony?**
No.

## AFTER THE CEREMONY

**Is there usually a reception after the ceremony?**

There is usually a one- to two-hour reception, with eating, drinking and toasting. Alcoholic beverages will probably be served. There may also be dancing and music.

It may be in a church hall, a catering facility or another place chosen by the bride and groom.

**Would it be considered impolite to neither eat nor drink?**

No.

**Is there a grace or benediction before eating or drinking?**

Depends on local preferences.

**Is there a grace or benediction after eating or drinking?**

No.

**Is there a traditional greeting for the family?**

Just offer your congratulations to the bride and groom and their immediate family.

**Is there a traditional form of address for clergy who may be at the reception?**

"Reverend," followed by the pastor's last name. In Canada, simply "Mr." or "Ms." followed by the minister's last name. Not "Reverend."

**Is it okay to leave early?**

Depends on local preferences.

## · Funerals and Mourning ·

Presbyterians believe that in heaven the souls of the faithful are reunited with God in a warm and loving relationship. They also believe that it is not for humans to judge the fate of the unfaithful.

The funeral follows the order for Sunday worship, with prayers added for both the deceased and for oneself. Scripture texts that are used convey assurances of eternal life. The funeral usually lasts about 30 to 60 minutes.

## BEFORE THE CEREMONY

**How soon after the death does the funeral usually take place?**

Usually within two to three days.

## What should a non-Presbyterian do upon hearing of the death of a member of that faith?

Telephone the bereaved to offer your condolences. Whether one visits the home of the bereaved varies with the mourners' preference and predisposition. Those who are known to be more "open" would probably welcome visitors. Those who are more private might prefer no visitors. One can certainly call the bereaved to get a sense of their preference.

## APPROPRIATE ATTIRE

**Men:** Jacket and tie. No head covering is required.

**Women:** Dresses or skirt and blouse. Open-toed shoes and modest jewelry permitted. Hems need not reach the knees nor must arms be covered. No head covering is required.

There are no rules regarding colors of clothing, but dark, somber colors are recommended.

## GIFTS

### Is it appropriate to send flowers or make a contribution?

Flowers are appreciated. They may be sent to the bereaved or to the funeral home before the funeral upon hearing the news of the death or shortly thereafter. Other contributions are not customary, although the family may suggest contributions to charity in lieu of flowers.

### Is it appropriate to send food?

Yes, to the home of the bereaved after the funeral.

## THE CEREMONY

### Where will the ceremony take place?

At a church or a funeral home.

### When should guests arrive and where should they sit?

Arrive on time. Sit wherever you wish.

### If arriving late, are there times when a guest should *not* enter the ceremony?

If you arrive late, wait to be seated.

### Will the bereaved family be present at the church or the funeral home before the ceremony?

It is not customary for the family to be publicly present before the service.

**Is there a traditional greeting for the family?**
Just offer your condolences.

**Will there be an open casket?**
Rarely.

**Is a guest expected to view the body?**
This is the individual's choice to make.

**What is appropriate behavior upon viewing the body?**
Silent prayer.

**Who are the major officiants at the ceremony and what do they do?**
◦ *The pastor or minister*, who officiates.

**What books are used?**
In the U.S., the two main books in the service are a hymnal and a Bible. Since there are no prescribed editions of either, hymnals and the version of the Bible may differ from one congregation to another. The most recent edition of the Old and New Testaments recommended for Presbyterians is the New Revised Standard Version, which is printed by several publishers. The most recent hymnal is the *Presbyterian Hymnal* (Louisville, Ky.: Westminster/John Knox Press, 1990). No individual Presbyterian or individual Presbyterian church is required to use these.

In Canada, the two main books in worship are *The Book of Praise* and the Bible. *The Book of Praise* contains the hymns sung by the congregation. There is also growing use of a Psalter (1997) that allows for the Psalms to be read or (in very few churches) chanted.

**To indicate the order of the ceremony:**
A program or bulletin will be distributed and the pastor or minister will announce the service.

**Will a guest who is not a Presbyterian be expected to do anything other than sit?**
Guests are not expected to do or say anything at the funeral.

**Are there any parts of the ceremony in which a guest who is not a Presbyterian should *not* participate?**
No.

**If not disruptive to the ceremony, is it okay to:**
◦ **Take pictures?** No.
◦ **Use a flash?** No.

◙ **Use a video camera?** No.
◙ **Use a tape recorder?** No.

**Will contributions to the church be collected at the ceremony?**
No.

## THE INTERMENT

**Should guests attend the interment?**
Yes.

**Whom should one ask for directions?**
The ushers.

**What happens at the graveside?**
The officiating pastor or minister recites prayers. The graveside service may last 10 to 15 minutes.

**Do guests who are not Presbyterians participate at the graveside service?**
No. They are simply present.

## COMFORTING THE BEREAVED

**Is it appropriate to visit the home of the bereaved after the funeral?**
This depends on the preferences of the bereaved. There is no set tradition. Frequently, mourners welcome visitors at their home after the funeral. This imparts a sense of community to the grieving process. Other mourners may prefer solitude and privacy.

**Will there be a religious service at the home of the bereaved?**
No.

**Will food be served?**
Possibly. This is at the discretion of the hosts.

**How soon after the funeral will a mourner usually return to a normal work schedule?**
This is left to the discretion of the mourner, but is usually about a week.

**How soon after the funeral will a mourner usually return to a normal social schedule?**
This is left to the discretion of the mourner, but is usually about a week.

**Are there mourning customs to which a friend who is not Presbyterian should be sensitive?**
No.

**Are there rituals for observing the anniversary of the death?**
No.

## V · HOME CELEBRATIONS

Not applicable to Presbyterians.

## Chapter 17 Contents

# 17

# Quaker
# (Religious Society of Friends)

## I · HISTORY AND BELIEFS

"Quaker" was originally a nickname for the Children of Light or the Friends of Truth, as they called themselves. Members of the group were said to tremble or quake with religious zeal, and the nickname stuck. In time, they came to be known simply as "Friends."

The central Quaker conviction is that the saving knowledge and power of God are present as divine influences in each person through what has been variously called the "inner light," the "light of the eternal Christ within" or "the Seed within." Many affirm their acceptance of Jesus as their personal savior. Others conceive of the inward guide as a universal spirit that was in Jesus in abundant nature and is in everyone to some degree.

This reliance on the Spirit within was a direct challenge to religions that relied on outward authority, such as Catholicism or mainstream Protestantism. Largely because of this, Quakers were persecuted from the time they were founded in England in the 1650s. This tapered off about four decades later, and the English Quakers continued to grow and establish Quaker meetings, or congregations, in many parts of the world, especially in the British colonies in North America.

Quakers do not have ordained ministers and do not celebrate outward Christian sacraments. They seek, instead, an inward reality and contend that all life is sacramental.

Belief in the "inner light" present in every person also accounts for the distinctive nature of unprogrammed Quaker worship, in which the congregation is silent except when individuals are moved to speak. This conviction also motivates Quaker confidence in working for the kingdom of God in this world and their emphasis over the years on nonviolence and peace, abolishing slavery, relieving suffering, improving housing, educational and employment opportunities, reforming prisons and eliminating prejudice and discrimination against minorities and the underprivileged.

Quakers are strongly opposed to war and conscription and seek to remove the causes of war and conflict. While a few Quakers have accepted the draft and fought in wars, most declare themselves to be conscientious objectors. A small minority are draft resisters, and refuse to register or in any way cooperate with the military system.

**U.S. meetings, or congregations:** 1,200
**U.S. membership:** 104,000
*(data from the* 1998 Yearbook of American and Canadian Churches*)*

**For more information, contact:**
The Friends World Committee for Consultation
Section of the Americas
1506 Race Street
Philadelphia, PA 19102
(215) 241-7250

**Canadian meetings or worship groups:** 57
**Canadian membership:** 1,126
*(data from Reports, Ottawa: Canadian Yearly Meeting, 1998)*

**For more information, contact:**
Canadian Yearly Meeting
Religious Society of Friends (Quakers)
91A Fourth Avenue
Ottawa, ON K1S 2L1
(613) 235-8553

## II · THE BASIC SERVICE

There are two types of Quaker "meetings," or worship events: "Unprogrammed" and "programmed." Unprogrammed meetings are held in the traditional manner of the Friends on the basis of silence. Worshippers sit and wait for divine guidance and inspiration. If so moved, they then speak. If so inspired, people may also sing. Either is called "vocal ministry."

Programmed meetings are planned in advance and may include hymn singing, vocal prayer, Bible reading, silent worship and a sermon. In many cases, worship is led by a pastor, who is generally paid and is responsible for other pastoral services in the meeting.

Either form of meeting usually lasts an hour.

## APPROPRIATE ATTIRE

**Men:** Jackets and ties are more often worn by older Friends; more casual clothes are usually worn by younger Friends, especially those around college age or below. In general, the emphasis at Quaker meetings is on casual attire. No head covering is required.

**Women:** A skirt and blouse or pants suit. Open-toed shoes and modest jewelry are permissible. More casual clothes are usually worn by younger Friends, especially those around college age or below. In general, the emphasis at Quaker meetings is on casual attire. No head covering is required.

There are no rules regarding colors of clothing.

## THE SANCTUARY

### What are the major sections of the meetinghouse?

Aside from the facing bench, where the elders traditionally sat, there is no undifferentiated section in the meetinghouse. In most meeting houses, the facing bench has now been integrated into the rest of the seating, although raised benches on the side of the meetinghouse may remain. In Canada, many small meetings are held in members' homes.

An elder is a spiritually sensitive person appointed by the monthly meeting to assist the recorded ministers in their work and to share with them discernment and spiritual concern for members of the meeting. In Canada, where the term elder is rarely used, a meeting of Ministry and Counsel is appointed by the monthly meeting to oversee its spiritual life and to coordinate pastoral care for its members.

## THE SERVICE

### When should guests arrive and where should they sit?

It is customary to arrive early. There are no restrictions on where to sit.

### If arriving late, are there times when a guest should *not* enter the service?

If someone is offering a vocal ministry, wait until he or she has finished.

### Are there times when a guest should *not* leave the service?

Ordinarily, no one leaves the meeting. If it is necessary to do so, do not leave when someone is offering vocal ministry.

### Who are the major officiants, leaders or participants and what do they do?

Two members of the meeting, who often belong to a Worship and Ministry Committee (or a committee with a similar function), will close the service by shaking hands with each other. This prompts all those attending to shake hands with those near them. This is often followed by introducing visitors and making announcements, and then by a coffee hour.

**What are the major ritual objects of the service?**
There are none.

**What books are used?**
In unprogrammed meetings, there is no collective oral or silent reading during the service. Bibles and hymnals may be available, as well as *Faith and Practice*, published by each yearly meeting, which is the overarching body that includes various monthly meetings, or congregations, in a specific geographic area. This book sets out the belief and the way of doing business of the yearly meeting.

Sometimes *Faith and Practice* is called *The Discipline*.

**To indicate the order of the service:**
In unprogrammed meetings, no announcements are made or programs provided. The "order" of the service is spontaneous and determined by who is present and what, if anything, they are moved to say. However, brochures that explain Quaker services may be available in the meetinghouse.

Some programmed meetings provide written programs, in addition to general brochures about Friends worship and belief.

## GUEST BEHAVIOR DURING THE SERVICE

**Will a guest who is not a Quaker be expected to do anything other than sit?**
No. Those attending an unprogrammed meeting for worship simply sit expectantly unless they are moved to speak or offer a prayer or message that comes out of the silence. All present, Quaker and non-Quaker, are welcome to give such "vocal ministry."

**Are there any parts of the service in which a guest who is not a Quaker should *not* participate?**
No.

**If not disruptive to the service, is it okay to:**
◼ **Take pictures?** No.
◼ **Use a flash?** No.
◼ **Use a video camera?** No.
◼ **Use a tape recorder?** Possibly. Ask permission in advance from the

meeting contact (clerk, pastor, secretary—whomever you can reach by phoning the meeting).

**Will contributions to the meeting be collected at the service?**

Possibly, depending on the meetinghouse and its practices. Contribution envelopes may be next to the facing bench where the elders sit; or at the table, usually in the front hallway of a meetinghouse, where literature and brochures about Friends are placed.

**How much is customary to contribute?**

Give as you feel led. Often, $1 to $5 is sufficient.

## AFTER THE SERVICE

**Is there usually a reception after the service?**

Yes, usually somewhere in the meeting building. It may last about 30 to 60 minutes. Usually, cookies, coffee and tea are served.

It is not considered impolite to neither eat nor drink. There is no grace or benediction before or after eating or drinking except before a full meal, when there is a blessing or silent grace.

**Is there a traditional form of address for clergy who may be at the reception?**

Quakers have no ordained clergy; pastors and ministers do not have a traditional form of address.

**Is it okay to leave early?**

Yes.

## GENERAL GUIDELINES AND ADVICE

If a visitor is moved to offer a vocal ministry, he or she should first consider their motivation for speaking. Those who speak should be mindful about how long they speak and respect the need for an interval of time for worshippers to receive and consider the previous message from another worshipper.

Do not speak unless deeply moved and certain that your message is one that needs to be shared with those present. Do not feel that you need to respond to a previous message. The messages offered at Quaker worship do not comprise a discussion.

## SPECIAL VOCABULARY

None provided.

## DOGMA AND IDEOLOGY

**Quakers believe:**

▪ "Meeting," or worship, is held in the presence of God and no intermediary is needed between individual worshippers and God.

▪ God can speak to—and potentially through—each person.

▪ The true sacraments are experiences of inner spiritual grace, not outward material symbols of that grace. For Quakers, all of life's activities have sacred potential.

**Some basic books to which a guest can refer to learn more about the Religious Society of Friends:**

*Quaker Spirituality: Selected Writings*, edited and introduced by Douglas V. Steere (Mahwah, N.J.: Paulist Press, 1984).

*Friends for 300 Years: The History and Beliefs of the Society of Friends Since George Fox Started the Quaker Movement*, by Howard Brinton (Wallingford, Pa.: Pendle Hill, 1964).

*The Dictionary of Friends Terms*, compiled by Beatrice Kimball and Joyce Holden (Richmond, Ind.: Friends United Press, 1986).

*Guide to Quaker Practice*, by Howard Brinton (Wallingford, Pa.: Pendle Hill, 1993).

Three periodicals would also be useful: "Friends Journal," an independent monthly magazine, is available from its offices at 1501 Cherry St., Philadelphia, PA 19102. "Quaker Life" is published 10 times yearly by the Friends United Meeting, 101 Quaker Hill Drive, Richmond, IN 47374. In Canada, *The Canadian Friend*, the bi-monthly magazine of the Canadian Yearly Meeting, is available from the Yearly Meeting Office at 91A Fourth Ave., Ottawa, ON K1S 2L1.

---

## III · HOLY DAYS AND FESTIVALS

Friends believe that every day is a holy day and that no one day is to be celebrated more than any other. Nevertheless, some Christmas and Easter celebrations do occasionally occur among Quakers through the influence of other Christian denominations. As with those denominations, Christmas, which always falls on December 25, celebrates the birth of Christ; and Easter, which usually occurs in April, commemorates the death and resurrection of Jesus. Easter always falls on the Sunday after the full moon that occurs on or after the spring equinox of March 21.

As with other Christian faiths, the traditional greetings among Quakers for these holidays are "Merry Christmas" and "Happy Easter."

## IV · LIFE CYCLE EVENTS

### · Birth Ceremony ·

While some Quaker meetings may hold a special or called meeting for worship to celebrate the birth of a child, there is generally no accepted way to commemorate a birth.

What transpires at a special, or called, meeting is the same at an ordinary meeting. It is just convened, in this instance, for the purpose of celebrating the birth of a child.

Meetings usually last about an hour.

### BEFORE THE CEREMONY

**Are guests usually invited by a formal invitation?**
Possibly. If no invitation is extended to the meeting as a whole, then there is a formal invitation.

**If not stated explicitly, should one assume that children are invited?**
Yes.

**If one can't attend, what should one do?**
If there is a formal invitation, RSVP with your regrets.

### APPROPRIATE ATTIRE

**Men:** Jackets and ties are more often worn by older Friends; more casual clothes are usually worn by younger Friends, especially those around college age or below. In general, the emphasis at Quaker meetings is on casual attire. No head covering is required.

**Women:** A skirt and blouse or pants suit. Open-toed shoes and modest jewelry are permissible. More casual clothes are usually worn by younger Friends, especially those around college age or below. In general, the emphasis at Quaker meetings is on casual attire. No head covering is required.

There are no rules regarding colors of clothing.

### GIFTS

**Is a gift customarily expected?**
Only if one is formally invited. There is no Quaker expectation about how

much should be spent on a gift. Many Friends prefer to give educational presents to youngsters rather than toys designed to generate children's interest in such media programming as Saturday morning cartoons.

**Should gifts be brought to the ceremony?**
They can either be brought to the ceremony or to the reception.

## THE CEREMONY

**Where will the ceremony take place?**
In the meetinghouse or the home of the parents.

**When should guests arrive and where should they sit?**
It is customary to arrive early. There are no restrictions on where to sit.

**If arriving late, are there times when a guest should *not* enter the ceremony?**
If someone is offering a vocal ministry, wait until he or she has finished.

**Are there times when a guest should *not* leave the ceremony?**
Ordinarily, no one leaves the meeting. If it is necessary to do so, do not leave when someone is offering vocal ministry.

**Who are the major officiants, leaders or participants at the ceremony and what do they do?**
The family and child are the center of attention. Those present at the meeting may comment about the child or the family.

**What books are used?**
Possibly a Bible or a hymnal.

**To indicate the order of the ceremony:**
Probably nothing is provided.

**Will a guest who is not a Quaker be expected to do anything other than sit?**
No. Those attending an unprogrammed meeting for worship simply sit expectantly unless they are moved to speak or offer a prayer or message that comes out of the silence. All present, Quaker and non-Quaker, are welcome to give such "vocal ministry."

**Are there any parts of the ceremony in which a guest who is not a Quaker should *not* participate?**
No.

**If not disruptive to the ceremony, is it okay to:**
◙ Take pictures? No.

◘ **Use a flash?** No.
◘ **Use a video camera?** No.
◘ **Use a tape recorder?** No.

**Will contributions to the meeting be collected at the ceremony?**
Probably not.

## AFTER THE CEREMONY

**Is there usually a reception after the ceremony?**
There is usually a reception at which food is served. The reception may last 30 to 60 minutes.

**Would it be considered impolite to neither eat nor drink?**
No.

**Is there a grace or benediction before eating or drinking?**
If the meeting is serving a full meal, there will probably be a blessing or silent grace. If there is only light food, there will not be a blessing.

**Is there a grace or benediction after eating or drinking?**
Not usually.

**Is there a traditional greeting for the family?**
No. Simply offer your best wishes.

**Is there a traditional form of address for clergy who may be at the reception?**
Quakers have no ordained clergy; pastors and ministers do not have a traditional form of address.

**Is it okay to leave early?**
Yes.

## · *Initiation Ceremony* ·

Quakers have no special celebration initiating an adolescent into the faith. Some meetings may present a young Friend who is between 13 and 16 years old with a Bible or a copy of his or her Yearly Meeting's *Faith and Practice*. This is usually done privately or at First Day School, the Quaker term for Sunday School.

## · *Marriage Ceremony* ·

From its beginnings, the Religious Society of Friends has stressed the belief that marriage is a binding relationship entered into in the presence of

God and of witnessing friends. Before this public commitment is made on the day of the wedding, the proposed marriage has already received the approval of the Monthly Meeting, which is given after careful consideration by an appointed committee.

A Quaker marriage ceremony has the form of a regular "meeting," or worship service, but during it the bride and groom exchange vows and sign a marriage certificate. The certificate, which is a religious document, is read aloud, and then the meeting continues. There is also a legal marriage certificate which is witnessed by two members of the meeting's oversight committee.

There are two types of Quaker meetings: "Unprogrammed" and "programmed." Unprogrammed meetings are held in the traditional manner of the Friends on the basis of silence. Worshippers sit and wait for divine guidance and inspiration. If so moved, they then speak to the group. This is called "vocal ministry."

Programmed meetings are planned in advance and usually include hymn singing, vocal prayers, Bible reading, silent worship and a sermon. In many cases, worship is led by a pastor, who is generally paid and is responsible for some other pastoral services in the meeting.

The marriage ceremony may last 30 to 60 minutes.

## BEFORE THE CEREMONY

**Are guests usually invited by a formal invitation?**
Yes.

**If not stated explicitly, should one assume that children are invited?**
Yes.

**If one can't attend, what should one do?**
RSVP with your regrets. Possibly send a gift.

## APPROPRIATE ATTIRE

**Men:** Jacket and tie or more informal clothing. Varies with each ceremony. No head covering is required.

**Women:** A dress or a skirt and blouse or a pants suit. Open-toed shoes and modest jewelry are permissible. Varies with each ceremony. No head covering is required.

There are no rules regarding colors of clothing.

## GIFTS

### Is a gift customarily expected?

Yes—anything the giver deems appropriate or which is requested by the newlyweds. Some couples may suggest that contributions be given to a certain charity or cause; others may register with a bridal registry.

### Should gifts be brought to the ceremony?

Usually they are sent to the home of the newlyweds.

## THE CEREMONY

### Where will the ceremony take place?

Depending on the wishes of the bride and groom, it may be in their meetinghouse or in a home or outdoors.

### When should guests arrive and where should they sit?

Arrive early. Ushers will probably advise guests on where to sit. The front rows tend to be reserved for immediate members of the two families.

### If arriving late, are there times when a guest should *not* enter the ceremony?

If someone is offering a vocal ministry, wait until he or she has finished.

### Are there times when a guest should *not* leave the ceremony?

It is inappropriate to leave, especially during vocal ministry.

### Who are the major officiants, leaders or participants and what do they do?

Members of the meeting or friends or relatives of the bride and groom will:

- Bring the wedding certificate to the couple, who are usually at the front of the room.
- Be appointed by the oversight committee in consultation with the couple to read the wedding certificate aloud to the guests.
- Be asked by the oversight committee in consultation with the couple to briefly explain the procedure of the ceremony to those assembled.
- Close the meeting. This is usually done by those at the front of the room who had explained the purpose of marriage shaking each other's hands. This is followed by guests shaking hands with those near them.

### What books are used?

A Bible or a hymnal.

### To indicate the order of the ceremony:

A verbal explanation of the service is usually sufficient.

## Will a guest who is not a Quaker be expected to do anything other than sit?

No, but guests are welcome to speak if moved to do so. All present should sign the marriage certificate afterward. This is usually placed in the meeting room and can be signed after the close of worship.

## Are there any parts of the ceremony in which a guest who is not a Quaker should *not* participate?

No.

## If not disruptive to the ceremony, is it okay to:

◙ **Take pictures?** No.
◙ **Use a flash?** No.
◙ **Use a video camera?** No.
◙ **Use a tape recorder?** Possibly. Ask permission from the couple.
(Photos and videos are usually taken after the ceremony.)

## Will contributions to the meeting be collected at the ceremony?

No.

### AFTER THE CEREMONY

## Is there usually a reception after the ceremony?

There is often a reception that may last one to two hours. It may be at a home, at a catering facility or at any other site chosen by the family. The extent of the food that is served varies from wedding to wedding. Some may have light food and beverages. Others may have a sit-down meal. Still others may have a pot-luck meal. Often, no alcohol is served, mostly because there was a Quaker tradition during most of the 19th century and the first half of the 20th century advising Friends to abstain from drinking alcohol.

Depending on the newlyweds' preferences, there may be music and/or dancing.

## Would it be considered impolite to neither eat nor drink?

No.

## Is there a grace or benediction before eating or drinking?

There may be a silent or spoken grace if the reception is a "sit-down" affair.

## Is there a grace or benediction after eating or drinking?

No.

## Is there a traditional greeting for the family?

Offer your congratulations.

**Is there a traditional form of address for clergy who may be at the reception?**

No.

**Is it okay to leave early?**

Yes, but usually only after the wedding cake is cut and served.

## · *Funerals and Mourning* ·

There are many Quaker attitudes about the possibility of life after death, since the Society of Friends is a religious body without creeds. Friends' beliefs about afterlife can be divided into three main areas:

■ There is no individual survival, but the good (and possibly the evil, also) that we do lives on in the lives of those who come after us.

■ The human spirit survives. This belief is not linked to the traditional duality of heaven or hell or to any theory of redemption by a savior figure. Instead, it sees survival after death as a continuation of this life, but with the possibility of progressing from one stage to another. Some Quakers also believe in rebirth or reincarnation.

■ An approach closer to the traditional Christian belief which accepts heaven and hell as places where souls go after the death of the physical body. One's destiny depends on the life led while on earth.

A Quaker funeral, or memorial meeting, is either "unprogrammed" or "programmed." Unprogrammed meetings are held in the traditional manner of the Friends on the basis of silence. Worshippers sit and wait for divine guidance and inspiration. If so moved, they then speak to the group. This is called "vocal ministry."

Programmed meetings are planned in advance and usually include hymn singing, vocal prayers, Bible reading, silent worship and a sermon. In many cases, worship is led by a pastor, who is generally paid and is responsible for some other pastoral services in the meeting.

Either form of meeting usually lasts an hour.

### BEFORE THE CEREMONY

**How soon after death does the funeral usually take place?**

This varies with the individual family. Scheduling the memorial service or meeting mostly depends on its convenience to the most people since it is independent of the actual burial, which may take place within two to three days after death.

**What should a non-Quaker do upon hearing of the death of a member of that faith?**

Telephone, visit or send letters of sympathy to the bereaved. There is no specific "ritual" for calling or expressing sympathy to someone who is mourning.

## APPROPRIATE ATTIRE

**Men:** Jacket and tie. No head covering is required.

**Women:** A dress or skirt and blouse. Clothing should be modest. Open-toed shoes and modest jewelry are permissible. No head covering is required.

There are no rules regarding colors of clothing, but dark, somber colors are recommended.

## GIFTS

**Is it appropriate to send flowers or make a contribution?**

Both are appropriate. Frequently, obituary notices in local newspapers will list specific charities to which contributions can be made in memory of the deceased.

**Is it appropriate to send food?**

Close friends and neighbors may bring food to the home of the bereaved.

## THE CEREMONY

**Where will the ceremony take place?**

Usually in a Quaker meetinghouse, sometimes in a funeral home, and very rarely in a home.

**When should guests arrive and where should they sit?**

Arrive early. Usually ushers will advise guests on where to sit.

**If arriving late, are there times when a guest should *not* enter the ceremony?**

Do not enter when anyone is speaking.

**Are there times when a guest should *not* leave the ceremony?**

It is inappropriate to leave, especially when anyone is speaking.

**Will the bereaved family be present at the meetinghouse or funeral home before the ceremony?**

No.

**Is there a traditional greeting for the family?**
No.

**Will there be an open casket?**
Very rarely.

**Is a guest expected to view the body?**
This is entirely optional.

**What is appropriate behavior upon viewing the body?**
Silence.

**Who are the major officiants at the ceremony and what do they do?**
A person appointed by a meeting's Oversight Committee may explain Quaker custom at a memorial meeting to the non-Quakers present. This person may close the meeting at the appropriate time with a handshake to those seated nearby.

**What books are used?**
The Bible or a hymnal.

**To indicate the order of the ceremony:**
A program may be distributed that includes an obituary.

**Will a guest who is not a Quaker be expected to do anything other than sit?**
No, especially since most Quakers simply sit during the service unless they are moved to speak or offer a prayer or message that comes out of the silence. All present, Quaker and non-Quaker, are welcome to speak if moved to do so.

**Are there any parts of the ceremony in which a guest who is not a Quaker should *not* participate?**
No.

**If not disruptive to the ceremony, is it okay to:**
- **Take pictures?** No.
- **Use a flash?** No.
- **Use a video camera?** No.
- **Use a tape recorder?** Yes. This is often done, but it is still important to get permission from the family.

**Will contributions to the meeting be collected at the ceremony?**
No.

## THE INTERMENT

### Should guests attend the interment?

No. Usually only close family members attend.

### Whom should one ask for directions?

See above.

### What happens at the graveside?

The body is committed to the ground. If there has been a cremation, the ashes are either buried or put in a vault. Sometimes, the ashes are scattered.

### Do guests who are not Quakers participate at the graveside ceremony?

No. They are simply present.

## COMFORTING THE BEREAVED

### Is it appropriate to visit the home of the bereaved after the funeral?

Yes, although there is no specific "ritual" for calling or expressing sympathy to someone who is mourning. Nor is there a "ritual" that guides the behavior of the mourners.

### Will there be a religious service at the home of the bereaved?

No.

### Will food be served?

Possibly.

### How soon after the funeral will a mourner usually return to a normal work schedule?

This varies according to one's personal needs. There is no doctrine on mourning.

### How soon after the funeral will a mourner usually return to a normal social schedule?

This varies according to one's personal needs. The Quaker emphasis is to resume the fabric of one's life.

### Are there rituals for observing the anniversary of the death?

No.

## V · HOME CELEBRATIONS

Not traditional for Quakers.

# Chapter 18 Contents

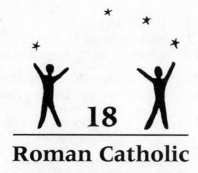

# 18

# Roman Catholic

## I · HISTORY AND BELIEFS

The term "catholic" was first applied around 100 A.D. to the Christian church, which was then one entity. It meant being geographically universal, continuous with the Christian past and transcending language, race and nation. The test of catholicity was communion with the universal church and with the See of Rome.

After the eastern and western wings of the church divided in 1054 A.D., "catholic" was more usually used to refer to the church in the west under the spiritual leadership of the Holy See based in Rome. (This is commonly known as the Vatican.) Since the 16th century, "Roman Catholic" has meant the religious body which acknowledges the pope's authority and the Vatican as the center of ecclesiastical unity.

In the 19th century, the church became increasingly centralized in Rome. In 1870, Vatican Council I declared that the pope has jurisdictional primacy over the entire church, and that under certain circumstances, he is infallible in proclaiming doctrines of faith and morals.

In Roman Catholic teaching, revelation is summed up in Jesus Christ, who commanded his apostles to teach the gospel. To preserve the living gospel, the apostles appointed bishops as their successors. Roman Catholics believe in the unity of God, who is understood as God the Father, God (Jesus Christ) the Son and God the Holy Spirit. Catholicism teaches that original sin—Adam and Eve's expulsion from the Garden of Eden for disobeying God—alienated humanity from God, but did not totally corrupt man and woman, and that grace can fully make a sinner just.

Catholics especially venerate Mary, the mother of Jesus. Catholics believe that Mary was conceived without original sin, and that she was a virgin when Jesus was conceived.

Roman Catholicism has about 900 million members in 2,000 dioceses around the world.

**U.S. churches:** 22,728
**U.S. membership:** 61.2 million
*(data from the* 1998 Yearbook of American and Canadian Churches*)*

**For more information, contact:**
The National Conference of Catholic Bishops
3211 Fourth Street
Washington, DC 20017-1194
(202) 541-3000

**Canadian churches:** 5,706
**Canadian membership:** 12.5 million
*(data from the* 1998 Yearbook of American and Canadian Churches*)*

**For more information, contact:**
Canadian Conference of Catholic Bishops
90 Parent Avenue
Ottawa, ON K1N 7B1
(613) 241-9461

## II · THE BASIC SERVICE

Sunday Mass lasts about 30 to 60 minutes. It consists of two principal divisions called the "Liturgy of the Word," which features the proclamation of the Word of God, and the Eucharistic Liturgy, which focuses on Jesus' sacrifice on behalf of humanity through the crucifixion.

During the Liturgy of the Word, passages from the Bible are read. If three readings are scheduled, the first is usually from Hebrew scriptures (the Old Testament), the second and the third from the New Testament. Also, the presiding priest delivers a homily, an explanation of some point in the readings. He and the congregants together recite "the creed," a profession of their faith, and "the prayers of the faithful," which are prayers of petition concerning the needs of the church, the salvation of the world, public figures, individuals in need, and the local community.

During the Eucharistic Liturgy, bread and wine are transubstantiated through consecration into the body and blood of Jesus Christ, and the priest administers communion (portions of the bread and wine) to congregants.

## APPROPRIATE ATTIRE

**Men:** Jacket and tie. No head covering required.

**Women:** Dress or a skirt and blouse or a pants suit. Jewelry and open-toed shoes are acceptable. Clothing should be modest, depending on the fashion and the locale. No head covering required.

There are no rules regarding colors of clothing.

## THE SANCTUARY

### What are the major sections of the church?

- *The sanctuary:* The part of the church where the altar is located and where priests lead congregants in prayer. It is set off from the body of the church by a distinctive structural feature, such as an elevation above the floor level, or by ornamentation. It is usually at the front of the church, but may be centrally located.
- *The pulpit or lectern:* The stand at which scriptural lessons and psalm responses are read and the word of God is preached.
- *Seating for congregants:* Seats and kneeling benches, usually in front and/or to the side of the altar.
- *Statues:* Images of Jesus, the Virgin Mary, Catholic saints and persons from the Old Testament. Generally, there is only one statue of any individual saint in a church.
- *Baptistery:* The place for administering baptism. Some churches have baptisteries adjoining or near their entrance. This position indicates that through baptism, one is initiated, or "enters," the church. Contemporary practice favors placing the baptistery near the sanctuary and altar, or using a portable font in the same position. This emphasizes the relationship of baptism to the Eucharist, and the celebration of the death and resurrection of Jesus Christ.
- *The confessional room:* A booth-like structure in which priests hear confession of sins from penitents. There are separate compartments for each, and a grating or screen between them. Since the Second Vatican Council in the mid-1960s, there has been a trend in the United States to replace or supplement confessional booths with small reconciliation rooms that are arranged so priest and penitent can converse face-to-face.
- *Holy water fonts:* Receptacles, usually at a church's entrance, containing holy water for Roman Catholics to use. It is customary for them, upon entering a church, to dip their first two fingers into a font and with them to make a sign of the cross. (Guests need not do this.)
- *Sanctuary lamp:* A lamp which is kept burning continuously before a

tabernacle in which the blessed sacrament is reserved, as a sign of the presence of Christ.

## THE SERVICE

**When should guests arrive and where should they sit?**
It is customary to arrive at the time called. Once you enter the sanctuary, sit wherever you like.

**If arriving late, are there times when a guest should *not* enter the service?**
No.

**Are there times when a guest should *not* leave the service?**
Unless it's an emergency, do not leave the service until it is over.

**Who are the major officiants, leaders or participants and what do they do?**
- *The priest,* who reads the Gospel, comments upon it and offers the sacrifice, also known as the Eucharist or communion.
- *The lector,* who reads the first two readings from the scriptures to congregants. Can also lead prayers.

**What are the major ritual objects of the service?**
- *Bread and wine,* which are transubstantiated through consecration into the body and blood of Jesus Christ.
- *The chalice and paten,* which, respectively, hold the consecrated bread and wine. Gold coating is required of the interior parts of sacred vessels.
- *Candles,* used for symbolic purposes. They represent Christ, the light and life of grace, at liturgical functions. Made of beeswax.

**What books are used?**
The New American Bible (or another authorized translation) or a lectionary that contains selections from the Bible, and a prayer book, which is also called a missal.

**To indicate the order of the service:**
Periodic announcements may be made by the lector or priest. Also, the basic outline of the service is usually provided in a printed program and prayers may be announced by a display located near the front of the sanctuary.

## GUEST BEHAVIOR DURING THE SERVICE

**Will a guest who is not a Catholic be expected to do anything other than sit?**
Yes. They are also expected to stand. It is optional for them for kneel with

the congregation, read prayers aloud and sing with congregants.

**Are there any parts of the service in which a guest who is not a Catholic should *not* participate?**

Such guests should not receive communion or say any prayers contradictory to the beliefs of their own faith.

**If not disruptive to the service, is it okay to:**

▪ **Take pictures?** Yes. Verify beforehand with the priest or usher.

▪ **Use a flash?** No. Verify beforehand with the priest or usher.

▪ **Use a video camera?** Yes. Verify beforehand with the priest or usher.

▪ **Use a tape recorder?** Yes. Verify beforehand with the priest or usher.

**Will contributions to the church be collected at the service?**

Yes, but guests are not expected to contribute.

**How much is customary to contribute?**

From $1 to $5.

## AFTER THE SERVICE

**Is there usually a reception after the service?**

Sometimes there is a 30- to 60-minute reception in the parish hall adjoining the sanctuary. Depending on the parish, light food may be served. It is not considered impolite to neither eat nor drink. Do not eat until a blessing is recited. Benedictions are also said after the reception.

**Is there a traditional form of address for clergy who may be at the reception?**

"Father" if greeting a priest. "Your excellency" if greeting a bishop. "Your eminence" if greeting a cardinal.

**Is it okay to leave early?**

Yes.

## GENERAL GUIDELINES AND ADVICE

None provided.

## SPECIAL VOCABULARY

None provided.

## DOGMA AND IDEOLOGY

**Roman Catholics believe:**

▪ Worship is directed toward God alone.

◧ All revelation is summed up in Jesus Christ, who was both human and divine and commanded His twelve apostles to preach the gospel.

◧ The pope has primacy of jurisdiction over the church. He and the body of bishops have infallibility when addressing religious issues.

◧ The Eucharist (or communion) is the center of church life. The mass is considered to make present Christ's one sacrifice of death and resurrection. During it, Christ is said to be present through the transubstantiation of the bread and wine of the Eucharist.

**A basic book to which a guest can refer to learn more about the Roman Catholic Church:**
*The Catechism of the Catholic Church* (New York: Doubleday, 1994).

---

## III · HOLY DAYS AND FESTIVALS

---

◧ *Christmas,* which always falls on December 25, celebrates the birth of Christ.

◧ *Easter,* which commemorates the death and resurrection of Jesus. Always falls on the Sunday after the full moon that occurs on or after the spring equinox of March 21.

◧ *Pentecost* occurs 50 days after Easter because this is when the Holy Ghost (the spirit of Jesus) descended on His apostles. Celebrates the power of the Holy Spirit and its manifestation in the early Christian church.

◧ *Ash Wednesday,* which occurs 40 days before Easter, commemorates the beginning of Lent, which is a season for preparation and penitence before Easter itself.

◧ *Maundy Thursday,* which falls four days before Easter. Commemorates the institution of the Eucharist (also known as communion) and Jesus' subsequent arrest and trial.

◧ *Good Friday,* three days before Easter. Commemorates the crucifixion, death and burial of Jesus.

---

## IV · LIFE CYCLE EVENTS

---

### · *Birth Ceremony* ·

Baptism is the sacrament of spiritual regeneration by which a person, usually a six- to eight-week old infant, is incorporated into Christ and made a member of His Mystical Body, given grace and cleansed of original sin. The virtues of faith, hope and charity are given with grace. The sacrament confers a character on the soul and can only be received once.

The 30- to 60-minute baptismal ceremony is sometimes part of a larger service, usually a mass. (For details on the mass, see "The Basic Service" section above.) During the ceremony, a bishop, priest or deacon pours water on the forehead of the person being baptized and says, "I baptize you in the name of the Father and of the Son and of the Holy Spirit."

Catholics must first be baptized before they can receive other sacraments from their church.

## BEFORE THE CEREMONY

**Are guests usually invited by a formal invitation?**
Yes.

**If not stated explicitly, should one assume that children are invited?**
Yes.

**If one can't attend, what should one do?**
RSVP with regrets and send a gift.

## APPROPRIATE ATTIRE

**Men:** Jacket and tie or more relaxed clothing. No head covering required.

**Women:** Dress or a skirt and blouse or a pants suit. Jewelry and open-toed shoes are acceptable. Clothing should be modest, depending on the fashion and the locale. No head covering required.

There are no rules regarding colors of clothing.

## GIFTS

**Is a gift customarily expected?**
Yes, the value of which depends solely on your socio-economic level.

**Should gifts be brought to the ceremony?**
Bring them to the reception afterward.

## THE CEREMONY

**Where will the ceremony take place?**
In the baptistery, which is usually near or adjoins the church entrance. Contemporary practice favors placing the baptistery near the sanctuary and altar, or using a portable font in the same position. This emphasizes the relationship of baptism to communion and, thus, to the celebration of the death and resurrection of Jesus Christ.

**When should guests arrive and where should they sit?**
Arrive on time. Sit wherever you wish.

**If arriving late, are there times when a guest should *not* enter the ceremony?**
No.

**Are there times when a guest should *not* leave the ceremony?**
Do not leave before the service ends.

**Who are the major officiants, leaders or participants at the ceremony and what do they do?**
◙ A priest, who will baptize the child.

**What books are used?**
The main books are the hymnal, the New American Bible (or another authorized translation) or a lectionary that contains selections from the Bible, and a prayer book, which is also called a missal.

**To indicate the order of the ceremony:**
Periodic announcements will be made by the lector or pastor. Also, the basic outline of the service is usually provided in a printed program and prayers will be announced by a display located near the front of the sanctuary.

**Will a guest who is not a Catholic be expected to do anything other than sit?**
Guests are expected to stand with the congregation. It is optional for them to kneel, read prayers aloud and sing with the congregation.

**Are there any parts of the ceremony in which a guest who is not a Catholic should *not* participate?**
Such guests should not receive communion or say any prayers contradictory to the beliefs of their own faith.

**If not disruptive to the ceremony, is it okay to:**
◙ **Take pictures?** Yes. Verify beforehand with the priest or usher.
◙ **Use a flash?** No. Verify beforehand with the priest or usher.
◙ **Use a video camera?** Yes. Verify beforehand with the priest or usher.
◙ **Use a tape recorder?** Yes. Verify beforehand with the priest or usher.

**Will contributions to the church be collected at the ceremony?**
No.

### AFTER THE CEREMONY

**Is there usually a reception after the ceremony?**
Yes, usually at the home of the baptized child. Food will be served. Alco-

holic beverages may be served. There may be music and dancing. The reception may last one to two hours.

**Would it be considered impolite to neither eat nor drink?**
No.

**Is there a grace or benediction before eating or drinking?**
Yes.

**Is there a grace or benediction after eating or drinking?**
Sometimes.

**Is there a traditional greeting for the family?**
No, just offer your congratulations.

**Is there a traditional form of address for clergy who may be at the reception?**
"Father" if greeting a priest. "Your excellency" if greeting a bishop. "Your eminence" if greeting a cardinal.

**Is it okay to leave early?**
Yes.

## · Initiation Ceremony ·

Confirmation is the sacrament by which a baptized early adolescent is endowed with the fullness of baptismal grace; is united more intimately with the church; is enriched with the special power of the Holy Spirit; and is committed to be an authentic witness to Christ in word and action.

Those being confirmed often receive the sacrament with their entire confirmation class. The ceremony is sometimes part of a larger service. It will last slightly more than one hour.

Confirmation may occur between the ages of seven and 18, depending on the policy of the local diocese.

### BEFORE THE CEREMONY

**Are guests usually invited by a formal invitation?**
Yes.

**If not stated explicitly, should one assume that children are invited?**
Yes.

**If one can't attend, what should one do?**
RSVP with regrets and send a gift.

## APPROPRIATE ATTIRE

**Men:** Jacket and tie or more relaxed clothing. No head covering required.

**Women:** Dress or a skirt and blouse or a pants suit. Jewelry and open-toed shoes are acceptable. Clothing should be modest, depending on the fashion and the locale. No head covering required.

There are no rules regarding colors of clothing.

## GIFTS

**Is a gift customarily expected?**
Yes. Often money is appropriate. The exact amount is totally discretionary.

**Should gifts be brought to the ceremony?**
Bring them to the reception afterward.

## THE CEREMONY

**Where will the ceremony take place?**
In the main sanctuary of the confirmand's church.

**When should guests arrive and where should they sit?**
It is customary to arrive at the time called. Sit wherever you wish.

**If arriving late, are there times when a guest should *not* enter the ceremony?**
No.

**Are there times when a guest should *not* leave the ceremony?**
Guests should remain until the ceremony ends.

**Who are the major officiants, leaders or participants at the ceremony and what do they do?**
The bishop, who anoints each confirmand with oil on the forehead.

**What books are used?**
The main books are the hymnal, the New American Bible (or another authorized translation) or a lectionary that contains selections from the Bible, and a prayer book, which is also called a missal.

**To indicate the order of the ceremony:**
Periodic announcements may be made by the lector or pastor. Also, the basic outline of the service is usually provided in a printed program and prayers will be announced by a display located near the front of the sanctuary.

**Will a guest who is not a Catholic be expected to do anything other than sit?**

Guests are expected to stand with the congregation. It is optional for them to kneel, read prayers aloud or sing with the congregation.

**Are there any parts of the ceremony in which a guest who is not a Catholic should *not* participate?**

Yes. Anything that implies a statement of faith that would violate their own beliefs.

**If not disruptive to the ceremony, is it okay to:**

- **Take pictures?** Yes. Verify beforehand with the priest or usher.
- **Use a flash?** No. Verify beforehand with the priest or usher.
- **Use a video camera?** Yes. Verify beforehand with the priest or usher.
- **Use a tape recorder?** Yes. Verify beforehand with the priest or usher.

**Will contributions to the church be collected at the ceremony?**
No.

## AFTER THE CEREMONY

**Is there usually a reception after the ceremony?**

There is a reception, usually at the home of the confirmand. Food and soft drinks will be served. Alcoholic beverages may be served. The reception may last between one and two hours.

**Would it be considered impolite to neither eat nor drink?**
No.

**Is there a grace or benediction before eating or drinking?**
No.

**Is there a grace or benediction after eating or drinking?**
No.

**Is there a traditional greeting for the family?**
Just offer your congratulations.

**Is there a traditional form of address for clergy who may be at the reception?**

"Father" if greeting a priest. "Your excellency" if greeting a bishop. "Your eminence" if greeting a cardinal.

**Is it okay to leave early?**
Yes.

## · *Marriage Ceremony* ·

Catholics consider married life, which was created by God, to have a decisive bearing on the continuation of the human race, on the personal development and eternal destiny of individual members of a family, and on the dignity, stability, peace and prosperity of families and society.

Love, the church teaches, is uniquely expressed and perfected through marriage. Children are the "gift of marriage," although marriage is not instituted solely for procreation. Rather, its essential nature as an unbreakable compact between man and wife and for the welfare of the children that come out of it both demand that the love of the respective spouses be embodied in a manner that grows, thrives and ripens.

The marriage ceremony may either be a ceremony unto itself and not part of a larger service or it may be part of a mass. (For details on the mass, see "The Basic Service" section above.) It may last between 30 and 60 minutes to more than one hour.

### BEFORE THE CEREMONY

**Are guests usually invited by a formal invitation?**
Yes.

**If not stated explicitly, should one assume that children are invited?**
Yes.

**If one can't attend, what should one do?**
RSVP with regrets and send a gift.

### APPROPRIATE ATTIRE

**Men:** Jacket and tie or more relaxed clothing. No head covering required.

**Women:** Dress or a skirt and blouse or a pants suit. Jewelry and open-toed shoes are acceptable. Clothing should be modest, depending on the fashion and the locale. No head covering required. It is recommended that black not be worn.

### GIFTS

**Is a gift customarily expected?**
Yes. Often money is most appropriate, with the exact amount subject to your discretion.

**Should gifts be brought to the ceremony?**
Gifts should be sent to the home or brought to the reception.

## THE CEREMONY

**Where will the ceremony take place?**
In the main sanctuary of the church.

**When should guests arrive and where should they sit?**
Arrive on time. An usher will show guests where to sit.

**Are there times when a guest should *not* enter the ceremony?**
Ushers may guide latecomers. Do not enter as the wedding party processes into the sanctuary.

**Are there times when a guest should *not* leave the service?**
Do not leave until it ends.

**Who are the major officiants, leaders or participants at the ceremony and what do they do?**
The priest, who witnesses the vows.

**What books are used?**
The hymnal, the New American Bible (or another authorized translation) or a lectionary that contains selections from the Bible, and a prayer book, which is also called a missal.

**To indicate the order of the ceremony:**
There will be a program.

**Will a guest who is not a Catholic be expected to do anything other than sit?**
Guests are expected to stand with the congregation. It is optional for them to kneel, read prayers aloud or sing with the congregation.

**Are there any parts of the ceremony in which a non-Catholic guest should *not* participate?**
Non-Catholics do not receive communion.

**If not disruptive to the ceremony, is it okay to:**
- **Take pictures?** Yes. Verify beforehand with the priest or usher.
- **Use a flash?** Yes. Verify beforehand with the priest or usher.
- **Use a video camera?** Yes. Verify beforehand with the priest or usher.
- **Use a tape recorder?** Yes. Verify beforehand with the priest or usher.

**Will contributions to the church be collected at the ceremony?**
No.

## AFTER THE CEREMONY

**Is there usually a reception after the ceremony?**
There is a reception that may last more than two hours. It is usually at a catering hall, where food and beverages will be served and there will be dancing and music.

**Would it be considered impolite to neither eat nor drink?**
No.

**Is there a grace or benediction before eating or drinking?**
Yes, the blessing before the meal.

**Is there a grace or benediction after eating or drinking?**
Usually not.

**Is there a traditional greeting for the family?**
Just offer your congratulations.

**Is there a traditional form of address for clergy who may be at the reception?**
"Father" if greeting a priest. "Your excellency" if greeting a bishop. "Your eminence" if greeting a cardinal.

**Is it okay to leave early?**
Yes.

## · *Funerals and Mourning* ·

Roman Catholicism deeply believes in immortality. Each human does not face utter spiritual dissolution since God loves him or her. Not only does all love desire immortality, but God's love *is* immortality. On the "last day" when the Messiah has arrived, one's physical body joins the spirit in the beatific vision of heaven or the damnation of hell.

A Catholic funeral may be part of a larger service or a ceremony unto itself. If it is part of another service, that will be a mass. (For details on the mass, see "The Basic Service" section above.)

The first day after a death is usually reserved for the family to make arrangements for the funeral. The second day is often reserved for a wake, which may last for possibly one to two days. It is most commonly held at the funeral home. The style of wake varies (i.e., food, beverages, mood, prayer) widely and usually depends on the ethnicity of the deceased and his or her family. However, common to all wakes is an opportunity for community, friends and relatives to gather, pray and express their sympathies to the family of the deceased, to whom they also pay their respects.

## BEFORE THE CEREMONY

**How soon after the death does the funeral usually take place?**
Usually within two to three days. Sometimes as much as one week later.

**What should a non-Catholic do upon hearing of the death of a member of that faith?**
Telephone the bereaved at home or visit them at the funeral home to express condolences.

## APPROPRIATE ATTIRE

**Men:** Jacket and tie. No head covering required.

**Women:** Dress or a skirt and blouse or a pants suit. Jewelry and open-toed shoes are acceptable. Clothing should be modest, depending on the fashion and the locale. No head covering required.

Black or equally sober colors are recommended.

## GIFTS

**Is it appropriate to send flowers or make a contribution?**
Flowers of any kind are appreciated. They may be sent upon hearing the news of the death or shortly thereafter. They may be sent to the home of the deceased before or after the funeral or to the funeral home before the funeral.

Contributions are not customary unless the family indicates they are appropriate.

**Is it appropriate to send food?**
Yes, to the home of the bereaved before or after the funeral.

## THE CEREMONY

**Where will the ceremony take place?**
At a church or a funeral home.

**When should guests arrive and where should they sit?**
Arrive on time. Sit wherever you like.

**If arriving late, are there times when a guest should *not* enter the ceremony?**
No.

**Will the bereaved family be present at the church or funeral home before the ceremony?**
Yes.

**Is there a traditional greeting for the family?**
Offer your condolences.

**Will there be an open casket?**
Usually.

**Is a guest expected to view the body?**
Yes.

**What is appropriate behavior upon viewing the body?**
Silent prayer.

**Who are the major officiants at the ceremony and what do they do?**
◙ The priest, who says the mass and the prayers at graveside.

**What books are used?**
The hymnal, the New American Bible (or another authorized translation), and a prayer book, which is also called a missal.

**To indicate the order of the ceremony:**
A program will be distributed.

**Will a guest who is not a Catholic be expected to do anything other than sit?**
Guests are expected to stand with the other mourners. It is optional for them to kneel, read prayers aloud and sing with the congregation.

**Are there any parts of the ceremony in which a non-Catholic guest should *not* participate?**
Such guests should not receive communion or say any prayers contradictory to the beliefs of their own faith.

**If not disruptive to the ceremony, is it okay to:**
◙ **Take pictures?** No. Verify beforehand with the priest or usher.
◙ **Use a flash?** No. Verify beforehand with the priest or usher.
◙ **Use a video camera?** No. Verify beforehand with the priest or usher.
◙ **Use a tape recorder?** No. Verify beforehand with the priest or usher.

**Will contributions to the church be collected at the ceremony?**
No.

## THE INTERMENT

**Should guests attend the interment?**
Yes.

**Whom should one ask for directions?**
The funeral director.

**What happens at the graveside?**
The priest leads prayers for the deceased.

**Do guests who are not Catholics participate at the graveside ceremony?**
No. They are simply present.

## COMFORTING THE BEREAVED

**Is it appropriate to visit the home of the bereaved after the funeral?**
Yes, briefly.

**Will there be a religious service at the home of the bereaved?**
No.

**Will food be served?**
Possibly. Given the broad ethnic mixture of Catholicism, some Catholics may have a "wake," at which food (and often, drink) is served.

**How soon after the funeral will a mourner usually return to a normal work schedule?**
Perhaps a week.

**How soon after the funeral will a mourner usually return to a normal social schedule?**
Perhaps a week.

**Are there mourning customs to which a friend who is not a Catholic should be sensitive?**
No.

**Are there rituals for observing the anniversary of the death?**
There is a mass on the annual anniversary of the death.

# V · HOME CELEBRATIONS

Not applicable to Roman Catholicism.

# Chapter 19 Contents

# Seventh-day Adventist

## I · HISTORY AND BELIEFS

The Seventh-day Adventist Church stemmed from a worldwide religious revival in the mid-1800s when people of many faiths fervently believed biblical prophecies that they interpreted as meaning that Jesus Christ's second coming, or "advent," was imminent.

When Christ did not come in the 1840s, a group of these disappointed Adventists in the U.S. concluded that they had misinterpreted prophetic events, and that the second coming was still in the future. This same group later became known as Seventh-day Adventists, which organized formally as a denomination in 1863.

Adventists anticipate and prepare for the world's end in conjunction with the second coming of Jesus Christ. They believe that the end of the world is near and that eternal hell for the wicked is not consistent with the concept of a "loving Father." Instead, they believe in eventual annihilation of the wicked and eternal bliss for the saved. After a thousand-year reign of the saints with Christ in Heaven, the wicked will be raised and, along with Satan, annihilated. Out of the chaos of the old earth will emerge a new earth, which the redeemed will inherit as their everlasting home.

Worldwide, there are about eight million Seventh-day Adventists. The movement grows by about seven percent annually and has more than 37,000 congregations in over 200 countries.

In addition to a mission program, the church has the largest worldwide Protestant parochial school system with over 800,000 elementary through college students in more than 5,400 schools. It also operates medical schools and hospitals.

**U.S. churches:** 4,363
**U.S. membership:** 809,000
*(data from the* 1998 Yearbook of American and Canadian Churches*)*

---

**For more information, contact:**
The Seventh-day Adventist Church
12501 Old Columbia Pike
Silver Spring, MD 20904-6600
(301) 680-6000

**Canadian churches:** 336
**Canadian membership:** 46,961
*(data from 1997)*

---

**For more information, contact:**
Seventh-day Adventist Church in Canada
1148 King Street East
Oshawa, ON L1H 1H8
(905) 433-0982

---

## II · THE BASIC SERVICE

The Adventists' basic religious service is held on Saturday mornings and lasts about 60 minutes. The service is strong on fellowship. About half of it is devoted to readings and teachings from the Old and New Testaments.

### APPROPRIATE ATTIRE

**Men:** Jacket and tie or more relaxed clothing. No head covering required.

**Women:** Suit, dress, skirt and blouse or conservative pants suits are acceptable. No head covering required. Clothing usually covers the arms and hems are below the knee, but neither is obligatory.

Although Adventists do not ordinarily wear jewelry, guests should feel comfortable wearing it.

There are no rules regarding colors of clothing.

### THE SANCTUARY

**What are the major sections of the church?**
- *The sanctuary,* where congregants sit.
- *The speakers' platform,* which is slightly elevated for speakers and, at times, the choir.

## THE SERVICE

### When should guests arrive and where should they sit?

It is customary to arrive at the time the service is scheduled. There will usually be someone to help you find a seat; if not, take any open seat.

### If arriving late, are there times when a guest should *not* enter the service?

If arriving late, do not enter during prayer.

### Are there times when a guest should *not* leave the service?

Do not leave during prayer.

### Who are the major officiants, leaders or participants and what do they do?

- *The elders,* who are elected lay leaders in charge of individual congregations. They are usually elected for one year.
- An ordained *pastor,* although not every congregation has one. Adventists only ordain men.

### What are the major ritual objects of the service?

There are no specific ritual objects.

### What books are used?

A hymnal and the Old and New Testaments.

### To indicate the order of the service:

A program will be distributed to congregants and guests.

## GUEST BEHAVIOR DURING THE SERVICE

### Will a guest who is not a Seventh-day Adventist be expected to do anything other than sit?

It is optional for guests to stand, kneel and sing with the congregation. It is also optional for them to join in the washing of feet. During this ritual, men and women will leave the sanctuary and go to rooms reserved, for the sake of modesty, for the separate genders. Guests may remain in the sanctuary, during which time the organist will be playing. The entire ritual may take about 10 minutes. The ritual is based on a passage in the New Testament (John 13:14-15) in which Jesus first washes the feet of his disciples at the Last Supper, then instructs them that they should do the same to one another. Adventists do this almost as a weekly mini-baptism.

**Are there any parts of the service in which a guest who is not a Seventh-day Adventist should *not* participate?**

Guests can participate in all aspects of the service, unless their own faith forbids it.

**If not disruptive to the service, is it okay to:**

◙ **Take pictures?** Yes.

◙ **Use a flash?** Yes.

◙ **Use a video camera?** Yes.

◙ **Use a tape recorder?** Yes.

**Will contributions to the church be collected at the service?**

An offering plate will be passed through the congregation. Donations by guests are optional.

**How much is customary to contribute?**

Contributions from $1 to $5 are customary.

## AFTER THE SERVICE

**Is there usually a reception after the service?**

Often, yes, lasting 30 to 60 minutes. A variety of foods may be served. Often, a pot luck luncheon is provided for members and guests, in an activity room. There is usually a benediction or prayer before eating. There will be no alcoholic beverages.

It is not considered impolite to neither eat nor drink, especially if one has dietary restrictions.

**Is there a traditional form of address for clergy who may be at the reception?**

"Elder" or "Pastor."

**Is it okay to leave early?**

Yes.

## GENERAL GUIDELINES AND ADVICE

None provided.

## SPECIAL VOCABULARY

**Key words or phrases which might be helpful for a visitor to know:**

◙ *Sabbath School,* the study service preceding the worship service.

◙ *Prayer Meeting,* the midweek service, usually held on Wednesday evenings.

## DOGMA AND IDEOLOGY

**Seventh-day Adventists believe:**

◼ The scriptures of both the Old and New Testaments are the final authority. The Saturday service focuses on the study of these scriptures and their exposition. (No specific translation of the Bible is used since 90 percent of Adventists live outside the United States and use hundreds of different translations of the Bible.)

**A basic book to which a guest can refer to learn more about the Seventh-day Adventist Church:**

*Seventh-day Adventists Believe* (Silver Spring, Md.: Ministerial Association, General Conference of Seventh-day Adventists).

## III · HOLY DAYS AND FESTIVALS

Seventh-day Adventists' only holy day is the Sabbath, which occurs each Saturday. This is Seventh-day Adventists' central day of worship on which they avoid labor and secular activities.

The faith recognizes no other holy days because the Sabbath is the only universal holy day mentioned in the scriptures.

## IV · LIFE CYCLE EVENTS

### · *Birth Ceremony* ·

Baptism initiates an adolescent or adult into the church. During the ceremony, which usually lasts less than 30 minutes, the person to be baptized enters a baptismal pool with a pastor or elder and is fully and briefly immersed under the water. The baptism is part of a public service, usually the basic Sabbath worship service.

Baptism is a sign of remission of sin and spiritual rebirth by symbolically participating in Christ's death, burial and resurrection.

### BEFORE THE CEREMONY

**Are guests usually invited by a formal invitation?**

There will be no formal invitation. All are welcome, including children.

**If not stated explicitly, should one assume that children are invited?**

Yes.

**If one can't attend, what should one do?**

One may offer their best wishes to the family.

## APPROPRIATE ATTIRE

**Men:** Jacket and tie or more relaxed clothing. No head covering required.

**Women:** Dress, skirt and blouse or conservative pant suit are acceptable. No head covering required. Clothing usually covers the arms and hems are below the knee, but neither is obligatory.

Although Adventists do not ordinarily wear jewelry, guests should feel comfortable wearing it.

There are no rules regarding colors of clothing.

## GIFTS

**Is a gift customarily expected?**

A gift is neither customary nor expected.

**Should gifts be brought to the ceremony?**

See above.

## THE CEREMONY

**Where will the ceremony take place?**

Generally, in the main sanctuary of the church. Sometimes, the baptismal immersion will be at an outdoor site, such as a lake, a stream or even the ocean.

**When should guests arrive and where should they sit?**

It is customary to arrive at the time the service is called. If arriving late, do not enter during prayer. There will usually be someone to help you find a seat; if not, you can take any open seat.

**Are there times when a guest should *not* enter the ceremony?**

If arriving late, do not enter during prayer.

**Are there times when a guest should *not* leave the ceremony?**

Do not leave during prayer.

**Who are the major officiants, leaders or participants at the ceremony and what do they do?**

◼ *The Elder or Pastor,* who performs the baptism by immersion.

**What books are used?**
None.

**To indicate the order of the ceremony:**
There may be a program.

**Will a guest who is not a Seventh-day Adventist be expected to do anything other than sit?**
It is optional for guests to stand, kneel and sing with the congregation.

**Are there any parts of the ceremony in which a guest who is not a Seventh-day Adventist should *not* participate?**
Guests can participate in all aspects of the service, unless their own faith forbids it.

**If not disruptive to the ceremony, is it okay to:**
◘ **Take pictures?** Yes.
◘ **Use a flash?** Yes.
◘ **Use a video camera?** Yes.
◘ **Use a tape recorder?** Yes.

**Will contributions to the church be collected at the ceremony?**
Normally baptism is a part of the regular worship service, during which an offering plate is passed through the congregation. No special offering will be taken in connection with the baptism itself. Donations by guests are optional.

**How much is customary to contribute?**
Contributions from $1 to $5 are customary.

### AFTER THE CEREMONY

**Is there usually a reception after the ceremony?**
No.

**Is there a traditional greeting for the family?**
No.

**Is there a traditional form of address for clergy whom a guest may meet?**
"Elder" or "Pastor."

## · Initiation Ceremony ·

Not applicable to Seventh-day Adventists.

# · *Marriage Ceremony* ·

Seventh-day Adventists believe that marriage was divinely established in Eden. To accomplish this most important part of Creation, God performed a miracle and brought forth Eve from the side of Adam, and gave her to Adam as his wife. Jesus later affirmed marriage to be a lifelong union between a man and a woman in loving companionship.

A marriage commitment is to God, as well as to the spouse. Marriage should be entered into only between partners who share a common religious faith. Mutual love, honor, respect and responsibility are the fabric of this relationship.

The marriage ceremony usually lasts between 30 and 60 minutes.

## BEFORE THE CEREMONY

### Are guests usually invited by a formal invitation?

Yes. Occasionally, there will be a general invitation in the local church bulletin.

### If not stated explicity, should one assume that children are invited?

Yes.

### If one can't attend, what should one do?

RSVP with your regrets and send a gift to the bride and groom.

## APPROPRIATE ATTIRE

**Men:** Jacket and tie. No head covering required.

**Women:** Dress or skirt and blouse. No head covering required. Clothing should cover the arms and hems should reach below the knee.

Although Adventists do not ordinarily wear jewelry, guests should feel comfortable wearing it.

There are no rules regarding colors of clothing.

## GIFTS

### Is a gift customarily expected?

Only if the celebrants are close friends or relatives. Money and other gifts are appropriate.

**Should gifts be brought to the ceremony?**

Gifts may be sent to the home before or after the wedding ceremony or brought to the ceremony and placed in the reception area.

## THE CEREMONY

**Where will the ceremony take place?**

In a variety of settings, although most commonly in the church sanctuary.

**When should guests arrive and where should they sit?**

Arrive shortly before the ceremony is scheduled to start.

**If arriving late, are there times when a guest should *not* enter the ceremony?**

Latecomers should not enter during the bride's entry.

**Are there times when a guest should *not* leave the ceremony?**

Do not leave during prayer.

**Who are the major officiants, leaders or participants at the ceremony and what do they do?**

◙ *The pastor,* who will deliver a few comments.

**What books are used?**

Only the clergyman uses a Bible.

**To indicate the order of the ceremony:**

A program will be distributed.

**Will a guest who is not a Seventh-day Adventist be expected to do anything other than sit?**

It is optional for guests to stand, kneel and sing with the congregation.

**Are there any parts of the ceremony in which a guest who is not a Seventh-day Adventist should *not* participate?**

Guests who belong to other faiths can participate in all aspects of the service, unless restricted from doing so by their own faith.

**If not disruptive to the ceremony, is it okay to:**

◙ **Take photographs?** Yes.

◙ **Use a flash?** Yes.

◙ **Use a video camera?** Yes.

◙ **Use a tape recorder?** Yes.

**Will contributions to the church be collected at the ceremony?**

No.

## AFTER THE CEREMONY

**Is there usually a reception after the ceremony?**
There is usually a 30- to 60-minute reception. The location varies, but will be announced in advance. Guests greet the participants, visit with other guests and enjoy the food. Usually, there is punch and cake. Sometimes, there is a sit-down meal. There will be no alcoholic beverages.

**Would it considered impolite to neither eat or drink?**
No, especially if a guest has dietary restrictions.

**Is there a grace or benediction before eating or drinking?**
Wait for a brief prayer of thanks for the food before eating.

**Is there a grace or benediction after eating or drinking?**
No.

**Is there a special greeting for the family?**
Just offer your congratulations.

**Is there a traditional form of address for clergy who may be at the reception?**
"Elder" or "Pastor."

**Is it okay to leave early?**
Yes.

## · *Funerals and Mourning* ·

Seventh-day Adventists believe that the deceased sleep until the resurrection of Jesus. A Seventh-day Adventist funeral usually lasts about 15 to 30 minutes.

## BEFORE THE CEREMONY

**How soon after the death does the funeral usually take place?**
Within one week of the death.

**What should someone who is not a Seventh-day Adventist do upon hearing of the death of a member of that faith?**
Telephone or visit to express sorrow. Express such words of comfort as "I sense your grief and share it with you." When speaking with each other, Adventists usually follow this phrase with, "We look for the coming resurrection." One should not consign the deceased to heaven or hell.

## APPROPRIATE ATTIRE

**Men:** Jacket and tie. No head covering required.

**Women:** Dress or skirt and blouse. No head covering required. Clothing should cover the arms, and hems should be below the knee.

No jewelry should be worn.

Somber colors are recommended.

## GIFTS

### Is it appropriate to send flowers or make a contribution?
It is not appropriate to make a donation, but it is appropriate to send flowers to the funeral or to the deceased's home before or after the funeral. The bereaved can also be helped by offering to transport incoming relatives from airports or bus or train stations or offering to help with errands.

### Is it appropriate to send food?
It is appropriate to bring food after the funeral to the home of the deceased or to the place of a memorial meal, which could be elsewhere.

## THE CEREMONY

### Where will the ceremony take place?
Either in a church or funeral home.

### When should guests arrive and where should they sit?
It is customary to arrive early. If there is no usher, sit in any seat.

### If arriving late, are there times when a guest should *not* enter the ceremony?
Do not enter during prayer.

### Will the bereaved family be present at the church or funeral home before the ceremony?
Often.

### Is there a traditional greeting for the family?
It is appropriate to offer the family a brief word of encouragement before the funeral.

### Will there be an open casket?
Usually.

### Is a guest expected to view the body?
This is optional.

**What is appropriate behavior upon viewing the body?**
Simply stand in silent observation.

**Who are the major officiants at the ceremony and what do they do?**
◪ *A clergyman,* who leads the service; possibly also an associate clergy or layperson; musician(s).

**What books are used?**
The clergy alone uses the Bible.

**To indicate the order of the ceremony:**
A program will be distributed.

**Will a guest who is not a Seventh-day Adventist be expected to do anything other than sit?**
You are not expected to do anything other than sit respectfully.

**Are there any parts of the ceremony in which a guest who is not a Seventh-day Adventist should *not* participate?**
No.

**If not disruptive to the service, is it okay to:**
◪ **Take pictures?** No.
◪ **Use a flash?** No.
◪ **Use a video camera?** No.
◪ **Use a tape recorder?** No.

**Will contributions to the church be collected at the ceremony?**
No.

## THE INTERMENT

**Should guests attend the interment?**
This is optional.

**Whom should one ask for directions?**
The funeral director.

**What happens at the the graveside?**
There will be a brief message of encouragement and prayer from the clergyman.

**Do guests who are not Seventh-day Adventists participate at the graveside ceremony?**
No. They are simply present.

## COMFORTING THE BEREAVED

### Is it appropriate to visit the home of the bereaved after the funeral?

Yes, especially during the first few days after the funeral. More than once is appropriate. One should visit briefly, perhaps ten minutes, to express words of encouragement or to offer to help with any difficulties the bereaved may encounter.

### Will there be a religious service at the home of the bereaved?

There are no special customs or religious services at the home.

### Will food be served?

No.

### How soon after the funeral will a mourner usually return to a normal work schedule?

This is left entirely to the discretion of individual mourners since the Bible does not mandate specific periods for mourning. Probably within days of the funeral.

### How soon after the funeral will a mourner usually return to a normal social schedule?

Probably within days of the funeral.

### Are there rituals for observing the anniversary of the death?

No, since the Bible does not mandate such rituals.

## V · HOME CELEBRATIONS

Not applicable to Seventh-day Adventists.

# Chapter 20 Contents

# 20

# United Church of Canada

## I · HISTORY AND BELIEFS

The United Church of Canada was created by an Act of Parliament in 1925 as a union of the country's Presbyterian, Methodist and Congregational denominations. In Western Canada, in communities unable to afford the luxury of separate churches, a number of informal Union churches had already formed, applying pressure on parent denominations to amalgamate.

Although Presbyterians provided the initial push for the three-denomination Union, in the end they also offered its greatest opposition; approximately one-third of Presbyterian congregations voted not to unite. The Methodist and Congregational denominations entered the Church Union as a whole.

The United Church sees itself as having a mandate to work toward further unions. In 1968, it was joined by the Evangelical United Brethren. A proposed union with the Anglican Church of Canada, however, foundered in the 1970s.

Its worship and policies are, inevitably, a product of its founding traditions. From the Methodists, the United Church inherited a passion for social justice; from the Presbyterians, a conciliar system for internal governance; from the Congregationalists, a stubborn refusal to be bound by arbitrary doctrine or dogma.

The United Church has been at the forefront of social change in Canada. It was the first mainline denomination in the world to ordain women as ministers. It welcomed draft dodgers during the Vietnam War, lobbied against alcohol and tobacco, urged recognition of the Republic of China, endorsed women's right to choice of abortion and, most recently, ruled that homosexuality is not, in and of itself, a bar to ordination.

The national court of the United Church is the General Council, which meets every three years. Only the General Council speaks for the United Church. Between Councils, elected officials of the church or various committees or Divisions may interpret or comment on the Council's policies. Surprisingly, there are few doctrinal statements. The *Basis of Union* of 1925 contains *Twenty Articles of Faith*, developed as a statement of the common faith of the three founding denominations. The only *Statement of Faith* issued by the United Church itself came in 1940, with a teaching *Catechism* in 1942. In 1968, the General Council authorized a "New Creed" as an authentic expression of the United Church's faith. This "Creed" has since been revised twice, to eliminate exclusively masculine language, and to add concern for the natural environment.

The Congregationalist openness to diverse viewpoints means that ministers are required only to be in "essential agreement" with the *Twenty Articles*. As a result, the church's ministry encompasses a wide variety of theological viewpoints.

As a national denomination, the United Church has no branches or subsidiaries in any other country. It does have working partnerships with a number of other churches in other parts of the world. The United Church maintains membership in the world associations to which its predecessors belonged, such as the World Alliance of Reformed Churches.

**Canadian churches:** 3,872
**Canadian membership:** 720,000
*(data from* The United Church of Canada Yearbook *and the*
1998 Yearbook of American and Canadian Churches*)*

---

**For more information, contact:**
The United Church of Canada
3251 Bloor Street West
Toronto, ON  M8K 2Y4
(416) 231-5931

---

## II · THE BASIC SERVICE

United Church congregations gather to worship God, to explore God's will and to celebrate the sacraments together. The United Church normally meets for worship Sunday mornings, although some congregations have experimented with midweek services, especially during holiday seasons. The traditional time was 11:00 A.M.; increasingly, services are moving to 10:00 or 10:30 A.M. Most services last about an hour. Children are welcome. Sunday school is commonly held at the same time as the worship service, with the children leaving partway through the service.

## APPROPRIATE ATTIRE

**Men:** Depends on local culture more than on religious standards. The further west, the more casual the standards; the further east and/or the bigger the church, the more formal. There are no requirements. Common sense and reasonably good taste are usually sufficient guidelines.

**Women:** Depends on local culture more than on religious standards. The further west, the more casual the standards; the further east and/or the bigger the church, the more formal. There are no requirements. Common sense and reasonably good taste are usually sufficient guidelines.

## THE SANCTUARY

### What are the major sections of the church?

- *The chancel*, at the front of the church, normally slightly raised. Worship is normally led by ministers, choir and lay members, from the chancel.
- *The nave*, where the people sit. Many churches have fixed pews; some have moveable seating.
- *The narthex or foyer*, usually the area just outside the sanctuary. Normally where people hang coats. In some buildings, also where refreshments are served after the service.
- *The Christian Education area*, rooms where the Sunday school and other groups meet.

## THE SERVICE

### When should guests arrive, and where should they sit?

Arrive at the time of the service, or earlier. Latecomers may have to sit near the front. If ushers do not guide visitors to a specific seat, visitors may take any vacant seat.

### If arriving late, are there times when a guest should *not* enter the service?

Yes. Ushers will seat you when it is appropriate.

### Are there times when a guest should *not* leave the service?

No.

### Who are the major officiants, leaders or participants and what do they do?

- *The worship leader*, who is usually a professional minister, male or female, presides, preaches and celebrates communion.

- *Lay members,* who may lead prayers, read the Bible or speak.
- *The choir, choir director and/or organist,* who provide leadership in music.

## What are the major ritual objects of the service?

- *The cross,* mounted on a wall and/or placed on the communion table.
- *The Christ candle* (usually one, sometimes several), lit at the beginning of the service.
- *The Bible,* sometimes carried in, commonly opened at the beginning of the service.
- *The communion table.*
- *Bread and wine,* for communion services. Practices for distribution vary. In some congregations members come forward to the chancel; others serve members in their seats. Some provide whole bread, and have members break off chunks; others provide pre-cut cubes or balls of bread. Most use small individual cups to serve wine (usually grape juice), for hygienic reasons; those that use a common cup may encourage "intinction," dipping the bread into the wine.

## What books are used?

Most congregations use *Voices United,* the United Church's hymnbook (Etobicoke, Ont.: The United Church Publishing House, 1996). Many, however, continue to use *The Hymn Book* (red) published 1971, and some use the *The Hymnary* (blue or black) published 1930. Most congregations also use *Songs for a Gospel People* (Winfield, B.C.: Wood Lake Books Inc., 1987), commonly referred to as "the green book," published as a supplement to the 1971 *Hymn Book.* Many congregations provide Bibles, in one of the modern translations. A few provide the Psalms, most often in the *Good News* translation.

## To indicate the order of the service:

Most congregations provide a printed program or bulletin, usually supplemented by announcements from the worship leader.

## GUEST BEHAVIOR DURING THE SERVICE

### Will a guest who is not a member of the United Church be expected to do anything other than sit?

Visitors are invited to participate along with the congregation in all aspects of a worship service. The United Church practices open communion, meaning that all who profess faith in Jesus Christ are welcome in the Service of the Word (ordinary worship) and at the Service of the Table (communion).

No one is excluded on the basis of denominational allegiance, age, race, color or for any reason other than personal choice.

**Are there any parts of the service in which a guest who is not a member of the United Church should *not* participate?**
No.

**If not disruptive to the service, is it okay to:**
- **Take pictures?** Possibly. But ask first.
- **Use a flash?** No, unless you have received permission.
- **Use a video camera?** Possibly. Ask first.
- **Use a tape recorder?** Probably.

**Will contributions to the church be collected at the service?**
Yes. Plates or baskets will be passed, usually after the sermon.

**How much is customary to contribute?**
Unless you're a child, you should consider $1 a minimum. Most visitors will contribute up to $10.

## AFTER THE SERVICE

**Is there usually a reception after the service?**
Many congregations do have some kind of reception after a service, usually in the narthex or an adjoining hall.

Food may or may not be available. There is normally coffee, sometimes tea or juices. You will not find alcoholic beverages. There is no obligation to take anything at a post-service reception. Visitors with dietary restrictions should simply avoid unsuitable foods and beverages.

Unless the reception is a sit-down meal for a special occasion, there will usually be no opening ritual or grace, or any formal closing. People will drift away when they have finished their conversations.

**Is there a traditional form of address for clergy whom a guest may meet?**
Formally, clergy should be addressed as "Mr.," "Mrs." or "Ms.," followed by their last name. It is impolite to refer to them simply as "Reverend." Informally, many prefer to be addressed by their first names.

**Is it okay to leave early?**
Yes.

## GENERAL GUIDELINES AND ADVICE

United Church congregations usually stand for hymns and sit for prayers.

There are no universal practices. Some have formal refrains or responses to readings; others do not. Some encourage congregations to clap; others discourage it.

The best guideline is simply to do as the people around you are doing. Pay particular attention to any instructions that are given for receiving communion.

## SPECIAL VOCABULARY

None. The United Church is probably the most colloquial denomination in Canada for its language and terminology. It places a greater emphasis than most other denominations on inclusive language, especially when referring to God—but even this varies widely from congregation to congregation, and from minister to minister.

## DOGMA AND IDEOLOGY

▪ The United Church is officially Trinitarian. That is, it believes in three primary manifestations of the divine: Father, Son and Holy Spirit. Some congregations and clergy prefer to formulate these as Creator, Sustainer and Nurturer (or some similar wording).

▪ Worship services typically move through a call to worship, confession of sins, assurance of pardon, two or more Bible readings, a sermon and the congregational response in prayers and offerings.

▪ As a general rule, the United Church is liberal in its theology. It emphasizes reason and scholarship along with piety. But individual congregations are highly diverse, ranging from conservative to radical.

**Some basic books to which a guest can refer to learn more about The United Church of Canada:**

*This United Church of Ours*, by Ralph Milton, 2nd ed. (Kelowna, B.C.: Wood Lake Books Inc., 1991).

*This Is Your Church*, by Steven Chambers (Etobicoke, Ont.: United Church Publishing House, various editions).

## III · HOLY DAYS AND FESTIVALS

▪ *Advent.* The four weeks preceding Christmas. A time of preparation for the coming of Christ. There are no particular religious observances, nor any traditional greetings.

▪ *Christmas.* December 25; includes Christmas Eve, December 24. Usually special services, similar in format to normal worship. Marks the birth of

Jesus, the revelation of God in human form (the "Incarnation"). Traditional greeting: "Merry Christmas."

- *Lent.* The seven weeks preceding Easter. Begins on Ash Wednesday. Traditionally a time for repentance and reflection. Abstinence and self-denial as a form of self-discipline are rarely practiced anymore. During the final week before Easter, called "Passion Week," there may be special services.
- *Good Friday.* Friday immediately preceding Easter. Services focus on the suffering of the crucifixion. The sanctuary is often stripped of its usual symbols. A few congregations celebrate Easter Vigil, Saturday night.
- *Easter.* The Sunday following the first full moon after the spring equinox. Celebrates the resurrection of Christ. Some congregations will have sunrise services. Traditional greeting: "Happy Easter!"
- *Christian Family Sunday.* Coincides with the secular Mother's Day in May.
- *Pentecost.* The seventh Sunday after Easter. Celebrates the coming of the Holy Spirit. Often considered the birthday of the Christian Church. No traditional greetings.
- *Thanksgiving.* Usually falls on the second Monday of October. Not to be confused with American Thanksgiving, which comes at the end of November. Many congregations celebrate Thanksgiving Sunday with lavishly decorated sanctuaries.

There are no restrictions on any person to participation in any of these services. The same guidelines for behavior apply as for ordinary worship services.

## IV · LIFE CYCLE EVENTS

### · *Birth Ceremony* ·

There is no celebration of birth as such, but many infants are baptized within months after birth.

Baptism initiates a person into the universal Christian church. It is a one-time event, recognized as valid in almost all mainline denominations. Persons may be baptized as adults, or as infants (when parents make the vows on the child's behalf). Adults seeking baptism, and parents seeking baptism for a child, normally attend one or more sessions of preparation and study.

Baptism is not an act of magic that protects a child from going to hell. The United Church teaches that God loves all children, baptized or not. Baptism is the affirmation by the person (or by the parents, on his/her behalf) to seek to live a Christian life, in the Christian community.

Some congregations include, as part of the baptismal ceremony, either or both of the following:

■ *Confirmation.* Historically the act of a bishop, confirming the actions of a parish priest who had done the actual baptism some time before. Now sometimes combined with baptism to confirm that this person is now a full member of the universal Christian church.

■ *Reaffirmation of faith.* A continuation of the baptismal ceremony in which members of the Christian church (that is, anyone who has already been baptized) are invited to renew their baptismal vows. Rarely, the symbolism of water in baptism is repeated by sprinkling the congregation with drops of water (called *aspersion*).

## BEFORE THE CEREMONY

### Are guests usually invited by a formal invitation?
The family may invite special guests, but the baptism normally takes place during a regular worship service, at which anyone is welcome.

### If not stated explicitly, should one assume that children are invited?
Yes.

### If one can't attend, what should one do?
Reply, expressing regrets. Telephone to offer good wishes. Send flowers or a gift to the home.

## APPROPRIATE ATTIRE

**Men:** Depends on local culture more than on religious standards. The further west, the more casual the standards; the further east and/or the bigger the church, the more formal. There are no requirements. Common sense and reasonably good taste are usually sufficient guidelines.

If you have been specifically invited to a baptismal celebration, greater formality may be expected.

**Women:** Depends on local culture more than on religious standards. The further west, the more casual the standards; the further east and/or the bigger the church, the more formal. There are no requirements. Common sense and reasonably good taste are usually sufficient guidelines.

If you have been specifically invited to a baptismal celebration, greater formality may be expected.

## GIFTS

### Is a gift customarily expected?

Only if you have been formally invited by the family. For infant baptism, gifts should be comparable to those you would give at a baby shower.

### Should gifts be brought to the ceremony?

Gifts should be brought to the reception or the home, not to the service.

## THE CEREMONY

### Where will the ceremony take place?

In the United Church of Canada, baptism is seen as initiation into a specific community of faith, a congregation. Therefore, baptism almost always takes place with a congregation present, during a regular worship service, in the home church of the parents (sometimes of the grandparents). It is performed privately only in exceptional circumstances.

The service as a whole will take slightly over one hour; the baptismal portion will probably take about ten minutes.

### When should guests arrive and where should they sit?

Invited guests should arrive early, not at the last minute, and will probably gather as a group before the service. Family and friends will be seated in a special block of reserved seats. Others may sit wherever they choose.

### If arriving late, are there times when a guest should *not* enter the service?

Yes. Ushers will seat you when it is appropriate.

### Are there times when a guest should *not* leave the service?

The baptismal party (family, friends and invited guests) is expected to be present for the whole service. Some congregations give opportunity for parents and infants (especially crying infants) to leave after the baptism itself, but it is considered discourteous for the whole baptismal party to leave.

### Who are the major officiants, leaders or participants at the ceremony and what do they do?

- *The minister(s)*, who will baptize the child or adult seeking baptism. A favorite minister from another congregation may be invited to take part in the ceremony, if the participants wish.
- *The person being baptized* (and his or her parents, if a child), who is the central participant. Baptism is not something done *to* this person, but something this person does as an affirmation of faith in the Triune God.

The United Church does not formally recognize *godparents*, but if parents wish to have godparents, they may be invited to come forward to stand with the parents during the baptism.

## What books are used?

*Voices United,* the United Church's hymnbook (Etobicoke, Ont.: The United Church Publishing House, 1996). Most congregations also use *Songs for a Gospel People* (Winfield, B.C.: Wood Lake Books Inc., 1987), commonly referred to as "the green book." Many congregations provide Bibles, in one of the modern translations. A few provide the Psalms, most often in the *Good News* translation.

## To indicate the order of the ceremony:

Most congregations provide a printed program or bulletin, usually supplemented by announcements from the worship leader.

## Will a guest who is not a member of the United Church be expected to do anything other than sit?

Visitors are invited to participate along with the congregation in all aspects of a baptismal service that do not violate their own personal beliefs.

No one is excluded on the basis of denominational allegiance, age, race, color or for any reason other than personal choice.

## Are there any parts of the ceremony in which a guest who is not a member of the United Church should *not* participate?

No.

## If not disruptive to the service, is it okay to:

- **Take pictures?** Possibly. But ask first.
- **Use a flash?** No, unless you have received permission.
- **Use a video camera?** Possibly. Ask first.
- **Use a tape recorder?** Probably.

## Will contributions to the church be collected at the ceremony?

Yes. Plates or baskets will be passed, usually after the sermon.

## How much is customary to contribute?

Unless you're a child, you should consider $1 a minimum. Most visitors will contribute up to $10.

## AFTER THE CEREMONY

## Is there usually a reception after the ceremony?

If there is a formal reception after a baptismal service, it will probably be held at the parents' or grandparents' home. If it is held at the church, it will probably be informal, open to all.

**Would it be considered impolite to neither eat nor drink?**
At the church, no.

**Is there a grace or benediction before eating or drinking?**
At a private reception, maybe. At the church, after the service, probably not.

**Is there a grace or benediction after eating or drinking?**
No.

**Is there a traditional greeting for the family?**
No.

**Is there a traditional form of address for clergy who may be at the reception?**
Formally, clergy should be addressed as "Mr.," "Mrs." or "Ms.," followed by their last name. It is impolite to refer to them simply as "Reverend." Informally, many prefer to be addressed by their first names.

**Is it okay to leave early?**
Yes.

## · Initiation Ceremony ·

Some United Church congregations continue to use Confirmation as a ceremony in which young people officially become members of the church. The candidates affirm for themselves the Christian faith and church into which they were baptized, usually as infants.

Other congregations combine Confirmation with Baptism and have, instead, a Service of Reaffirmation of Baptismal Faith for young people wishing to affirm their baptismal vows as their own.

Either ceremony takes about 10 minutes, as part of a regular worship service, which lasts about an hour.

### BEFORE THE CEREMONY

**Are guests usually invited by a formal invitation?**
The family may invite special guests, but the ceremony normally takes place during a regular worship service, at which anyone is welcome.

**If not stated explicitly, should one assume that children are invited?**
Yes.

**If one can't attend, what should one do?**
Reply, expressing regrets.

## APPROPRIATE ATTIRE

**Men:** Depends on local culture more than on religious standards. The further west, the more casual the standards; the further east and/or the bigger the church, the more formal. There are no requirements. Common sense and reasonably good taste are usually sufficient guidelines.

If you have been specifically invited by the family, greater formality may be expected.

**Women:** Depends on local culture more than on religious standards. The further west, the more casual the standards; the further east and/or the bigger the church, the more formal. There are no requirements. Common sense and reasonably good taste are usually sufficient guidelines.

If you have been specifically invited by the family, greater formality may be expected.

## GIFTS

**Is a gift customarily expected?**
No.

**Should gifts be brought to the ceremony?**
No.

## THE CEREMONY

**Where will the ceremony take place?**
At the front of the main sanctuary of the church.

**When should guests arrive and where should they sit?**
Invited guests should arrive early, not at the last minute. Ushers may indicate where to sit. The candidates themselves will probably sit in a block of reserved seats. Otherwise, there are no restrictions on where to sit.

**If arriving late, are there times when a guest should *not* enter the ceremony?**
Yes. Ushers will seat you when it is appropriate.

**Are there times when a guest should *not* leave the ceremony?**
No.

**Who are the major officiants, leaders or participants at the ceremony and what do they do?**
- *The minister(s),* who will preside at the ceremony.
- *The candidates,* who are the central participants.

◘ *Lay persons or mentors,* who may participate in laying on of hands.

## What books are used?

*Voices United,* the United Church's hymnbook (Etobicoke, Ont.: The United Church Publishing House, 1996). Most congregations also use *Songs for a Gospel People* (Winfield, B.C.: Wood Lake Books Inc., 1987), commonly referred to as "the green book." Many congregations provide Bibles, in one of the modern translations. A few provide the Psalms, most often in the *Good News* translation.

## To indicate the order of the ceremony:

Most congregations provide a printed program or bulletin, usually supplemented by announcements from the worship leader.

## Will a guest who is not a member of the United Church be expected to do anything other than sit?

Visitors are invited to participate along with the congregation in all aspects of the service that do not violate their own personal beliefs.

No one is excluded on the basis of denominational allegiance, age, race, color or for any reason other than personal choice.

## Are there any parts of the ceremony in which a guest who is not a member of the United Church should *not* participate?

No.

## If not disruptive to the service, is it okay to:
◘ **Take pictures?** Possibly. But ask first.
◘ **Use a flash?** No, unless you have received permission.
◘ **Use a video camera?** Possibly. Ask first.
◘ **Use a tape recorder?** Probably.

## Will contributions to the church be collected at the ceremony?

Yes. Plates or baskets will be passed, usually after the sermon.

## How much is customary to contribute?

Unless you're a child, you should consider $1 a minimum. Most visitors will contribute up to $10.

### AFTER THE CEREMONY

## Is there usually a reception after the ceremony?

Rarely, other than the usual gathering for coffee, tea, etc.

## Would it be considered impolite to neither eat nor drink?

No.

**Is there a grace or benediction before eating or drinking?**
No.

**Is there a grace or benediction after eating or drinking?**
No.

**Is there a traditional greeting for the family?**
No.

**Is there a traditional form of address for clergy who may be at the reception?**
Formally, clergy should be addressed as "Mr.," "Mrs." or "Ms.," followed by their last name. It is impolite to refer to them simply as "Reverend." Informally, many prefer to be addressed by their first names.

**Is it okay to leave early?**
Yes.

## · *Marriage Ceremony* ·

Marriage is the formal ceremony in which a couple make lifetime vows of commitment to each other, in the presence of God and of their families and friends. The ceremony is rarely combined with a regular worship service. It is both a civil and a religious ceremony, and may last anywhere from 15 minutes to an hour, depending on the number of musical numbers performed, the length of the minister's address to the couple and the time required for signing the official register.

### BEFORE THE CEREMONY

**Are guests usually invited by a formal invitation?**
Yes. Anyone may attend the religious ceremony of marriage, without requiring an invitation. But an invitation is required for the reception that follows the wedding ceremony.

**If not stated explicitly, should one assume children are invited?**
No.

**If one cannot attend, what should one do?**
Reply with regrets, and send a gift.

### APPROPRIATE ATTIRE

**Men:** Generally, a suit or jacket and tie.

**Women:** A dress or pants suit. Clothing and jewelry should be relatively modest.

Dress for both men and women depends more on the local culture than on religious standards. The more elaborate the wedding ceremony, the more formal attire should be. There are no religious rules applicable to attire at wedding ceremonies.

## GIFTS

### Is a gift ordinarily expected?

Yes, if you have received a formal invitation. If you are simply attending a public ceremony, a gift would be appreciated, but is not necessary. Items suitable for helping the couple set up their home—small appliances, bedding, sheets, towels and other household gifts—are appropriate.

### Should gifts be brought to the ceremony?

No. Gifts should be sent to the home of the newlyweds.

## THE CEREMONY

### Where will the ceremony take place?

Normally, in the sanctuary, the place of worship. However, United Church clergy have shown themselves remarkably adaptable, and may be willing to perform the ceremony outside the church—for example, in a garden or on a beach.

If the ceremony is held in a church, the actual ceremony will take place in front of the congregation, immediately before the chancel.

### When should guests arrive and where should they sit?

Arrive early. In most weddings, ushers will show guests where to sit. It is still traditional, in many places, to have friends of the groom sit on one side of the sanctuary, and friends of the bride on the other side.

### If arriving late, are there times when a guest should *not* enter the ceremony?

Ushers will assist latecomers.

### Are there times when a guest should *not* leave the ceremony?

It is considered poor taste to leave before the ceremony is completed.

### Who are the major officiants, leaders or participants at the ceremony and what do they do?

- *The minister(s)*, who leads the service.
- *The couple*, who exchange vows.
- *The wedding party*, who provide support and witness the vows.

### What books are used?

Most likely the congregation's normal hymnbook(s). Often the hymns and other responses are printed out in a special program or bulletin.

**To indicate the order of the ceremony:**
Usually a printed program or bulletin will be provided, supplemented by announcements from the minister.

**Will a guest who is not a member of the United Church be expected to do anything other than sit?**
Guests are invited to participate in all aspects of a marriage ceremony that do not violate their own personal beliefs.

**If not disruptive to the service, is it okay to:**
◘ **Take pictures?** Possibly. But ask first.
◘ **Use a flash?** No, unless you have received permission.
◘ **Use a video camera?** Possibly. Ask first.
◘ **Use a tape recorder?** Probably.

**Will contributions to the church be collected at the ceremony?**
No.

## AFTER THE CEREMONY

**Is there usually a reception after the ceremony?**
Yes. Sometimes it is held in a hall or room adjacent to the church sanctuary. More commonly, it is catered in an entirely separate location. Food and beverages may be served; there may be dancing or other activities. Alcoholic beverages may be served, if the reception is not on church premises. The reception may last anywhere from an hour to most of a night.

**Would it be considered impolite to neither eat nor drink?**
No. Guests should feel free to apply their own dietary standards.

**Is there a grace or benediction before eating or drinking?**
Sometimes. It depends on the family's preferences.

**Is there a grace or benediction after eating or drinking?**
No.

**Is there a traditional greeting for the family?**
No.

**Is there a traditional form of address for clergy who may be at the reception?**
Formally, clergy should be addressed as "Mr.," "Mrs." or "Ms.," followed by their last name. It is impolite to refer to them simply as "Reverend." Informally, many prefer to be addressed by their first names.

**Is it okay to leave early?**

Yes, but it's usually expected that you will stay until at least the toasts have been made and the wedding cake served.

## · Funerals and Mourning ·

In the United Church of Canada, traditional funerals are often replaced by memorial services, which celebrate the life and faith of the departed person. Funerals, with a casket present, are increasingly rare. If a casket is present, it will more often be closed than open.

More and more, United Church members choose cremation rather than burial.

Beliefs about life after death vary widely across the United Church of Canada. Some believe that after death they will be reunited with their loved ones. Others may believe that this life is all we have, and that death is final.

Officially, the United Church of Canada teaches that the resurrection of Jesus is symbolic of the resurrection that is possible for all who believe in him.

### BEFORE THE CEREMONY

**How soon after the death will the funeral usually take place?**

Between a few days and a week. There are no religious requirements to have a funeral immediately. A memorial service may be held several weeks after a death, to allow time for mourners to gather from across the country.

**What should someone who is not a member of the United Church do upon hearing of the death of a member of that church?**

Telephone or visit the bereaved to offer sympathy. In some parts of the country, visits are made directly to the family's home. In others, visits are made at specified times to the funeral parlor. Check the obituary notice; if it makes no reference to visiting times at a funeral parlor, then visits may be made at any (reasonable) time in the home.

### APPROPRIATE ATTIRE

Funerals call for more formality in dress than almost any other religious occasion in the United Church of Canada.

**Men:** Mainly suit and tie, dark colors preferred. In more casual cultures, slacks and sweaters may be acceptable.

**Women:** Dresses, dark colors, plain fabrics. Pants suits may be permissible, again, in darker colors. Arms and heads may be uncovered. Subdued jewelry is permissible.

## GIFTS

### Is it appropriate to send flowers or to make a contribution?

Check the obituary notice to see if the family wants to have donations made to a charity or cause in lieu of flowers.

If they accept flowers, the flowers should usually go to the church or funeral parlor rather than to the family home.

If donations are preferred, send them directly to the chosen charity, marked "In Memory of [name]." Some charities send notification of such gifts to the bereaved family; some don't. If you want the bereaved to know that you've made a donation, include a note providing their address so the charity will know where to send a notification.

### Is it appropriate to send food?

Yes. Send or take it to the home of the bereaved.

## THE CEREMONY

### Where will the ceremony take place?

In a church or in a funeral parlor.

### When should guests arrive and where should they sit?

Arrive early. Family and friends will be seated in a special block of reserved seats. Ushers will advise where to sit. If there are no ushers, guests may sit wherever they choose.

### If arriving late, are there times when a guest should *not* enter the service?

Yes. Ushers will seat you when it is appropriate.

### Will the bereaved family be present at the church or funeral home before the ceremony?

Possibly.

### Is there a traditional greeting for the family?

No. Express sympathy. If time permits, invite the bereaved to talk about their feelings, and how they're coping with their loss. Share your favorite memories of the deceased person. Funny memories are just as acceptable as sorrowful ones.

Avoid preaching. Don't offer pat answers about the meaning of life or about God's promises of eternal life. Don't suggest that this is all God's will and will work out for the best in the end.

### Will there be an open casket?
In the United Church, less and less often.

### Is a guest expected to view the body?
This is optional, but if it is a memorial service, there will be no body to view.

### What is appropriate behavior upon viewing the body?
Silence, or silent prayer.

### Who are the major officiants at the ceremony and what do they do?
◼ *The minister(s)*, who will lead the service.

### What books are used?
*Voices United*, the United Church's hymnbook (Etobicoke, Ont.: The United Church Publishing House, 1996). Most congregations also use *Songs for a Gospel People* (Winfield, B.C.: Wood Lake Books Inc., 1987), commonly referred to as "the green book." Many congregations provide Bibles, in one of the modern translations. A few provide the Psalms, most often in the *Good News* translation.

### To indicate the order of the ceremony:
There will be a printed program or bulletin, and the minister will make announcements or give instructions.

### Will a guest who is not a member of the United Church be expected to do anything other than sit?
Visitors are invited to participate along with the congregation in all aspects of a funeral or memorial service that do not violate their own personal beliefs.

### Are there any parts of the ceremony in which a guest who is not a member of the United Church should *not* participate?
No.

### If not disruptive to the service, is it okay to:
◼ **Take pictures?** No, unless you have received prior permission.
◼ **Use a flash?** No, unless you have received permission.
◼ **Use a video camera?** No, unless you have received prior permission.
◼ **Use a tape recorder?** Possibly, but ask first.

**Will contributions to the church be collected at the ceremony?**
No.

## THE INTERMENT

With the increasing trend to cremation and memorial services, there may not be an interment. If there is, it may take place months later, as a private ceremony for the immediate family.

**Should guests attend the interment?**
This is optional. If it immediately follows a funeral service, probably yes. After a memorial service, no.

**Whom should one ask for directions?**
The funeral director.

**What happens at the graveside?**
If there is a formal interment or burial, of the casket or of ashes, you are simply expected to be present and to participate in the ceremony as you are able. The minister or presider will offer prayers. If responses are expected, they will either be familiar or will be printed in a program or bulletin. The casket or ashes will be lowered into the ground or placed in a vault. Guests may be invited to assist in sprinkling earth or sand; you are not obliged to participate if you do not wish to.

The rites of a fraternal order or of the military may be part of a graveside service.

**Do guests who are not members of the United Church participate at the graveside ceremony?**
Guests are invited to participate along with the congregation in all aspects of an interment or burial that do not violate their own personal beliefs.

## COMFORTING THE BEREAVED

**Is it appropriate to visit the home of the bereaved after the funeral?**
Yes. At any mutually convenient time, and as often as you feel appropriate. Too often, families are expected to return to normal right after the ceremony. Grieving takes a lot longer than that. Visiting allows people to talk about their experience, turning painful memories into memories of painful memories.

How long you stay depends on your closeness to the bereaved. An average visit might be 15 to 30 minutes.

**Will there be a religious service at the home of the bereaved?**
No.

**Will food be served?**
Often, refreshments or a light meal will be served at a reception immediately following the memorial, funeral or interment service.

**How soon after the funeral will a mourner usually return to a normal work schedule?**
Depends on the person and the situation. There are no customs requiring a certain period of isolation, or a certain number of days off work. Most mourners will return to work within a week.

**How soon after the funeral will a mourner usually return to a normal social schedule?**
Depends on the person and the situation. Remember that grieving is a process. It can't, and shouldn't, be hurried.

**Are there mourning customs to which a friend who is not a member of the United Church should be sensitive?**
No.

**Are there rituals for observing the anniversary of the death?**
No.

## V · HOME CELEBRATIONS

Not applicable to the United Church of Canada.

# Chapter 21 Contents

# 21
# United Church of Christ

## I · HISTORY AND BELIEFS

Formed in 1957 by the merger of two churches, the United Church of Christ is one of the newer Protestant denominations in the United States.

The merger was between the Congregational Christian Churches, whose roots date back to 16th century England and to the Puritan and Separatist movements that settled New England; and the Evangelical and Reform Church, which had previously been formed by combining the German Reformed Church and the Evangelical Synod of North America.

According to the constitution of the United Church of Christ, Jesus Christ is the "sole Head" of the Church and each local congregation is its "basic unit." Local churches choose their own pastors and determine policy regarding membership, worship, budget and programs. Congregations cooperate in area groupings called "associations" and in larger regional bodies called "conferences." The General Synod, the Church's central deliberative body, meets biennially to conduct denominational business. More than half the Church's membership is in the New England and Midwestern states.

**U.S. churches:** 6,110
**U.S. membership:** 1.5 million
*(data from the 1998 Yearbook of American and Canadian Churches)*

**For more information, contact:**
The United Church of Christ
700 Prospect Avenue
Cleveland, OH 44115
(216) 736-2100
langa@ucc.org
www.apk.net/ucc/

## II · THE BASIC SERVICE

The primary components of the Sunday morning service are a "call to worship," which is usually read responsively by the minister and congregants; the reading of Scriptures; a sermon, which may last about 20 minutes and, in some ways, is the centerpiece of the service; prayers, including the Lord's Prayer, some of which are said by the congregation and some by the minister on behalf of the congregation; and a closing benediction, or a "sending forth," said by the minister. The service usually lasts about one hour.

### APPROPRIATE ATTIRE

**Men:** A jacket and tie would never be out of place, although many congregations welcome more casual attire. No head covering is required.

**Women:** A dress or a skirt and blouse or a pants suit, although many congregations welcome casual attire. Clothing need not cover the arms and hems need not reach below the knees. Open-toed shoes and modest jewelry are permissible. No head covering is required.

There are no rules regarding colors of clothing.

### THE SANCTUARY

**What are the major sections of the church?**
- *The foyer or narthex:* Where worshippers are greeted and receive a church bulletin.
- *The pews:* Where congregants and guests sit.
- *The chancel:* A raised section at the front of the sanctuary for an altar, pulpit and lectern and where ministers and other worship leaders sit.
- *The choir loft:* Where the choir or other musicians sit. Depending on the architecture of the church, this may be to one (or both) side(s) of the chancel or in a balcony at the rear of the sanctuary.

### THE SERVICE

**When should guests arrive and where should they sit?**
Arrive about five minutes before the scheduled start of the service. In many churches, ushers will advise guests where to sit.

**If arriving late, are there times when a guest should *not* enter the service?**
Do not enter while prayers are being recited, during the reading of Scriptures or during the sermon.

**Are there times when a guest should *not* leave the service?**

Do not leave while prayers are being recited, during the reading of Scriptures or during the sermon.

**Who are the major officiants, leaders or participants and what do they do?**

- *The minister(s) or pastor(s)*, the primary leader of the service. He or she preaches a sermon and presides over the communion and baptism.
- *Lector(s) or reader(s)*, who read the Scriptures aloud to the congregants.
- *Ushers*, who greet worshippers in most churches and distribute church bulletins and offering plates. In some churches, they also seat worshippers and guests.
- *Lay leaders*, who may greet congregants and guests, make announcements about church activities and lead prayers.
- *Deacons*, who help serve communion in some churches.

**What are the major ritual objects of the service?**

- *A Bible*, which is on the altar or pulpit and which worship leaders read during the service.
- *A cross*, which is usually displayed on the altar and reminds worshippers of the suffering, death and resurrection of Christ.
- *Candles*, which remind worshippers of God's illuminating presence.
- *Bread and wine or grape juice*, which are served to worshippers during communion. Most United Church of Christ congregations believe that Christ is spiritually present at communion. Unlike certain other Christian churches, they do not believe that the bread and wine or grape juice are transubstantiated into the actual body and blood of Christ.
- *The baptismal font*, which contains water used during services that include baptisms.

**What books are used?**

The most commonly used of several Protestant Bibles is The Holy Bible, New Revised Standard Version (New York: National Council of Churches, 1989). Also used is *The New Century Hymnal* (Cleveland, Ohio: The Pilgrim Press, 1995).

**To indicate the order of the service:**

A program will be distributed and the minister will make periodic announcements.

## GUEST BEHAVIOR DURING THE SERVICE

**Will a guest who is not a member of the United Church of Christ be expected to do anything other than sit?**

Guests are expected to join congregants when they stand during the service. It is entirely optional for them to read prayers aloud and sing with the congregation. In most United Church of Christ congregations, congregants do not kneel. In those churches where kneeling occurs, it is optional for guests to join in. Those guests who do not kneel should remain seated.

**Are there any parts of the service in which a guest who is not a member of the United Church of Christ should *not* participate?**
No, except that local practices regarding the sacrament of communion vary. In most congregations, communion is open to all who wish to receive it; in some, it is preferred that only baptized Christians and/or only adults receive it. If you wish to know the practice of a local congregation on this or any other matter, ask the local minister in advance.

**If not disruptive to the service, is it okay to:**
◘ **Take pictures?** No.
◘ **Use a flash?** No.
◘ **Use a video camera?** No.
◘ **Use a tape recorder?** No.

**Will contributions to the church be collected at the service?**
Yes. Ushers pass offering plates through the congregation during the service.

**How much is customary to contribute?**
It is entirely optional for guests to contribute. If they choose to do so, contributions between $1 and $10 are appropriate.

## AFTER THE SERVICE

**Is there usually a reception after the service?**
Yes. Some churches serve no food during the reception; some serve such light foods as coffee, tea, juice and pastry; some serve a complete lunch. The reception may last 30 to 60 minutes.

**Is there a traditional form of address for clergy who may be at the reception?**
Some are addressed as "Pastor." Some prefer to be addressed as "Mr." or "Ms." or, if the church bulletin distributed at services so indicates, as "Dr." Many United Church of Christ clergy prefer being addressed by their first name.

**Is it okay to leave early?**
If necessary.

## GENERAL GUIDELINES AND ADVICE

Take your cues from those around you. Do not remain standing when congregants have re-seated themselves. In many congregations, "amen" is not said or sung at the conclusion of each hymn or prayer.

## SPECIAL VOCABULARY

### Key words or phrases which might be helpful for a visitor to know:

- *"And also with you."* The proper response if someone says, "The peace of God be with you."
- *"That they may all be one."* This quote from the Gospel according to John (17:21) appears in the logo of the United Church of Christ. It is part of Jesus' prayer for unity among those who believe in Him.

## DOGMA AND IDEOLOGY

### Members of the United Church of Christ believe:

- In the trinitarian concept of the Divinity. This consists of God the Father, God the Son (Jesus) and God the Holy Spirit.
- Each person who believes and trusts in Jesus, who is the "head" of the church, has their sins forgiven, is endowed with "courage in the struggle for justice and peace," and is granted "eternal life in Your realm which has no end."

### Some basic books to which a guest can refer to learn more about the United Church of Christ:

*We Believe*, by Roger L. Shinn and Daniel Day Williams (Philadelphia: United Church Press, 1966).

*A History of the Evangelical and Reform Church*, by David Dunn and Lowell H. Zuck (New York and Cleveland, Ohio: The Pilgrim Press, 1990).

## III · HOLY DAYS AND FESTIVALS

- *Advent*. Occurs four weeks before Christmas. The purpose is to begin preparing for Christmas and to focus on Christ. There is no traditional greeting for this holiday.
- *Christmas*. Occurs on the evening of Dec. 24 and the day of Dec. 25. Marks the birth of Jesus and the incarnation of God as a human.
- *Lent*. Begins on Ash Wednesday, which occurs six weeks before Easter. The purpose is to prepare for Easter. There is no traditional greeting for Lent. Between Lent and Easter, abstention from entertainment is

encouraged, as is increased giving to the poor. Often, there are mid-week worship services. Few members of the United Church of Christ engage in a moderate fast (abstaining from certain foods) during Lent.

■ *Easter*. Always the Sunday following the first full moon on or after March 21. Celebrates the Resurrection of Jesus Christ. In worship services, the pastor may greet congregants with, "Christ is risen!" Congregants respond with "Christ [or "He"] is risen, indeed!"

■ *Pentecost Sunday*. The seventh Sunday after Easter. Celebrates the coming of the Holy Spirit, which is the empowering spirit of God in human life. This is often considered the birth of the Christian church. There is no traditional greeting for this holiday.

## IV · LIFE CYCLE EVENTS

### · *Birth Ceremony* ·

The baptism or "dedication" service is the same for males and females. Baptism celebrates the birth of a person into the church, and can occur anytime from birth onward through adulthood. The ceremony is usually integrated into a regular church service and may last about 15 minutes. In the United Church of Christ, baptism is administered only once. Baptism initiates an individual into the Church and is the sign and seal of God's grace upon that person through the power of the Holy Spirit. During the ceremony, the pastor pours or sprinkles water over the candidate's head or dips or immerses him or her in water. Another method of baptism is "immersion," in which the person being baptized is lowered into the water and raised up again.

Baptism is almost always part of a larger Sunday morning service. The baptism itself may last about 15 minutes, while the entire service may last about one hour.

#### BEFORE THE CEREMONY

**Are guests usually invited by a formal invitation?**
Invitations are usually oral.

**If not stated explicitly, should one assume that children are invited?**
Yes.

**If one can't attend, what should one do?**
RSVP with regrets. While appreciated, gifts are not expected.

## APPROPRIATE ATTIRE

**Men:** A jacket and tie would never be out of place, although many congregations accept more casual attire. No head covering is required.

**Women:** A dress or a skirt and blouse or a pants suit. Many congregations welcome casual attire. Clothing need not cover the arms and hems need not reach below the knees. Open-toed shoes and modest jewelry are permissible. No head covering is required.

There are no rules regarding colors of clothing.

## GIFTS

**Is a gift customarily expected?**
While not inappropriate, gifts are not expected. Should one decide to give a gift, such items as clothing or toys are appropriate for an infant being baptized and books are appropriate for adults being baptized.

**Should gifts be brought to the ceremony?**
No, they should be sent to the home of the person being baptized.

## THE CEREMONY

**Where will the ceremony take place?**
Almost always in the church's main sanctuary. Only occasionally does a baptism occur at the parents' home or outdoors.

**When should guests arrive and where should they sit?**
Arrive about ten minutes before the scheduled start of the service. In many churches, ushers will advise guests where to sit.

**If arriving late, are there times when a guest should *not* enter the ceremony?**
Do not enter while prayers are being recited, during the reading of Scriptures or during the sermon.

**Are there times when a guest should *not* leave the ceremony?**
Do not leave while prayers are being recited, during the reading of Scriptures or during the sermon.

**Who are the major officiants, leaders or participants at the ceremony and what do they do?**
- *The minister(s) or pastor(s)*, the primary leader of the service; presides over the baptism.
- *The person being baptized.*

- *The parents* (in the case of a child), who present the child and pledge to raise him or her in Christ's faith.
- *The sponsor(s) or godparents*, who may accompany the child to the baptismal font and pledge to offer special support for him or her.
- *The congregation*, which welcomes the person being baptized into the community of faith.

**What books are used?**

The most commonly used of several Protestant Bibles is The Holy Bible, New Revised Standard Version (New York: National Council of Churches, 1989). Also used is *The New Century Hymnal* Cleveland, Ohio: The Pilgrim Press, 1995).

**To indicate the order of the ceremony:**

A program will be distributed and the minister will make periodic announcements.

**Will a guest who is not a member of the United Church of Christ be expected to do anything other than sit?**

Upon request of the family of the person being baptized, a guest may be asked to stand at the front of the sanctuary as a sponsor, a family member or a friend. If so, consult the family or the pastor for instructions.

Ordinarily, guests are expected to join congregants when they stand during the service. It is entirely optional for them to read prayers aloud and sing with the congregation. In most United Church of Christ congregations, congregants do not kneel. In those churches where kneeling occurs, it is optional for guests to join in. Those guests who do not kneel should remain seated.

**Are there any parts of the ceremony in which a guest who is not a member of the United Church of Christ should *not* participate?**

No.

**If not disruptive to the ceremony, is it okay to:**

- **Take pictures?** Practice varies. Ask the pastor in advance.
- **Use a flash?** Practice varies. Ask the pastor in advance.
- **Use a video camera?** Practice varies. Ask the pastor in advance.
- **Use a tape recorder?** Practice varies. Ask the pastor in advance.

**Will contributions to the church be collected at the ceremony?**

Yes. Ushers pass offering plates through the congregation during the service.

**How much is customary to contribute?**

It is entirely optional for guests to contribute. If they choose to do so, contributions between $1 and $10 are appropriate.

## AFTER THE CEREMONY

### Is there usually a reception after the ceremony?

Sometimes there is a reception. If so, it may be at the home of the person being baptized or in the same building as the baptismal ceremony. There may be a reception line and light food such as coffee, tea, punch and pastries may be served. Sometimes, a full meal is served. If the reception is not in the church, there may be alcoholic beverages and/or music and dancing.

If at the church, the reception may last 30 to 60 minutes. If at home or elsewhere, it may last two hours or more.

### Would it be considered impolite to neither eat nor drink?

No.

### Is there a grace or benediction before eating or drinking?

Grace will be said only if a full meal is served.

### Is there a grace or benediction after eating or drinking?

No.

### Is there a traditional greeting for the family?

Just offer your congratulations.

### Is there a traditional form of address for clergy who may be at the reception?

Some are addressed as "Pastor." Some prefer to be addressed as "Mr." or "Ms." or, if the church bulletin distributed at services so indicates, as "Dr." Many United Church of Christ clergy prefer being addressed by their first name.

### Is it okay to leave early?

Yes.

## · Initiation Ceremony ·

Confirmation is celebrated for teenagers who had been baptized as infants. It offers one who was baptized as an infant the opportunity to publicly assent to the baptismal promises and celebrates the affirmation of baptism in the life of the individual. One is usually confirmed with other teens who had been in the same confirmation class.

The confirmation is usually part of the regular Sunday worship service. It may last about 15 minutes, although the entire service may last about an hour.

## BEFORE THE CEREMONY

**Are guests usually invited by a formal invitation?**
Invitations are usually issued orally.

**If not stated explicitly, should one assume that children are invited?**
Yes.

**If one can't attend, what should one do?**
RSVP with regrets. While appreciated, gifts are not expected.

## APPROPRIATE ATTIRE

**Men:** A jacket and tie would never be out of place, although many congregations accept more casual attire. No head covering is required.

**Women:** A dress or a skirt and blouse or a pants suit. Many congregations welcome casual attire. Clothing need not cover the arms and hems need not reach below the knees. Open-toed shoes and modest jewelry are permissible. No head covering is required.

There are no rules regarding colors of clothing.

## GIFTS

**Is a gift customarily expected?**
While not inappropriate, gifts are not expected. Should one decide to give a gift, appropriate items are a Bible or a book (either fiction or non-fiction).

**Should gifts be brought to the ceremony?**
Either bring or send gifts to the home of the confirmand.

## THE CEREMONY

**Where will the ceremony take place?**
In the church's main sanctuary.

**When should guests arrive and where should they sit?**
Arrive about ten minutes before the scheduled start of the service. In many churches, ushers will advise guests where to sit.

**If arriving late, are there times when a guest should *not* enter the ceremony?**
Do not enter while prayers are being recited, during the reading of Scriptures or during the sermon.

**Are there times when a guest should *not* leave the ceremony?**
Do not leave while prayers are being recited, during the reading of Scriptures or during the sermon.

**Who are the major officiants, leaders or participants at the ceremony and what do they do?**
- *The confirmand(s)*, the person(s) being confirmed.
- *The minister(s) or pastor(s)*, the primary leader of the service. He preaches a sermon and presides over the communion and baptism.
- *Lector(s) or reader(s)*, who read the Scriptures aloud to the congregants.
- *Ushers*, who greet worshippers in most churches and distribute church bulletins and offering plates. In some churches, they also seat worshippers and guests.
- *Lay leaders*, who may greet congregants and guests, make announcements about church activities and lead prayers.
- *Deacons*, who help serve communion in some churches.

**What books are used?**
The most commonly used of several Protestant Bibles is The Holy Bible, New Revised Standard Version (New York: National Council of Churches, 1989). Also used is *The New Century Hymnal* (Cleveland, Ohio: The Pilgrim Press, 1995).

**To indicate the order of the ceremony:**
A program will be distributed and the minister will make periodic announcements.

**Will a guest who is not a member of the United Church of Christ be expected to do anything other than sit?**
If the family or the confirmand has specifically asked you to join them while standing in front of the congregation, then do so.

Ordinarily, guests are expected to join congregants when they stand during the service. It is entirely optional for them to read prayers aloud and sing with the congregation. In most United Church of Christ congregations, congregants do not kneel. In those churches where kneeling occurs, it is optional for guests to join in. Those guests who do not kneel should remain seated.

**Are there any parts of the ceremony in which a guest who is not a member of the United Church of Christ should *not* participate?**
No.

**If not disruptive to the ceremony, is it okay to:**
- **Take pictures?** Practice varies. Ask the pastor in advance.

◪ **Use a flash?** Practice varies. Ask the pastor in advance.
◪ **Use a video camera?** Practice varies. Ask the pastor in advance.
◪ **Use a tape recorder?** Practice varies. Ask the pastor in advance.

**Will contributions to the church be collected at the ceremony?**
Yes. Ushers pass offering plates through the congregation during the service.

**How much is customary to contribute?**
It is entirely optional for guests to contribute. If they choose to do so, contributions between $1 and $10 are appropriate.

## AFTER THE CEREMONY

**Is there usually a reception after the ceremony?**
Yes. Some churches serve no food during the reception; some serve such light foods as coffee, tea, juice and pastry; some serve a complete lunch. Grace will be recited only if a meal is served—and then only before the meal, not after it. The reception may last 30 to 60 minutes.

**Would it be considered impolite to neither eat nor drink?**
No.

**Is there a grace or benediction before eating or drinking?**
Grace will be said if a full meal is served.

**Is there a grace or benediction after eating or drinking?**
No.

**Is there a traditional greeting for the family?**
Just offer your congratulations.

**Is there a traditional form of address for clergy who may be at the reception?**
Some are addressed as "Pastor." Some prefer to be addressed as "Mr." or "Ms." or, if the church bulletin distributed at services so indicates, as "Dr." Many United Church of Christ clergy prefer being addressed by their first name.

**Is it okay to leave early?**
Yes.

## · *Marriage Ceremony* ·

The United Church of Christ teaches that the essence of marriage is a covenanted commitment that has its foundation in the faithfulness of God's love. The marriage ceremony is the occasion on which two people unite as husband and wife in the mutual exchange of covenant promises. The presiding official represents the Church and gives the marriage the Church's blessing. The congregation joins in affirming the marriage and in offering support and thanksgiving for the new family.

Usually, the wedding is a ceremony unto itself. Only rarely is it part of a regular Sunday worship service. It may last 30 minutes to one hour.

### BEFORE THE CEREMONY

**Are guests usually invited by a formal invitation?**
Yes.

**If not stated explicitly, should one assume that children are invited?**
No.

**If one can't attend, what should one do?**
RSVP with regrets and send a gift.

### APPROPRIATE ATTIRE

**Men:** A jacket and tie. No head covering is required.

**Women:** A dress or a skirt and blouse. Clothing need not cover the arms and hems need not reach below the knees. Open-toed shoes and modest jewelry are permissible. No head covering is required.

There are no rules regarding colors of clothing.

### GIFTS

**Is a gift customarily expected?**
Yes. Cash or bonds or household items (such as sheets, kitchenware or small appliances) are appropriate.

**Should gifts be brought to the ceremony?**
Bring gifts to the reception that follows the wedding ceremony.

### THE CEREMONY

**Where will the ceremony take place?**
In the church's main sanctuary or a special room in the church, or in a home, a catering hall or outdoors.

**When should guests arrive and where should they sit?**
Arrive shortly before the time for which the wedding has been scheduled. Usually, ushers will advise guests where to sit.

**If arriving late, are there times when a guest should *not* enter the ceremony?**

Do not enter during the processional or recessional of the wedding party or during the recitation of wedding vows. Follow the ushers' guidance for entering the ceremony.

**Are there times when a guest should *not* leave the ceremony?**

Do not leave during the processional or recessional of the wedding party or during the recitation of wedding vows. Follow the ushers' guidance for leaving the ceremony.

**Who are the major officiants, leaders or participants at the ceremony and what do they do?**

- *The minister(s) or pastor(s)*, who preside over the ceremony.
- *The bride and groom.*
- Other members of the wedding party.
- *Lector(s) or reader(s)*, who, at some weddings, may read the Scriptures aloud to those present.
- *Deacons*, who help serve communion, which is not served at all weddings.
- *Ushers*, who greet and seat guests at most weddings.

**What books are used?**

The most commonly used of several Protestant Bibles is The Holy Bible, New Revised Standard Version (New York: National Council of Churches, 1989). Also used is *The New Century Hymnal* (Cleveland, Ohio: The Pilgrim Press, 1995).

**To indicate the order of the ceremony:**

The minister will make periodic announcements.

**Will a guest who is not a member of the United Church of Christ be expected to do anything other than sit?**

Guests are expected to join congregants when they stand during the service. It is entirely optional for them to read prayers aloud and sing with the congregation. In most United Church of Christ congregations, congregants do not kneel. In those churches where kneeling occurs, it is optional for guests to join in. Those guests who do not kneel should remain seated.

**Are there any parts of the ceremony in which a guest who is not a member of the United Church of Christ should *not* participate?**

No.

**If not disruptive to the ceremony, is it okay to:**

- **Take pictures?** Practice varies. Ask the pastor in advance.
- **Use a flash?** Practice varies. Ask the pastor in advance.
- **Use a video camera?** Practice varies. Ask the pastor in advance.

▣ **Use a tape recorder?** Practice varies. Ask the pastor in advance.

**Will contributions to the church be collected at the ceremony?**
Only if the wedding is part of a regular Sunday worship service. If so, ushers will pass offering plates through the congregation during the service.

**How much is customary to contribute?**
If guests choose to do so, contributions between $1 and $10 are appropriate.

## AFTER THE CEREMONY

**Is there usually a reception after the ceremony?**
Yes. It is usually in a catering hall, at a home or in a church reception hall. There is usually a reception line and a full meal is served. If the reception is not in the church, there may be alcoholic beverages and/or music and dancing. The reception may last two hours or more.

**Would it be considered impolite to neither eat nor drink?**
No.

**Is there a grace or benediction before eating or drinking?**
Grace will be said if a full meal is served.

**Is there a grace or benediction after eating or drinking?**
No.

**Is there a traditional greeting for the family?**
Just offer your congratulations.

**Is there a traditional form of address for clergy who may be at the reception?**
Some are addressed as "Pastor." Some prefer to be addressed as "Mr." or "Ms." or, if the church bulletin distributed at services so indicates, as "Dr." Many United Church of Christ clergy prefer being addressed by their first name.

**Is it okay to leave early?**
Yes.

## · Funerals and Mourning ·

A United Church of Christ funeral service, states the Church's *Book of Worship*, "recognizes both the pain and sorrow of the separation that accompanies death and the hope and joy of the promises of God to those who die and are raised in Jesus Christ. The service celebrates the life of the deceased, gives thanks for that person's life, and commends that life to God....Its purpose is to affirm once more the powerful, steadfast love of God from which people cannot be separated, even by death."

The funeral service is almost always a service unto itself. Ordinarily, it lasts about 15 to 30 minutes, although it may sometimes last up to 60 minutes.

## BEFORE THE CEREMONY

**How soon after the death does the funeral usually take place?**
Within one week.

**What should someone who is not a member of the United Church of Christ do upon hearing of the death of a member of that faith?**
Telephone or visit the bereaved family or send a card to them to express your condolences.

## APPROPRIATE ATTIRE

**Men:** A jacket and tie. No head covering is required.

**Women:** A dress or a skirt and blouse. Clothing need not cover the arms and hems need not reach below the knees. Open-toed shoes and modest jewelry are permissible. No head covering is required.

Dark, somber colors of clothing are advised. Bright, flashy tones are strongly discouraged.

## GIFTS

**Is it appropriate to send flowers or make a contribution?**
Flowers may be sent to the home of the bereaved upon hearing of the death or after the funeral or they may be sent to the church or funeral home where the funeral service will be held. Contributions to a church or organization designated by the family may be made after the funeral.

**Is it appropriate to send food?**
Yes. This may be sent to the home of the bereaved.

## THE CEREMONY

**Where will the ceremony take place?**
Either in a church or a funeral home.

**When should guests arrive and where should they sit?**
Arrive fifteen minutes before the time for which the service has been scheduled. Sit wherever you wish, unless a specially marked section has been reserved for immediate family.

**If arriving late, are there times when a guest should *not* enter the ceremony?**

Do not enter during prayers, the sermon or the eulogy. Follow ushers' guidance about entering the service.

**Will the bereaved family be present at the church or funeral home before the ceremony?**

Not usually, though sometimes family members do greet guests beforehand.

**Is there a traditional greeting for the family?**

No. Just offer your condolences.

**Will there be an open casket?**

Rarely. This depends on local customs and the preference of the family. "Viewing" time is sometimes scheduled in the days or hours before the funeral. "Viewing" may also be offered during or at the end of the funeral service itself.

**Is a guest expected to view the body?**

This is entirely optional. If there is a "viewing" at the funeral and you do not wish to participate, excuse yourself from the line that forms to pass the casket. If you happen to be in the line that passes the casket and you do not wish to view the body, simply avert your eyes.

**What is appropriate behavior upon viewing the body?**

View it silently and somberly. Do not touch it or place any flowers or memorabilia in the casket.

**Who are the major officiants at the ceremony and what do they do?**

- *A minister or pastor*, who officiates and delivers the sermon.
- Possibly a family member or a close friend, who may also deliver a eulogy.

**What books are used?**

The minister will use a Bible. Of several Protestant Bibles, the most commonly used in the United Church of Christ is The Holy Bible, New Revised Standard Version (New York: National Council of Churches, 1989). Also used is *The New Century Hymnal* (Cleveland, Ohio: The Pilgrim Press, 1995).

**To indicate the order of the ceremony:**

Usually a program will be distributed; sometimes the minister will make periodic announcements.

**Will a guest who is not a member of the United Church of Christ be expected to do anything other than sit?**

Guests are expected to join congregants when they stand during the service. It is entirely optional for them to read prayers aloud and sing with the congregation. In most United Church of Christ congregations, congregants do not kneel. In those churches where kneeling occurs, it is optional for guests to join in. Those guests who do not kneel should remain seated.

**Are there any parts of the service in which a guest who is not a member of the United Church of Christ should not participate?**

No.

**If not disruptive to the ceremony, is it okay to:**

◘ **Take pictures?** No.
◘ **Use a flash?** No.
◘ **Use a video camera?** No.
◘ **Use a tape recorder?** No.

**Will contributions to the church be collected at the ceremony?**

No.

## THE INTERMENT

**Should guests attend the interment?**

Yes, unless the minister announces at the funeral service that the interment is only for the family.

**Whom should one ask for directions?**

The minister or funeral director.

**What happens at the graveside?**

Scriptures are read and the casket is placed in the ground.

**Do guests who are not members of the United Church of Christ participate at the graveside ceremony?**

No, they are simply present—although rarely, guests may be invited to say a few words about the deceased.

## COMFORTING THE BEREAVED

**Is it appropriate to visit the home of the bereaved after the funeral?**

Often, there is a reception at the home of the bereaved after the funeral. If not, visiting a few days after the funeral is appropriate.

**Will there be a religious service at the home of the bereaved?**

No.

**Will food be served?**

Yes, possibly a dinner if there is a reception immediately after the interment.

**How soon after the funeral will a mourner usually return to a normal work schedule?**

The Church has no religious prescriptions specifying the number of days that one should formally be in mourning. Local, ethnic and cultural customs are more relevant than any particular religious tradition of the Church.

**How soon after the funeral will a mourner usually return to a normal social schedule?**

The Church has no religious prescriptions specifying the number of days that one should formally be in mourning. Local, ethnic and cultural customs are more relevant than any particular religious tradition of the Church.

**Are there mourning customs to which a friend who is not a member of the United Church of Christ should be sensitive?**

No. Local, ethnic and cultural customs are more relevant than any particular religious tradition of the Church.

**Are there rituals for observing the anniversary of the death?**

No. Local, ethnic and cultural customs are more relevant than any particular religious tradition of the Church.

## V · HOME CELEBRATIONS

Not applicable for the United Church of Christ.

# Glossary

**Aliyah** ("ah-lee-YAH"): [Hebrew] Literally translated as "going up," it is the honor of being called to participate in the reading of the Torah in a synagogue/temple.

**Apostles' Creed:** The most widely used creed, or declaratory affirmation, in the Christian church in the West. Based on a creed used in Rome in the third century and given its present form in France in the sixth or seventh century. States that one believes in God, "the Father Almighty"; in Jesus Christ, the "Son of the Lord," who was conceived in a virgin birth and eventually rose to heaven after His crucifixion, where He shall judge the dead; and in "the Holy Ghost;...the Forgiveness of sins; the Resurrection of the body; and the Life everlasting."

**Atman** ("AHT-mahn"): [Sanskrit] In Hinduism, the individual soul.

**Baptism:** In Christianity, a ritual washing for initiation; a sign of remission of sin and of spiritual rebirth by symbolically participating in Christ's death, burial and resurrection. Depending on the specific Christian denomination, baptism may occur at birth, during the pre-teen or teen years or as an adult.

**Baptistery:** The place for administering baptism. Some churches have baptisteries adjoining or near their entrance. This position indicates that through baptism, one is initiated, or "enters," the church.

**Bhagavad-Gita** ("BAHG-ah-vahd GEE-tah"): [Sanskrit] The epic Hindu poem in which Krishna, a god, expounds on the nature of reality.

**Bible:** As used by Judaism, applies to the Hebrew scriptures and ascribes primary authority to the Torah (the first five books of the Bible); secondary authority to the Books of the Prophets; and tertiary authority to the Kethubim, whose 13 books include Psalms, Proverbs and Daniel. As used by Christianity, "Bible" refers to the Hebrew and Christian scriptures known as the Old and New Testaments.

**Bimah** ("BEE-mah"): [Hebrew] The part of the sanctuary in a Jewish synagogue or temple from where the service is led and where the rabbi and cantor stand and sit. It is usually raised above the level where congregants sit and is at the front or in the middle of the sanctuary.

**Book of Mormon:** Joseph Smith's translation of God's revelations. First published in 1830.

**Brahman** ("BRAH-mahn"): [Sanskrit] In Hinduism, the One, All-Encompassing soul.

**Brit** ("breet"): [Hebrew] The Jewish birth ceremony. The term literally means "covenant." For boys, the *brit milah* ("breet mee-LAH"), or the "covenant of circumcision," occurs on the eighth day of a male child's life. The *brit bat* or *brit hayyim* ("breet baht" or "breet hy-YEEM"), the "covenant of a daughter" or the "covenant of life," is a naming ceremony for a girl.

**Censer:** An incense burner holder. Smoke from the incense represents prayers being carried to heaven. Used in Greek Orthodox churches.

**Chalice:** In Christianity, a cup, sometimes covered with gold and often with a tall stem. Held by a priest or other clergy and contains the holy wine, which, depending on the Christian denomination, either symbolizes the blood of Christ or is believed to have become transubstantiated into the actual blood of Christ.

**Christian Greek Scriptures:** The term Jehovah's Witnesses use for the scriptures written in the time of the early Christian church; see "New Testament."

**Congregation Elders:** Deliver talks on the Bible and lead Bible discussions with congregants at meetings of Jehovah's Witnesses.

**Chumash** ("KOOH-mahsh"): [Hebrew] The first five books of the Torah, also known as the Five Books of Moses. These are the biblical books of Genesis, Exodus, Leviticus, Numbers and Deuteronomy. It also contains the traditional sections from Prophets that are associated with each Torah section and which are read after the Torah reading.

**Communion:** A rite through which Christians believe they receive either the symbolic or the real body and blood of Christ as assurance that God has forgiven their sins.

**Confirmation:** Confirmation is a church rite in which one who was previously baptized expresses his or her faith in Jesus Christ.

**Creed:** A statement of belief. The Christian church generally uses one of the early Christian creeds, either the Apostles' Creed or the Nicene Creed.

**Epistles:** Generally refers to the letters of St. Paul or another New Testament writer.

**Error:** The Christian Science term for "evil."

**Eucharist:** The most widely accepted name for communion, the central act of Christian worship, in which Christians believe they receive either the symbolic or the real body and blood of Christ as assurance that God has forgiven their sins.

**First Reader:** The man or woman who conducts a Christian Science service. Reads mainly from *Science and Health* on Sunday and equally from the King James Bible and *Science and Health* on Wednesday. The Second Reader, who is elected by members to read from the Bible at the Sunday Service, shares the platform with the First Reader and presides in the absence of the First Reader.

**Gospel:** The New Testament Books of Matthew, Mark, Luke or John, which record the life and ministry of Jesus. "Gospel" literally means "good news." For Christians, the "good news" is that the Son of God became a man in the person of Jesus and suffered for the sins of humanity so people will not have to undergo that suffering.

**Haftarah** ("hahf-TOH-rah"): [Hebrew] In Judaism, the Torah reading during a service in a synagogue or temple.

**Haggadah** ("hah-GAH-dah"): [Hebrew] The Jewish text, usually in Hebrew and English, which tells the Passover story and its meaning for each generation. Read at the Passover *seder*.

**Hajj** ("hahj"): [Arabic] A pilgrimage to Mecca that a Muslim must make at least once in his or her lifetime if physically and financially able.

**Healing:** In Christian Science, a realization of God's goodness and the perfection of humanity; regeneration of thought reflected on the body.

**Holy Spirit:** In Christianity, the empowering spirit of God; the third person of the Triune God.

**Huppah** ("hoo-PAH"): [Hebrew] The canopy under which a Jewish wedding ceremony takes place. Symbolizes the canopy of the heavens under which all life transpires.

**Icons:** Two-dimensional artistic images of saints. Found primarily in Greek Orthodox churches.

**Imam** ("EE-mahm"): [Arabic] In Islam, the person who leads prayers and delivers a sermon.

**Jehovah:** According to Jehovah's Witnesses, the one true name for God.

**Jumma** ("JUH-mah"): [Arabic] In Islam, noon prayer on Friday. This congregational prayer is recited at a central mosque designated for that purpose.

**Kaddish** ("KAH-dish"): [Hebrew] The Jewish prayer for the dead.

**Kiddush cup** ("kee-DOOSH"): [Hebrew] Used to drink ritual wine at certain Jewish ritual events, such as the *shabbat* meal or by the bridal couple during a wedding ceremony.

**Kingdom Halls:** The name of Jehovah's Witnesses' meeting halls.

**Kosher** ("KOH-sher"): [Hebrew] Food deemed fit for consumption according to Jewish dietary laws, which prohibit such foods as pork or shellfish and the mixing of dairy and meat products at the same meal or within several hours after eating either one of these dishes.

**Meeting:** The Quaker term for worship service.

**Menorah** ("min-OHR-ah"): [Hebrew] A seven-branched candelabra, which has become a central motif in the consciousness of the Jewish people. Often placed on the *bima*, or pulpit, in a synagogue or temple.

**Mohel** ("MOH-hail"): [Hebrew] A specially trained male who performs a ritual Jewish circumcision. The *mohel* may also be a rabbi or physician.

**Muazzin** ("MOO-ah-zin"): [Arabic] In Islam, the person who calls Muslims to prayer.

**New Testament:** Scriptures written in the time of the early Christian church. Comprised of four Gospels, the Acts of the Apostles, 21 epistles, and the Apocalyptic revelations of John.

**Nicene Creed:** A declaratory affirmation in the Christian church that states the full deity of Jesus Christ.

**Nirvana** ("neer-VAH-nah"): [Sanskrit] In Buddhism, the extinction of worldly illusions and passions.

**Old Testament:** The Christian name for the collection of writings sacred to Christians and Jews. Its 39 books, beginning with Genesis and ending with Malachi, include history, law and poems.

**Ordinance:** The term used by the Assemblies of God Church for water baptism and Communion because they were practices ordained or established by Jesus.

**Paten:** Holds the consecrated bread or wafer of the Eucharist during a Christian service. Depending on the denomination, the wafer either symbolizes the body of Christ or is believed to have been transubstantiated into the actual body of Christ.

**Prasad** ("PRAH-sahd"): [Sanskrit] In Hinduism, sacramental food served to those present at certain rituals and ceremonies.

**Puja** ("POO-jah"): [Sanskrit] In Hinduism, a ritual worship held before a specific deity.

**Qiblah** ("KIHB-lah"): [Arabic] In Islam, the direction to which the imam, or prayer leader, faces while praying.

**Quran** ("koo-RAHN"): [Arabic] Islam's holy book, also known as *The Recitation*. Consists of 114 chapters or suras and a total of 6,000 verses. Divinely revealed to the Prophet Muhammad during the 22 years from 610 to 632 A.D.

**Raka'ah** ("RAH-kah"): [Arabic] In Islam, a way to "greet" and honor the mosque upon entering it. A full *raka'ah* consists of recitations during which one first stands, then makes one bow, followed by two prostrating motions (separated by a short sitting). Each prayer time requires a specific number of *raka'ah*.

**Requiem:** All or part of a Christian funeral service. In the Episcopal Church, if a funeral service is part of a larger service, it is called a "requiem."

**Sacrament Meeting:** Mormons' term for their basic service.

**Samsara** ("SAHM-sah-rah"): [Sanskrit] In Buddhism and Hinduism, recurrent birth-and-death from which one is finally liberated.

**Scriptures:** A general term for holy writings in Christianity.

**Seder** ("SAY-dihr"): [Hebrew] The festive dinner during the Jewish holiday of Passover during which the story of the Jewish people's liberation from slavery in Egypt is told. Rituals precede and follow the meal.

**Shabbat** ("shah-BAHT"): [Hebrew] The Jewish word for "Sabbath." Commemorates the day on which God rested after creating the world during the previous six days. *Shabbat* begins at sundown on Friday and ends at sundown on Saturday.

**Shahadah** ("SHAH-hah-dah"): [Arabic] The Islamic Declaration of Faith. One becomes a Muslim by saying and believing the *shahadah*: "There is no god but God and Muhammad is the Messenger of God."

**Shraddha** ("SHRAD-dah"): [Sanskrit] A Hindu ceremony held 10 to 30 days after death intended to liberate the soul of the deceased for its ascent to heaven.

**Shiva** ("SHIH-vah"): [Hebrew] The seven days immediately after the burial of a family member during which Jews sit in mourning.

**Torah** ("TOH-rah"): [Hebrew] Most commonly used to refer to the scroll of the Five Books of Moses, but its broader meaning includes the full body of rabbinic contributions to Judaism.

**Wadu** ("WAH-doo"): [Arabic] In Islam, ablutions of the hands, face and feet performed before prayer.

**Yahrzeit** ("YAHR-tzite"): [Hebrew] In Judaism, the yearly anniversary of the death of a member of the immediate family. Upon the *yahrzeit*, a wife, husband and/or children attend services at synagogue and light a *yahrzeit* candle at home.

**Yoga** ("YOH-gah"): [Sanskrit] Specific disciplines in Hinduism to achieve enlightenment that address the intellect, emotions and labor and service to others.

# Calendar of
# Religious Holidays and Festivals

The Gregorian calendar, in use throughout the world, was first introduced in 1582 by Pope Gregory XIII as a corrected form of the old Julian calendar.

The Hindu calendar is lunisolar and governs Hindu religious life and almost all Indian festivals.

The Jewish calendar is the official calendar of the Jewish religious community and is used to mark the dates of annual religious events and holidays.

The Muslim calendar is the official calendar in many Muslim countries, and is used throughout the Islamic world to mark religious events and festivals.

The following chart describes the basic structure of these calendars. Each list begins with the first month of the year.

## GREGORIAN

The solar year of the Gregorian calendar consists of 365 days, except in a leap year—occuring every fourth even-numbered year—which has 366 days. (Centenary years are leap years only if they are evenly divisible by 400).

| Month | Number of Days |
|---|---|
| January | 31 |
| February | 28 |
| in leap year | 29 |
| March | 31 |
| April | 30 |
| May | 31 |
| June | 30 |

July ...............................................31
August............................................31
September.....................................30
October ........................................31
November ....................................30
December.....................................31

## HINDU

In the Hindu calendar, the solar year is divided into 12 lunar months in accordance with the successive entrances of the sun into the signs of the zodiac; the months vary in length from 29 to 32 days. An intercalary month is inserted after every month in which two new moons occur (once in three years), and this intercalary month has the name of the month that precedes it. The months correspond approximately to the Gregorian months shown in parentheses in this chart.

### Months

Chai (March-April)

Baisakh (April-May)

Jeth (May-June)

Asarh (June-July)

Sawan (July-August)

Bhadon (August-September)

Asin (September-October)

Kartik (October-November)

Aghan (November-December)

Pus (December-January)

Magh (January-February)

Phagun (February-March)

## JEWISH

The Jewish calendar is based on both the solar and the lunar cycles. The lunar year, averaging 354 days, is adjusted to the solar year by periodic leap years, occuring approximately once every three years, which contain an intercalary month and ensure that the major religious holidays fall in the proper season. The months correspond approximately to the Gregorian months shown in parentheses in this chart.

| Month | Number of Days |
|-------|----------------|
| Tishrei (September-October) | 30 |
| Chesvan (October-November) | 29 |
| in some years | 30 |
| Kislev (November-December) | 29 |
| in some years | 30 |
| Tevet (December-January) | 29 |
| Shevat (January-February) | 30 |
| Adar (February-March) | 29 |
| in some years | 30 |
| Adar II | 29 |
| (intercalary month in leap year only) | |
| Nisan (March-April) | 30 |
| Iyar (April-May) | 29 |
| Sivan (May-June) | 30 |
| Tammuz (June-July) | 29 |
| Av (July-August) | 30 |
| Elul (August-September) | 29 |

## MUSLIM

The Muslim calendar is based on the lunar year. Each year consists of 354 days or 355 days (in leap years). The number of days per month is adjusted throughout the year, in accordance with each lunar cycle. The beginning of the Muslim year retrogresses through the solar year; it completes a full cycle every 32½ years.

| Month | Number of Days |
|-------|----------------|
| Muharram | 29 or 30 |
| Safar | 29 or 30 |
| Rabi I | 29 or 30 |
| Rabi II | 29 or 30 |
| Jumada I | 29 or 30 |
| Jumada II | 29 or 30 |
| Rajab | 29 or 30 |
| Sha'ban | 29 or 30 |
| Ramadan | 29 or 30 |

Shawwal ...........................29 or 30
Dhu al-Qa'dah ....................29 or 30
Dhu al-Hijjah ....................29 or 30

The list below presents the dates, on the Gregorian calendar, of major religious holidays and festivals of Buddhists, Christians, Hindus, Jews and Muslims.

Since, in the Muslim calendar, the actual beginning of the new month is determined by the appearance of the new moon, the Gregorian dates given here may vary slightly.

In Orthodox churches that use the old Julian calendar, observances are held thirteen days later than the dates that are listed below.

B: Buddhist
H: Hindu
J: Jewish
M: Muslim
O: Orthodox Churches (Christian)
W: Western Churches (Christian)

| Religious Holiday/Festival | 1999 | 2000 | 2001 |
|---|---|---|---|
| New Year's Day (B, O, W) | Jan. 1 | Jan. 1 | Jan. 1 |
| Epiphany (O, W) | Jan. 6 | Jan. 6 | Jan. 6 |
| Christmas (O—Armenian) | Jan. 6 | Jan. 6 | Jan. 6 |
| Id al-Fitr (M) | Jan. 17 | Jan. 8/ Dec. 27 | * |
| Nirvana Day (B) | Feb. 15 | Feb. 15 | Feb. 15 |
| Shiva Ratri (H) | Feb. 14 | * | * |
| Ash Wednesday (W) | Feb. 17 | Mar. 8 | Feb. 28 |
| Lent begins (O) | Feb. 22 | Mar. 13 | Feb. 26 |
| Purim (J) | Mar. 2 | Mar. 21 | Mar. 9 |
| Rama Navami (H) | Mar. 25 | * | * |
| Id al-Adha (M) | Mar. 28 | Mar. 16 | Mar. 5 |
| Hanamatsuri/Buddha Day (B) | Apr. 8 | Apr. 8 | Apr. 8 |
| Palm Sunday (W) | Mar. 28 | Apr. 16 | Apr. 8 |
| Holy Thursday (W) | Apr. 1 | Apr. 20 | Apr. 12 |
| Good Friday (W) | Apr. 2 | Apr. 21 | Apr. 13 |
| First Day of Passover (J) | Apr. 1 | Apr. 20 | Apr. 8 |

| Religious Holiday/Festival | 1999 | 2000 | 2001 |
|---|---|---|---|
| Easter (W) | Apr. 4 | Apr. 23 | Apr. 15 |
| Palm Sunday (O) | Apr. 4 | Apr. 23 | Apr. 8 |
| Holy Thursday (O) | Apr. 8 | Apr. 27 | Apr. 12 |
| Holy (Good) Friday (O) | Apr. 9 | Apr. 28 | Apr. 13 |
| Easter (O) | Apr. 11 | Apr. 30 | Apr. 15 |
| Ascension Day (W) | May 13 | June 1 | May 24 |
| First Day of the Month of Muharram (M) | * | * | * |
| Ascension Day (O) | May 13 | June 1 | May 24 |
| First Day of Shavuot (J) | May 21 | June 9 | May 28 |
| Pentecost (W) | May 30 | June 18 | June 3 |
| Pentecost (O) | May 30 | June 18 | June 3 |
| Mawlid al-Nabi (M) | June 26 | June 14 | * |
| Krishna Janmashtami (H) | Sept. 2 | * | * |
| Buddhist Churches of America Founding Day (B) | Sept. 1 | Sept. 1 | Sept. 1 |
| Duhsehra/Durga Puja (H) | Mar. 25 | * | * |
| First Day of Rosh Hashanah (J) | Sept. 11 | Sept. 30 | Sept. 18 |
| Yom Kippur (J) | Sept. 20 | Oct. 9 | Sept. 27 |
| First Day of Sukkot (J) | Sept. 25 | Oct. 14 | Oct. 2 |
| Shemini Atzeret (J) | Oct. 2 | Oct. 21 | Oct. 9 |
| Simchat Torah (J) | Oct. 3 | Oct. 22 | Oct. 10 |
| Reformation Sunday (W—Lutheran) | Oct. 24 | Oct. 29 | Oct. 28 |
| Reformation Day (W—Lutheran) | Oct. 31 | Oct. 31 | Oct. 31 |
| First Sunday of Advent (O, W) | Nov. 28 | Dec. 3 | Dec. 2 |
| Bodhi Day (B) | Dec. 8 | Dec. 8 | Dec. 8 |
| First Day of Hannukah (J) | Dec. 4 | Dec. 22 | Dec. 10 |
| First Day of the Month of Ramadan (M) | Dec. 9 | Nov. 27 | * |
| Christmas (O, except Armenian; W) | Dec. 25 | Dec. 25 | Dec. 25 |

EDITOR'S NOTE: *As both the Hindu and Muslim calendars are lunar-based, the dates starred above are not currently available.*

# About SKYLIGHT PATHS Publishing

Through spirituality, our religious beliefs are increasingly becoming *a part of* our lives, rather than *apart from* our lives. Nevertheless, while many people are more interested than ever in spiritual growth, they are less firmly planted in *traditional* religion. To deepen their relationship to the sacred, people want to learn from their own and other faith traditions, in new ways.

SkyLight Paths sees both believers and seekers as a community that increasingly transcends traditional boundaries of religion and denomination. Many people want to learn from each other, *walking together, finding the way.*

The SkyLight Paths staff is made up of people of many faiths. We are a small, highly committed group of people, a reflection of the religious diversity that now exists in most neighborhoods, most families. We will succeed only if our books make a difference in your life.

We at SkyLight Paths take great care to produce beautiful books that present meaningful spiritual content in a form that reflects the art of making high quality books. Therefore, we want to acknowledge those who contributed to the production of this book.

PRODUCTION
Bridgett Taylor & David Wall

EDITORIAL & PROOFREADING
Jennifer Goneau & Martha McKinney

COVER DESIGN
Chelsea Dippel

PRINTING AND BINDING
Lake Book, Melrose Park, Illinois

## AVAILABLE FROM BETTER BOOKSTORES.
## TRY YOUR BOOKSTORE FIRST.

# *Some Other Interesting Books—Spirituality*

### A HEART OF STILLNESS
### A Complete Guide to Learning the Art of Meditation
by *David A. Cooper*

**The only complete, nonsectarian guide to meditation, from
one of our most respected spiritual teachers.**

To experience what mystics have experienced for thousands of years,
*A Heart of Stillness* helps you acquire on your own, with minimal guidance, the skills of various styles of meditation. Draws upon the wisdom
teachings of Christianity, Judaism, Buddhism, Hinduism and Islam as
it teaches you the processes of purification, concentration, and mastery
in detail.

5½" x 8½", 272 pp. Quality Paperback, ISBN 1-893361-03-9 **$16.95**

### SILENCE, SIMPLICITY & SOLITUDE
### A Complete Guide to Spiritual Retreat
by *David A. Cooper*

**The classic personal spiritual retreat guide that enables
readers to create their own self-guided spiritual retreat.**

Award-winning author David Cooper traces personal mystical retreat in
all of the world's major traditions, describing the varieties of spiritual
practices for modern spiritual seekers. Cooper shares the techniques and
practices that encompass the personal spiritual retreat experience, allow-
ing readers to enhance their meditation practices and create an effective,
self-guided spiritual retreat in their own homes—without the instruction
of a meditation teacher.

5½" x 8½", 336 pp. Quality Paperback, ISBN 1-893361-04-7 **$16.95**

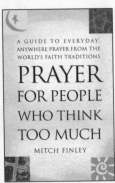

### PRAYER FOR PEOPLE WHO THINK TOO MUCH
### A Guide to Everyday, Anywhere Prayer
### from the World's Faith Traditions
by *Mitch Finley*

*Available
June 1999*

**A nonsectarian look at prayer
that helps people take prayer beyond worship services
to become a natural part of daily living.**

Takes away the stigma attached to prayer as a part of life to help people
pray holistically—with body, mind, heart and spirit—to make prayer
more than just something reserved for worship services. Examines the
concepts behind prayer in the world's major faith traditions.

5½" x 8½", 176 pp. (est) Hardcover, ISBN 1-893361-00-4 **$21.95**

*Or phone, fax or mail to:* **SKYLIGHT PATHS** Publishing
Sunset Farm Offices, Route 4 • P.O. Box 237 • Woodstock, Vermont 05091
Tel: (802) 457-4000 • Fax: (802) 457-4004 • www.skylightpaths.com
*Credit card orders* **(800) 962-4544** (9AM–5PM ET Monday–Friday)
*Generous discounts on quantity orders. SATISFACTION GUARANTEED. Prices subject to change.*

# Other Interesting Books—Spirituality

## VOICES FROM GENESIS
### Guiding Us Through the Stages of Life
by *Norman J. Cohen*

A brilliant blending of modern midrash and the life stages of Erik Erikson's developmental psychology. Shows how the pathways of our lives are quite similar to those of the leading figures of Genesis who speak directly to us, telling of their spiritual and emotional journeys.

6" x 9", 192 pp. HC, ISBN 1-879045-75-3 **$21.95**

---

## SELF, STRUGGLE & CHANGE
### Family Conflict Stories in Genesis and Their Healing Insights for Our Lives
by *Norman J. Cohen*

The people described by the biblical writers of Genesis were in situations and relationships very much like our own. We identify with them. Their stories still speak to us because they are about the same problems we deal with every day. Here a modern master of biblical interpretation brings us greater understanding of the ancient text and of ourselves in this intriguing re-telling of conflict between husband and wife, father and son, brothers, and sisters.

6" x 9", 224 pp. Quality Paperback, ISBN 1-879045-66-4 **$16.95**
HC, ISBN -19-2 **$21.95**

---

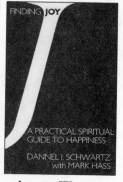

## FINDING JOY
### A Practical Spiritual Guide to Happiness
by *Dannel I. Schwartz* with *Mark Hass*

Searching for happiness in our modern world of stress and struggle is common; *finding* it is more unusual. This guide explores and explains how to find joy through a time-honored, creative—and surprisingly practical—approach based on the teachings of Jewish mysticism and *Kabbalah*.

"Lovely, simple introduction to Kabbalah....
A singular contribution."
—*American Library Association's* Booklist

• AWARD WINNER •

6" x 9", 192 pp. Quality PB, ISBN 1-58023-009-1 **$14.95**
HC, ISBN 1-879045-53-2 **$19.95**

---

## MOSES—THE PRINCE, THE PROPHET
### His Life, Legend & Message for Our Lives
by *Rabbi Levi Meier, Ph.D.*

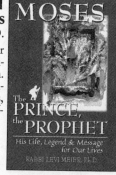

How can the struggles of a great biblical figure teach us to cope with our own lives today? A fascinating portrait of the struggles, failures, and triumphs of Moses, a central figure in Jewish, Christian, and Islamic tradition. Drawing upon stories from *Exodus*, midrash (finding contemporary meaning from ancient Jewish texts), the teachings of Jewish mystics, modern texts, and psychotherapy, Meier offers new ways to create our own path to self-knowledge and self-fulfillment—and face life's difficulties head-on.

6" x 9", 224 pp. HC, ISBN 1-58023-013-X **$23.95**

# Spiritual Inspiration . . .
## The Kushner Series

### EYES REMADE FOR WONDER
### A Lawrence Kushner Reader
Introduction by *Thomas Moore*

A treasury of insight from one of the most creative spiritual thinkers in America. Whether you are new to Kushner or a devoted fan, this is the place to begin. With samplings from each of Kushner's works, and a generous amount of new material, this is a book to be savored, to be read and reread, each time discovering deeper layers of meaning in our lives. Offers something unique to both the spiritual seeker and the committed person of faith.

6" x 9", 240 pp. Quality PB, ISBN 1-58023-042-3 **$16.95**
HC, ISBN -014-8 **$23.95**

---

## GOD WAS IN THIS PLACE & I, i DID NOT KNOW
### Finding Self, Spirituality & Ultimate Meaning
by *Lawrence Kushner*

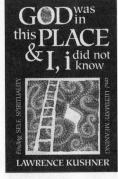

Who am I? Who is God? Kushner creates inspiring interpretations of Jacob's dream in Genesis, opening a window into Jewish spirituality for people of all faiths and backgrounds. In a fascinating blend of scholarship, imagination, psychology and history, seven Jewish spiritual masters ask and answer fundamental questions of human experience.

**"Rich and intriguing."**
—*M. Scott Peck, M.D.,*
*author of* The Road Less Traveled

6" x 9", 192 pp. Quality Paperback, ISBN 1-879045-33-8 **$16.95**

---

### HONEY FROM THE ROCK
### An Easy Introduction to Jewish Mysticism
by *Lawrence Kushner*

**"Quite simply the easiest introduction to Jewish mysticism you can read."**

An introduction to the ten gates of Jewish mysticism and how they apply to daily life.

6" x 9", 176 pp. Quality Paperback, ISBN 1-879045-02-8 **$14.95**

---

### THE RIVER OF LIGHT
### Spirituality, Judaism, Consciousness
by *Lawrence Kushner*

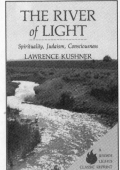

A "manual" for all spiritual travelers who would attempt a spiritual journey in our times. Taking us step by step, Kushner allows us to discover the meaning of our own quest: "to allow the river of light—the deepest currents of consciousness—to rise to the surface and animate our lives."

6" x 9", 192 pp. Quality Paperback, ISBN 1-879045-03-6 **$14.95**

# Spiritual Inspiration . . .
## The Kushner Series

## INVISIBLE LINES OF CONNECTION
### Sacred Stories of the Ordinary
by *Lawrence Kushner*

Through his everyday encounters with family, friends, colleagues and strangers, Kushner takes us deeply into our lives, finding flashes of spiritual insight in the process. This is a book where literature meets spirituality, where the sacred meets the ordinary, and, above all, where people of all faiths, all backgrounds can meet one another and themselves. Kushner ties together the stories of our lives into a roadmap showing how everything "ordinary" is supercharged with meaning—*if* we can just see it.

6" x 9", 160 pp. Quality Paperback, ISBN 1-879045-98-2 **$15.95**
HC, ISBN -52-4 **$21.95**

## THE BOOK OF WORDS
### Talking Spiritual Life, Living Spiritual Talk
by *Lawrence Kushner*

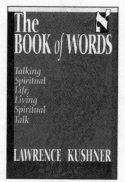

Kushner lifts up and shakes the dust off primary religious words we use to describe the spiritual dimension of life. The *Words* take on renewed spiritual significance, adding power and focus to the lives we live every day. For each word Kushner offers us a startling, moving and insightful explication, and pointed readings from classical Jewish sources that further illuminate the concept. He concludes with a short exercise that helps unite the spirit of the word with our actions in the world.

6" x 9", 160 pp. Beautiful two-color text.
Quality Paperback, ISBN 1-58023-020-2 **$16.95**
HC, ISBN 1-879045-35-4 **$21.95**

## THE BOOK OF LETTERS
### A Mystical Hebrew Alphabet
by *Lawrence Kushner*

In calligraphy by the author. Folktales about and exploration of the mystical meanings of the Hebrew Alphabet. Open the old prayerbook-like pages of *The Book of Letters* and you will enter a special world of sacred tradition and religious feeling. More than just symbols, all twenty-two letters of the Hebrew alphabet overflow with meanings and personalities of their own.

Rabbi Kushner draws from ancient Judaic sources, weaving talmudic commentary, Hasidic folktales, and kabbalistic mysteries around the letters.

**"A book which is in love with Jewish letters."**
—*Isaac Bashevis Singer* (ל״ז)
**• Popular Hardcover Edition •**
6" x 9", 80 pp. Hardcover, two colors, inspiring new Foreword
ISBN 1-879045-00-1 **$24.95**

**• Also available in a Deluxe Gift Edition** *($79.95)* **and Collector's Limited Edition** *($349.00)* **•**
*Call 1-800-962-4544 for more information.*

**ENDORSED BY CATHOLIC, PROTESTANT, AND JEWISH RELIGIOUS LEADERS**

# *Children's Spirituality*

## BUT GOD REMEMBERED
### Stories of Women from Creation to the Promised Land

**For ages 8 and up**

by *Sandy Eisenberg Sasso*
Full-color illustrations by *Bethanne Andersen*

NONDENOMINATIONAL, NONSECTARIAN

A fascinating collection of four different stories of women only briefly mentioned in biblical tradition and religious texts, but never before explored. Award-winning author Sasso brings to life the intriguing stories of Lilith, Serach, Bityah, and the Daughters of Z, courageous and strong women from ancient tradition. All teach important values through their faith and actions.

9" x 12", 32 pp. HC, Full-color illus., ISBN 1-879045-43-5 **$16.95**

**For ages 4 and up**

## IN GOD'S NAME

by *Sandy Eisenberg Sasso*
Full-color illustrations by *Phoebe Stone*

**Selected by Parent Council, Ltd.™**

MULTICULTURAL, NONDENOMINATIONAL, NONSECTARIAN

Like an ancient myth in its poetic text and vibrant illustrations, this modern fable about the search for God's name celebrates the diversity and, at the same time, the unity of all the people of the world. Each seeker claims he or she alone knows the answer. Finally, they come together and learn what God's name really is, sharing the ultimate harmony of belief in one God by people of all faiths, all backgrounds.

9" x 12", 32 pp. HC, Full color illus., ISBN 1-879045-26-5 **$16.95**

## GOD IN BETWEEN

**For ages 4 and up**

by *Sandy Eisenberg Sasso*
Full-color illustrations by *Sally Sweetland*

NONDENOMINATIONAL, NONSECTARIAN, MULTICULTURAL

*If you wanted to find God, where would you look?*
A magical, mythical tale that teaches that God can be found where we are: within all of us and the relationships between us.

9" x 12", 32 pp. HC, Full-color illus., ISBN 1-879045-86-9 **$16.95**

**For ages 4 and up**

## GOD'S PAINTBRUSH

by *Sandy Eisenberg Sasso*
Full-color illustrations by *Annette Compton*

MULTICULTURAL, NONDENOMINATIONAL, NONSECTARIAN

Invites children of all faiths and backgrounds to encounter God openly in their own lives. Wonderfully interactive, provides questions adult and child can explore together at the end of each episode.

11" x 8½", 32 pp. HC, Full-color illus., ISBN 1-879045-22-2 **$16.95**

**ENDORSED BY CATHOLIC, PROTESTANT, AND JEWISH RELIGIOUS LEADERS**

# Children's Spirituality

## A PRAYER FOR THE EARTH
### The Story of Naamah, Noah's Wife
by *Sandy Eisenberg Sasso*  **For ages 4 and up**
Full-color illustrations by *Bethanne Andersen*

NONDENOMINATIONAL, NONSECTARIAN

This new story, based on an ancient text, opens readers' religious imaginations to new ideas about the well-known story of the Flood. When God tells Noah to bring the animals of the world onto the ark, God *also* calls on Naamah, Noah's wife, to save each plant on Earth.

9" x 12", 32 pp. HC, Full-color illus., ISBN 1-879045-60-5 **$16.95**

---

## THE 11TH COMMANDMENT
### Wisdom from Our Children
**For all ages**  by *The Children of America*

MULTICULTURAL, NONDENOMINATIONAL, NONSECTARIAN

*"If there were an Eleventh Commandment, what would it be?"*
Children of many religious denominations across America answer this question—in their own drawings and words—in *The 11th Commandment.*

8" x 10", 48 pp. HC, Full-color illus., ISBN 1-879045-46-X **$16.95**

---

## IN OUR IMAGE
### God's First Creatures
by *Nancy Sohn Swartz*  **For ages 4 and up**
Full-color illustrations by *Melanie Hall*

NONDENOMINATIONAL, NONSECTARIAN

A playful new twist to the Creation story. Celebrates the interconnectedness of nature and the harmony of all living things.

9" x 12", 32 pp. HC, Full-color illus., ISBN 1-879045-99-0 **$16.95**

---

## PARENTING AS A SPIRITUAL JOURNEY
### Deepening Ordinary & Extraordinary Events into Sacred Occasions
by *Rabbi Nancy Fuchs-Kreimer*

A perfect gift for the new parent, and a helpful guidebook for those seeking to re-envision family life.

Draws on experiences of the author and over 100 parents of many faiths, revealing the transformative spiritual adventure that parents can experience while bringing up their children. Rituals, prayers, and passages from sacred Jewish texts—as well as from other religious traditions—are woven throughout the book.

"This is really relevant spirituality. I love her book."
—*Sylvia Boorstein, author of*
It's Easier Than You Think
*and mother of four*

6" x 9", 224 pp. Quality Paperback, ISBN 1-58023-016-4 **$16.95**

# AVAILABLE FROM BETTER BOOKSTORES.
# TRY YOUR BOOKSTORE FIRST.

## *Other Interesting Books—Spirituality*

### HOW TO BE A PERFECT STRANGER, In 2 Volumes
### A Guide to Etiquette in Other People's Religious Ceremonies
Edited by *Stuart M. Matlins* &

BEST REFERENCE BOOK OF THE YEAR

Explains the

helping an int

extent possib

Answers prac

nominations,

**VOL. 1 COV**

Church (Disci

Episcopalian/

Witnesses • J

Quaker • Ro

Canada • Unit

6" x 9",

**VOL. 2 COV**

Alliance • Cl

Evangelical F

Pentecostal H

Churches • P

Wesleyan

nd Missionary

e Nazarene •

International

s • Orthodox

Universalist •

The *Ar*

## Publ

## Pray

*Not for Clerg*

second edition

Lawrence A. Ho

ardened

irituality.

is ecumenical

o cares about

$17.95

*Or*

Sunset F

Tel:

lishing

ont 05091

ths.com

### Credit card orders (800) 962-4544 (9AM–5PM ET Monday–Friday)
*Generous discounts on quantity orders. SATISFACTION GUARANTEED. Prices subject to change.*

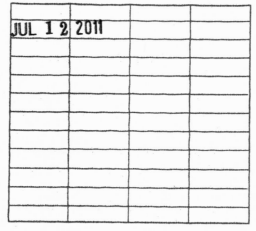

291.28
H847
v.1

3223500001539

How to be a perfect stranger : a
guide to etiquette in other people's
religious ceremonies

DATE DUE

JUL 1 2 2011

BEAL COLLEGE LIBRARY
P.O. BOX 450
BANGOR, ME 04402-0450

DEMCO